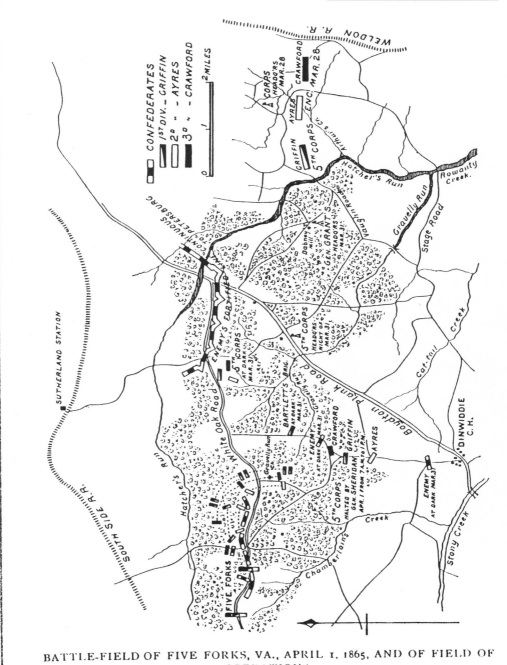

BATTLE-FIELD OF FIVE FORKS, VA., APRIL 1, 1865, AND OF FIELD OF OPERATIONS.

Showing the operations of the 5th Army Corps.

"BAYONET! FORWARD"
My Civil War Reminiscences

"General, you have the soul of the lion and the heart of the woman."

— General Horatio G. Sickel to General
Joshua Chamberlain at the Quaker
Road, Virginia, March 29, 1865

Joshua L. Chamberlain, ca. 1878
(Courtesy Pejepscot Historical Society)

"BAYONET! FORWARD"
MY CIVIL WAR REMINISCENCES

JOSHUA LAWRENCE CHAMBERLAIN

 Stan Clark Military Books
Gettysburg, Pennsylvania

SECOND EDITION

Published in 1994 by:
STAN CLARK MILITARY BOOKS
915 Fairview Avenue
Gettysburg, Pennsylvania 17325
(717) 337-1728

Cover artwork: "General Joshua Lawrence Chamberlain"
courtesy of Michael Gnatek, Jr., S. A. H. A.
A very special thanks to Mike for permission to use his
magnificent portrait on the cover of this publication.

ISBN: 1-879664-21-6

Printed and bound in the United States of America

Contents

List of Maps

List of Photographs

INTRODUCTION

Joshua Lawrence Chamberlain spent less than four of his eighty-five years in the service of the Army of the Potomac during the War Between the States. However, it is this short period of his life for which he is best known.

Little is said of his pre and post-war accomplishments. But his contributions in civilian life were typically as important as those years he spent in the war. He attended Bowdoin College and graduated in 1852 with honors in all departments. He continued his studies at the Theological Seminary at Bangor and served as Supervisor of the Brewer Schools. Later, he was appointed professor of rhetoric, oratory, and modern language at Bowdoin College. After the war he launched his political career with a stunning landslide victory that catapulted him into four terms as governor of Maine. Following his profession in government Chamberlain was named President of Bowdoin College. Still later, the President of the United States appointed him as Commissioner of Education to the World's Exposition in Paris. In this capacity, he was awarded the French medal of honor. Returning home, he rose to become the president of a railroad construction company and was later appointed by President McKinley as Surveyor of Customs for the Port of Portland. This was the position he held until his death in 1914. It is interesting to note that General Chamberlain has been and will undoubtedly continue to be venerated by writers and journalists.

After the war, his stirring orations were in great demand. He was often called upon to deliver the key-note address for a variety of occasions, but especially for gatherings of the Military Order of the Loyal Legion of the United States. At these affairs, General Chamberlain reminisced about his most memorable and poignant experiences in the war. The intention of this publication, is to make available to the reader, some of his most remarkable published articles, official reports and addresses. Presented herewith is a variety of the General's rare, popular and descriptive accounts written about his activities during the war. They reveal his intense, often passionate feelings for his country, the stirring accounts of his wartime experiences and the love he shared for the men who served under him. But his empathy did not end with those who fought with him. He also showed compassion and sensitivity to the Confederate soldiers who had opposed him. The qualities and values he held were esteemed far above many of his contemporaries. These same virtues commanded tremendous respect from his men, making Chamberlain one of the finest officers ever to serve in the Army of the Potomac.

The general served in over twenty engagements, representing battles considered to embrace the most ferocious fighting of the war, including: Fredericksburg, Chancellorsville, Gettysburg, Spotsylvania, Cold Harbor, Petersburg and Five Forks. He was wounded six times and two of these were nearly fatal. He entered the war in August, 1862 as Lieutenant Colonel of the Twentieth Regiment of Maine Volunteers. By May, 1863 he had been promoted to full Colonel. Two months later, he led his regiment to fame and glory with his epic struggle to defend Little Round Top at Gettysburg. His heroic actions at this battle resulted in his being awarded the coveted Medal of Honor.

After becoming seriously ill at Rappahannock Station, he was forced to convalesce, yet returned to fight again in May, 1864, in time to participate in the Spotsylvania, Cold Harbor and Petersburg Campaigns. It was at Petersburg, in June, 1864, after being severely wounded, that Ulysses S. Grant promoted him, in the field, to Brigadier General. General Grant did not expect Chamberlain to live and wanted to pay homage to this subordinate and allow him to die at that rank. But, to everyone's surprise, the tenacious fighter cheated death and returned to fight with General Sheridan on the battle for Quaker Road, where he was again wounded.

On March 29, 1865, Chamberlain was brevetted Major General, in time to take part in the bitter struggle on the White Oak Road. Here he received additional wounds on the battlefield, but stubbornly chose to remain with his beloved Fifth Corps to fight at Five Forks, where he distinguished himself once again.

Grant, in his admiration for Chamberlain, designated him to receive the first flag of surrender at Appomattox Courthouse, April 12, 1865. He was chosen to receive the formal surrender of arms and colors of the Confederate Army. At that time he rendered one of the most memorable and gallant acts of the war by giving a final salute to the soldiers of the Confederacy as they laid down their arms. General Chamberlain closed the war in a most fitting manner, by leading the Grand Review of the Army of the Potomac down Pennsylvania Avenue in Washington.

It is not surprising so many people are attracted to the great strength in the personality that made up this magnificent man. Nor is it any wonder that he is fast becoming one of America's greatest loved folk heros. There have been few men who have captured the hearts and imagination of America as has Joshua Lawrence Chamberlain. It is to his memory that this compilation is dedicated, in the hopes that it will inspire in this and generations to come, a sense of patriotism and love of country that was ever present and exemplified in the life of this beloved General. It is with this in mind, that we offer the following literary selections, compiled for you...and for generations to come.

Stan Clark
Gettysburg, PA

1

MY STORY OF FREDERICKSBURG

December of 1862 found the Army of the Potomac not in the best of cheer. After the hard-fought battle of Antietam, McClellan thought chiefly to recruit his army, and moved but slowly to follow the discomfited Lee. Before we had left that field, President Lincoln came to look over the pitiable scene and the heroic men who had made it, its dead, and themselves immortal. Being a guest at our Fifth Corps headquarters, we had the opportunity to discern something more of that great spirit than was ordinarily revealed in those rugged features and deep, sad eyes. The men conceived sympathy and an affection for him that was wonderful in its intensity. To cheer him and them, a grand review of the battered army was given. Lincoln was a good horseman, and this showed him to new advantage. He took in everything with earnest eyes. As the reviewing cavalcade passed along our lines, where mounted officers were stationed in front of their commands, he checked his mount to draw McClellan's attention to my horse, whose white-dappled color and proud bearing made me almost too conspicuous on some occasions.

Impatience at McClellan's slowness and irresolution, or some other influence at Washington, prompted the removal of this commander and the substitution of Burnside; and, as somehow a sequence of this, the removal of Fitz John Porter from command of the Fifth Corps and the appointment of Hooker to the place. Whatever justification there was for these changes, the sundering of long-familiar ties brought a strain on the heart-strings of many men, but it must be remarked in their honor that no murmuring or lack of loyal and cheerful

obedience ever betrayed their sorrow. Things were not bright-
ened when Burnside, in taking command, modestly but un-
wisely intimated his unfitness for it. There was a tendency to
take him at his word—especially among the high-ranking
generals—and the men could not help knowing it.

For another change, the army was reorganized in three
grand divisions: the right, consisting of the Second and Ninth
Corps, commanded by Sumner; the center, the Third and Fifth
Corps, commanded by Hooker; and the left, the First and Sixth
Corps, commanded by Franklin.

We were soon aware of a decided division of opinion
about the best plan for the prosecution of the campaign. Burnside
proposed to give up the pursuit of Lee's army, then gathered
mainly in the vicinity of Culpeper, and to strike for Petersburg
and Richmond. Halleck, general-in-chief, did not approve of
this, as it exposed Washington to a back stroke from Lee. Nor
did the President. Burnside then offered a compromise plan: to
cross the fords of the Rappahannock above Fredericksburg and
seize the heights around that city, making his line of supplies
the railroad between Fredericksburg and Acquia Creek on the
Potomac. Halleck still disapproved, and the President only reluctantly assented. But to the astonishment of both, Burnside,
instead of crossing at the upper fords, moved down the north
bank of the river and took position directly confronting
Fredericksburg.

LEE PREPARES A DEATH-TRAP

Burnside's intention was now manifest—to cross the
Rappahannock at this front. This would require the service of
pontoons, and the demand for them went promptly to Washington. This, of course, displeased the authorities there, a direct assault on Fredericksburg being no part of the plan approved; and there was a long wait for pontoons. In turn, this
gave Lee time to confront our purpose with his usual promptitude and skill. He seemed to have had perfect knowledge of
Burnside's movements and plans. He lost no time in seizing
the crests and wooded slopes which surround Fredericksburg,
where he strongly posted his infantry, covered by breastworks
and rifle pits. The ground afforded every advantage for his
artillery, both for cover and efficiency, and enabled him to
dispose his whole line so as to bring a front and flank fire upon

any possible assault of ours. His chief of artillery said to scrutinizing Longstreet: "Our guns are so placed that we can rake the whole field as with a fine-tooth comb. A chicken could not live on that field!" Other batteries were so directed as to sweep every pontoon bridge we could lay. At the base of the principal crest behind the city, some of Lee's best troops manned a breast-high stone wall, before which after history lays direful memories.

At last, on the 25th of November, the pontoons began to arrive. It requires skill and level heads to lay a pontoon bridge. But our brave engineers found their skill baffled and the level of their heads much disturbed by the hot fire from the well-manned rifle-pits on the opposite shore, and from the sharp-shooters in the houses above them, and had to give up the task. Then our nearest batteries opened a terrific fire on those offensive shelters and their occupants, under which some of the houses were set afire, the smoke and flame giving a wild background to the tense and stirring scene. In the tumult and shadow of this, some daring men of the 7th Michigan and the 19th Massachusetts forged to the front, manned the forsaken boats, and pushed across, driving all before them. Howard's Division soon crossed over and seized and held that portion of the town.

I may present an incident of this bombardment which impressed me at the time, and has stood vividly in memory ever since. I was near one of our upper batteries—I think Benjamin's, of the 2d Regular—observing the effect of the fire, when a staff officer of Sumner's rode up and, pointing across, bent low in his saddle and said with softened voice, "Captain, do you see that white shaft over yonder in the green field above those houses?" "I do, sir," was the reply. "That is the tomb of Washington's mother," rejoined the staff-officer. "Let your guns spare that!" "They will, sir!" was the answer, as if the guns themselves knew. I turned away, thoughtful of many things.

Next morning the bridges were laid without opposition; Lee doubtless thought his guns would do better work when crowds of men were crossing. Two bridges were in front of our right, Sumner's ground; one for us, in Hooker's front, just opposite the lower city—one being thought enough, as we were not expected to make our principal crossing there; two a mile or more below, in Franklin's front. Lee's dispositions for an offensive-defensive battle were such that it became necessary for us to cover his entire front with artillery for possible chances; so 149 guns were put in position on the north bank of the Rappahannock.

BURNSIDE'S PLAN OF BATTLE

The plan of battle was now made known to us. Sumner was to make an attack and secure a lodgement in the upper and central portion of the town; Franklin was to make the main assault a mile or two below, turn Lee's right, and take his main position in flank. To support Franklin in this, two divisions of our Third Corps were sent him, thus giving him sixty thousand effective men. Hooker, with the rest of our grand division, was to move up to the north bank, near the middle pontoon bridge, ready to cross there or to go to the support of either right or left as should be needed.

So we were held in reserve. It may be thought that we were glad to be kept out of the fight, at least for the present. But I take occasion to say that in forming for a great fight it is not regarded as a very special favor to be "held in reserve." The "holding" is, most likely, not for long; and it holds in itself peculiar stress and strain. Waiting and watching, intent and anxious, stirred by the pulse of manhood and the contagion of comradeship, conscious of strength to help, but forbidden to strike, all this wears sorely on every generous spirit. And that other not unmanly impulse—if the worst is coming, let us meet it—may have its part, too, in the drama. It is really less trying to go in first and deliver your blow in the flush of spirit and strength, with the feeling that if the worst comes you will be reenforced or "relieved," than to be held back till some dire disaster calls, when the life-and-death grapple clinches, and you must recover the lost ground or die trying. Or, on the other hand, to be called to advance in triumph over a field already carried—something then is lacking to the manly sense of service rendered according to strength.

THE DEATH-DELIVERING STONE WALL

Our division, Griffin's, of the Fifth Corps, was massed near the Lacy house, opposite the city. We could plainly see the fierce struggle of our Second and Ninth Corps; to surmount those flaming crests behind the city. Lines first steadily moving forward in perfect order and array, the flag high poised and leading; checked and broken somewhat on each successive rise under the first range of shot and shell; no musket replying—for this would have been worse than useless—but bright bayonets fixed, ready at the final reach to sweep like a sharp wave-crest over the enemy's rock-like barrier. Right on! Then, reaching the last slope before and beneath the death-delivering stone wall, suddenly illumined by a sheet of flame, and in an instant the whole line sinking as if swallowed up in earth, the bright flags quenched in gloom, and only a writhing mass marking that high-tide halt of uttermost manhood and supreme endeavor. Then a slow back-flowing, with despairing effort here and there to bear back broken bodies of the brave glorified by the baptism of blood. Again and again the bold essay repeated by other troops, with similar experience, and thickening ridges of the fallen marking the desperate essays.

There we stood for an hour, witnessing five immortal charges. Tears ran down the cheeks of stern men, waiting, almost wishing, to be summoned to the same futile, glorious work. We harkened intensely for the sound of Franklin's guns. Now was heard the exclamation of some veteran commander of ours unable to endure the agony of suspense: "For God's sake, where is Franklin! Where are the sixty thousand that were so quickly to decide this day!"

We had heard for a little while the boom of guns and a dull roar through the woods below, but all had died away, and a strange boding silence in that quarter desolated our hearts. The rumor came that Meade's Division alone had cut through the stubborn lines of Lee's right flank but, unsupported, had been driven back; and thereafter a brave onset by Gibbon's Division had met quickly a similar fate—and nothing more seemed attempted; or if so, but in vain.

Now came the call for the reserves! Burnside, despairing of the left and seeing the heroic valor on the right, at last exhausted in unavailing sacrifice, ordered in the Fifth Corps, Griffin's Division to lead. First came the silent departure of our First and Second Brigades, whose course our eyes could not follow. We waited in tremulous expectation. Not in fear, for that has little place in manhood when love and duty summon; but eager to do our best and make the finish. Few words were

spoken among officers, however endeared to each other by
confidences deepened by such pressure of life on the borders of
death as war compels; the sense of responsibility silenced all
else. Silence in the ranks, too; one little word, perhaps, telling
whom to write to. Griffin gave us a searching, wistful look, not
trusting his lips and we not needing more. Now rang forth the
thrilling bugle-cry, "Third Brigade, to the front!"

OVER THE RIVER AND UP THE HILL

We pushed for the nearby middle pontoon bridge. The
enemy's cannoneers knew the ranges perfectly. The air was
thick with the flying, bursting shells; whooping solid shot swept
lengthwise our narrow bridge, fortunately not yet plowing a
furrow through the midst of us, but driving the compressed air
so close above our heads that there was an unconquerable
instinct to shrink beneath it, although knowing it was then too
late. The crowding, swerving column set the pontoons swaying, so that the horses reeled and men could scarcely keep
their balance. Forming our line in the lower streets, the men
were ordered to unsling knapsacks, and leave them to be cared
for by our quartermaster. We began the advance. Two of our
regiments had failed to hear the last bugle-calls in the din and
roar around, and did not overtake us: we were thus the right
of the line. Our other two brigades, we heard, had gone to the
relief of Sturgis' Division of the Ninth Corps. We were directed straight forward, toward the left of the futile advance
we had seen so fearfully cut down. The fences soon compelled
us to send our horses back. The artillery fire made havoc.
Crushed bodies, severed limbs, were everywhere around, in
streets, dooryards, and gardens. Our men began to fall, and
were taken up by the faithful surgeons and hospital attendants, who also bring courage to their work.

Soon we came out in an open field. Immediately, through
the murky smoke, we saw to our right a battery swing into
position to sweep our front. It opened on us. "God help us
now! Colonel take the right wing; I must lead here!" calmly
spoke our brave Colonel Ames to me, and went to the front,
into the storm.

Now we reached the lines we were to pass for the farther goal. We picked our way amid bodies thickly strewn, some
stark and cold; some silent with slowly ebbing life; some in

sharp agony that must have voice, though unavailing; some
prone from sheer exhaustion or by final order of hopeless commander.   The living from their close-clung bosom of earth
strove to dissuade us: "It's no use, boys; we've tried that.
Nothing living can stand there; it's only for the dead!"

On we pushed, up slopes slippery with blood, miry with
repeated, unavailing tread. We reached that final crest, before
that all-commanding, countermanding stone wall.   Here we
exchanged fierce volleys at every disadvantage, until the muzzle-
flame deepened the sunset red, and all was dark. We stepped
back a little behind the shelter of this forlorn, foremost crest,
and sank to silence, perhaps—such is human weakness—to
sleep.

A BIVOUAC WITH THE DEAD

It was a cold night. Bitter, raw north winds swept the
stark slopes. The men, heated by their energetic and exciting
work, felt keenly the chilling change. Many of them had neither overcoat nor blanket, having left them with the discarded
knapsacks. They roamed about to find some garment not needed
by the dead. Mounted officers all lacked outer covering. This
had gone back with the horses, strapped to the saddles. So we
joined the uncanny quest. Necessity compels strange uses. For
myself it seemed best to bestow my body between two dead
men among the many left there by earlier assaults, and to
draw another crosswise for a pillow out of the trampled, blood-
soaked sod, pulling the flap of his coat over my face to fend off
the chilling winds, and, still more chilling, the deep, many-
voiced moan that overspread the field. It was heart-rending; it
could not be borne. I rose at midnight from my unearthly
bivouac, and taking our adjutant for companion went forth to
see what we could do for these forsaken sufferers. The deep
sound led us to our right and rear, where the fiercest of the
fight had held brave spirits too long. As we advanced over
that stricken field, the grave, conglomerate monotone resolved
itself into its diverse, several elements: some breathing inar-
ticulate agony; some dear home names; some begging for a
drop of water; some for a caring word; some praying God for
strength to bear; some for life; some for quick death. We did
what we could, but how little it was on a field so boundless for
feeble human reach! Our best was but to search the canteens

of the dead for a draft of water for the dying; or to ease the posture of a broken limb; or to compress a severed artery of fast-ebbing life that might perhaps so be saved, with what little skill we had been taught by our surgeons early in learning the tactics of saving as well as of destroying men. It was a place and time for farewells. Many a word was taken for far-away homes that otherwise might never have had one token from the field of the lost. It was something even to let the passing spirit know that its worth was not forgotten here.

Wearied with the sense of our own insufficiency, it was a relief at last to see through the murk the dusky forms of ghostly ambulances gliding up on the far edge of the field, pausing here and there to gather up its precious freight, and the low-hovering, half-covered lantern, or blue gleam of a lighted match, held close over a brave, calm face to know whether it were of the living or the dead.

We had taken bearings to lead us back to our place before the stone wall. There were wounded men lying there also, who had not lacked care. But it was interesting to observe how unmurmuring they were. That old New England habit so reluctant of emotional expression, so prompt to speak conviction, so reticent as to the sensibilities—held perhaps as something intimate and sacred—that habit of the blood had its corollary or after-glow in this reticence of complaint or murmur under the fearful sufferings and mortal anguish of the battle-field. Yet never have I seen such tenderness as brave men show to comrades when direst need befalls. I trust I show no lack of reverence for gracious spirits nor wrong to grateful memories, when confessing that this tenderness of the stern and strong recalls the Scripture phrase, "passing the love of women."

NIGHT ON THE BATTLEFIELD

Down again into our strange companionship of bed! The uncanny quest for covering was still going on around, and coming near. Once a rough but cautious hand lifted the dead man's coat-flap from my face, and a wild, ghoul-like gaze sought to read whether it was of the unresisting.

All night the winds roared. The things that caught their beat were such as were rooted to earth, or broken and shivered by man's machinery. One sound whose gloomy insistence impressed my mood was the flapping of a loosened window-blind in a forsaken brick house to our right, desolate but for a few daring or despairing wounded. It had a weird rhythm as it swung between the hoarse-answering sash and wall. To my wakened inner sense it struck a chord far deepening the theme of the eternal song of the "old clock on the stairs": "*Never—forever; forever—never!*" I still seem to hear, in lonely hours with the unforgotten, that dark refrain sounding across the anguished battlefield.

Wakened by the sharp fire that spoke the dawn, as I lifted my head from its restful though strange pillow, there fell out from the breast pocket a much-worn little New Testament written in it the owner's name and home. I could do no less than take this to my keeping, resolved that it should be sent to that home in the sweet valley of the Susquehanna as a token that he who bore it had kept the faith and fought the fight. I may add that sparing mercy allowed the wish to be fulfilled, and this evidence gave the stricken mother's name a place in the list of the nation's remembered benefactors.

Soon came a storm of bullets from front and flank to rout us from our slight shelter in the hollow between the two outermost crests of the manifold assault. This not sufficing, the artillery took up the task, trying to rain shell down upon us and sweep solid shot through our huddled group. We had to lie flat on the earth, and only by careful twisting could any man load and fire his musket against the covered line in front. Before long we saw two or three hundred of the enemy creep out from the right of their stone wall and take advantage of a gully-bank where the ground fell away from our left, to get a full flank fire on us.

The situation was critical. We took warrant of supreme necessity. We laid up a breastwork of dead bodies, to cover that exposed flank. Behind this we managed to live through the day. No man could stand up and not be laid down again hard. I saw a man lift his head by the prop of his hands and forearms, and catch a bullet in the middle of his forehead. Such recklessness was forbidden. We lay there all the long day, hearing the dismal "thud" of the bullets into the dead flesh of our life-saving bulwarks. No relief could dare to reach us: reenforcement we did not wish. We saw now and then a staff officer trying to bring orders, and his horse would be shot from under him the moment he reached the crest behind us.

We had to take things as they came, and do without the rest.

ORDERED BACK TO FREDERICKSBURG

Night came again, and midway of it the order to remove and take respite within the city. Our wounded were borne to shelter and care back near the pontoon bridge. We got our bodies ready to go, but not our minds. Our dead lay there. We could not take them where we were going, nor would we leave them as they lay. We would bury them in the earth they had made dear. Shallow graves were dug with bayonets and fragments of shell and muskets that strewed the ground. Low head-boards, made of broken fence-rails or musket-butts, rudely carved under sheltered match-light, marked each name and home.

We had to pick our way over a field strewn with incongruous ruin; men torn and broken and cut to pieces in every indescribable way, cannon dismounted, gun-carriages smashed or overturned, ammunition-chests flung wildly about, horses dead and half-dead still held in harness, accouterments of every sort scattered as by whirlwinds. It was not good for the nerves, that ghastly march, in the lowering night! We were moved to the part of the town first occupied by Sumner's troops, and bivouacked in the streets, on the stone flagging. Little sleep that night, or rest next morning. Troops of all commands were crowded in without pretension of military use or position. Consequently the Confederates began to bombard their own town. Toward night rumors came through prisoners that Stonewall Jackson was coming down from the right upon our huddled mass to crush us where we were or sweep us into the river. No doubt he could have done it. But we afterward learned that Lee did not favor the proposition, not feeling quite sure of the issue. He thought we might fight with our backs to walls as he had seen us fight before them, in the open. Rumor came also that Burnside, in his desperation, had ordered a new assault on the stone-wall front, and proposed to lead his Ninth Corps in person. But, as we afterward learned, Lincoln, hearing of this, wired, forbidding it.

Just after midnight of this miserable day we were summoned—three regiments of us—to set forth on some special service, we knew not what or where, something very serious, we must believe. Some extensive operations were

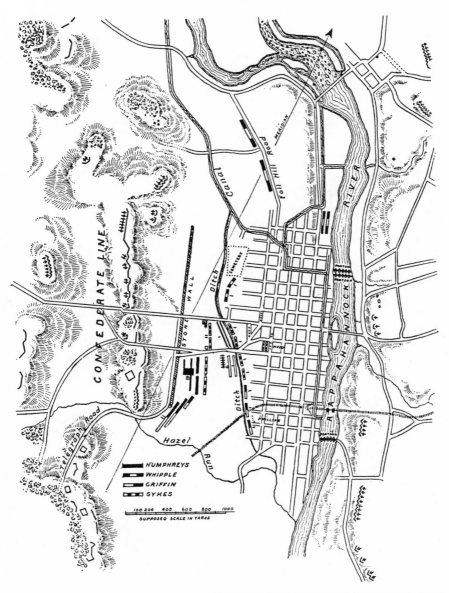

POSITION OF THE DIVISIONS OF HUMPHREYS, WHIPPLE, GRIFFIN, AND
SYKES AT THE BATTLE OF FREDERICKSBURG ON DEC. 13TH, 1862.

Lieutenant Colonel Joshua L. Chamberlain, August 1862
(Courtesy Pejepscot Historical Society)

contemplated—we were aware of that from the decided manner and movements of officers and men of all commands. But we were soon assured as to our part. We were bound for the extreme front, to form a picket-line to cover the center of the field while the army was to take some important action. Colonel Ames commanded our line, the regiment coming under my charge. The last order came in low tones, "Hold this ground at all hazards, and to the last!" A strange query crossed our minds: Last of what? No dictionary held that definition. As a general term, this reached the infinite!

REBUKED BY A REBEL PICKET

So we went to work, silently, but intently. Groping about, we laid hold of some picks and spades strewn rather hurriedly around a little to our rear earlier in the night. The men were told to settle themselves into the ground, and let it hold them for a good turn; each two, or each for himself, to throw up a little earthwork, elbow-like, behind which the morning's test might be withstood for a while. We were so near the enemy's rifle-pits that we could hear something of their conversation, from which it appeared that they were about as anxious as we were. We spoke only in whispers. The night was pitch dark. To be sure of the proper direction of our line I had to feel my way along by such tokens as instinct and prudence could provide. Hearing the gravel going at a lively rate a little out of what I thought conformity to instructions, I approached the sound and said in a very confidential tone to the invisible performer, "Throw to the other side, my man; that's where the danger is!" "Golly!" came back the confident answer, "don't ye s'pose I know which side them Yanks be? They're right onto us now." I was rebuked and instructed, but must preserve my dignity as a Confederate on "grand rounds." "Dig away then, but keep a right sharp lookout!" I said—then obeyed my own suggestion and "dug away" as calmly as my imperfect lookout would permit.

We were pretty well buried, and braced for the coming dawn, when a strange clatter came up from the left rear, and a gasping voice called, "Where is the commander of these troops?" I acknowledged that responsibility. "Get yourselves out of this quick as God will let you! The whole army is across the river!" was the message—heard, no doubt, by the whole hostile picket-line. This was a critical moment. Something must be said and done quickly. "Steady in your places, my men!" I ordered. "One or two of you arrest this stampeder! This is a ruse of the enemy! We'll give it to them in the morning!" This was spoken with no suppressed nor hesitating tone, but pitched for the benefit of our astonished neighbors in double darkness in our front. My men caught the keynote of my policy, trusted my discretion, and held themselves quiet. I stepped back to the staff officer, and rebuked him severely for his rashness, pointing out to him the state of things, vexed at having to moderate even my stress of voice. He explained. He had had such a time getting over that field and up to this front line he had almost lost his wits. I could understand this; and told him to follow for himself his message to us, and I would not report his misdemeanor.

HOW WE FINALLY LEFT THE FIELD

I sought out Ames, and we made up a manner of withdrawal: to keep up appearances; to hold the line for a time, with pretended zeal but redoubled caution; then to withdraw under a new form of tactics: every even-numbered man to resume his digging and make it lively; every odd-numbered man to step softly to the rear and form line under the second officer of the company; this half of the regiment to move back a hundred yards or so and halt in line of battle, faced to the front, and hold there till the other half, formed in like manner, should come up and pass them to a like distance; then the reciprocal movement to be repeated till we got well to the rear. These tactics proved to be wise, for the enemy, after a short, puzzled hesitation, came out from their entrenchments and followed us up as closely as they deemed safe, the same traits of human nature in them as in us causing little "nervousness" when moving in darkness and in the presence of an alert enemy, also moving.

Thus we made our way over that stricken field, with stooping walk and muskets at a "trail." It had been a misty night, with fitful rains. Just as our first reach was attained, the clouds broke apart in rifts here and there. Through one of these came a sudden gleam from the weird, waning moon, which struck full upon our bright musket-barrels, and revealed us clearly to our watchful pursuers. A bullet or two sang past us. "To the ground, every man of you!" went the quick order, and only a scattering volley sent its baffled greeting over our heads. We had to watch now for favoring clouds.

It was a dreary retreat down those wreck-strewn slopes. It was hard enough to be stumbling over torn-up sods, groups of the dead or forms of the solitary dying, muskets dropped with quick relax, or held fast with death's convulsive clutch, swords, bayonets, cartridge-boxes, fragments of everything, everywhere, but when a ghastly gleam of moonlight fell on the pale faces, fixed and stark, and on open eyes that saw not but reflected uttermost things, it sent a shiver through us.

Reaching the pontoon bridge-head just at dawn, we found that the bridge-floor had been muffled by sods and brush, that our expected night-tread might not disclose our passing to the pressing foe. We gathered what we could of what had belonged to us, taking along those of our wounded that had not gone before. But the piteous spectacle of others not of our command but belonging to us by the bond of a great brotherhood so moved our large-hearted surgeon, Doctor Hersom, that he begged permission to stay among them. This he did at the cost of being taken prisoner with dire experience of suffering for himself. Sorrowfully but proudly we left him for his ministry of mercy.

So we crossed again that bridge we had passed three days before with strange forebodings but unswerving resolution, little dreaming that we should be put to shame, but now little imputing to ourselves the blame. While waiting for the pontoons some of us had frequently ridden along the bank in full view of the Confederates across the river and through field-glasses studied the construction of their works with curious interest and the natural common-sense inference that we would never be called upon to assault just where Lee had prepared for and wished us.

WHY THE BATTLE WAS LOST

Over the river, then, we marched, and up that bank, whence we now looked back across at Fredericksburg and saw the green slopes blue with the bodies of our dead. It was raining drearily when I brought the regiment to rest by the dismal wayside. General Hooker came riding slowly by. We had not seen him during the terrible three days. Indeed, he

had no business to be where we were. We supposed he and
our corps commander, Butterfield, were somewhere controlling
and observing their commands. Hooker caught sight of me
sitting in the rain leaning back against a tree, and gave
kindly greeting. "You've had a hard chance, Colonel; I am
glad to see you out of it!" I was not cheerful, but tried to be
bright. "It was chance, General; not much intelligent design
there!" "God knows I did not put you in!" came the rather
crisp reply. "That was the trouble, General. You should have
put us in. We were handled in piecemeal, on toasting-forks."
It was plain talk. And he did not reprove me.

But the general's remark led to wide inferences. It
disclosed perhaps the main cause of this great disaster. The
commander of the center grand division "did not put his men
in!" They were sent by superior orders, in detachments, to
support other commands, or as a "forlorn hope," at various
times and places during the unexpected developments—or rather
the almost inevitable accidents—of the battle. It should not
have been a disaster; Franklin with his 60,000 men should
have turned Lee's right; whereas he attacked with only two
divisions, and one at a time, and did not follow up with his
whole force their splendid initiative. When Franklin failed, it
was rashness to expect Sumner to carry the formidable heights
behind the city, made impregnable by Lee's best skill and
valor. That front might have been held still under menace,
while Sumner, reenforced perhaps by the main body of Hooker's
grand division, might have concentrated upon Lee's left, above
the city, and flanked the formidable bastions crowning the
heights that entrenched his front with all that earth and manhood could do.

That the battle was not fought according to Burnside's
intention, and that his plan was mutilated by distrust and
disharmony among his subordinate commanders, does not ex-
onerate him. It is part of the great trust and place of a chief
commander to control reluctant and incongruous elements and
to make subordinates and opponents submit to his imperial
purpose.

Burnside attempted a vindication somewhat on these
lines; but too late. He prepared an order removing from command several of his high-ranking but too little subordinate
generals, and made ready to prefer charges against them for
trial by court-martial. But Lincoln again interposed his com-

mon-sense advice, and the matter was passed over.

Not long after, at his own request, Burnside was relieved from command of the army, and magnanimously resumed his place with his old Ninth Corps.

2

THROUGH BLOOD AND FIRE
AT GETTYSBURG

Editor's Note,—Around the little Pennsylvania town of Gettysburg, fifty years ago in July, was staged the greatest conflict ever fought on American soil. There for three days the red gods demanded homage and took toll of treasure. There the Confederacy reached its high tide; on the morrow of Gettysburg the South could only gather her broken forces and dread the certain end. But where fate would place her favor was not decided until the third day's thunder of guns had ceased to echo over the field where 6600 men had died. Each succeeding day's battle had been more desperate than the one before. On the first day only a part of each army was engaged. July 2nd witnessed the inferno of the Peach Orchard and the Round Tops. The last day was the most thrilling in our history. In this one battle was enough glory of heroism to immortalize the American soldier. The following article deals with the second day, when the slopes of the Round Tops were bathed in blood. The author, then colonel of the Twentieth Maine, was later given a Medal of Honor for his defense of these vital positions.

Nightfall brought us to Hanover, Pennsylvania, and to a halt. And it was the evening of the first day of July, 1863. All day we had been marching North from Maryland, searching and pushing out on all roads for the hoped-for collision with Lee—eagerly, hurriedly, yet cautiously, with skirmishers and flankers out to sound the first challenge, and our main body ready for the call. Fanwise our divisions had been spread out to cover Washington, but more was at stake than the

16

capitol city of the Union; there was that important political and international question, the recognition of the Southern Confederacy as independent by France and England. This recognition, denying the very contentions of the North from the beginning, would have been almost fatal to it. And Lee need not win a decided victory in the field to bring about the recognition; his capture and occupation of an important and strategic point in the North would have been enough.

All day, ever and again, we had seen detachments of Lee's cavalry; even as we passed an outlying field to our encampment the red slanting sunlight fell softly across the grim relics of a cavalry fight of the afternoon, the survivors of which had swept on, flying and pursuing.

Worn and famished we stacked arms in camping order, hoping to bivouac beside them, and scampered like madcaps for those two prime factors of a desultory supper—water and fence-rails; for the finding of which the Yankee volunteer has an aptitude which should be ranked among the spiritual intuitions, though in their old-school theology most farmers of our acquaintance were inclined to reckon the aptitude among the carnal appetites of the totally depraved. Some of the forage wagons had now got up, and there was a brief rally at their tail ends for quick justice to be dispensed. But the unregenerate fires had hardly blackened the coffee-dippers, and the hardtack hardly been hammered into working order by the bayonet-shanks, when everything was stopped short by whispers of disaster away on the left: the enemy had struck our column at Gettysburg, and driven it back with terrible loss; Reynolds, the commander, had been killed, and the remnant scarcely able to hold on to the hillsides unless rescue came before morning. These were only rumors flitting owl-like in the gathering shadows. We could not quite believe them, but they deepened our mood.

TO THE MARCH! ON TO GETTYSBURG!

Suddenly the startling bugle-call from unseen headquarters! "The General!" it rang! "To the march! No moment of delay!"

Word was coming, too. Staff officers dashed from corps, to division, to brigade, to regiment, to battery—and the order flew like the hawk, and not the owl. "To Gettysburg!" it said, a forced march of sixteen miles. But what forced it? And what opposed? Not supper, nor sleep nor sore feet and aching limbs.

In a moment, the whole corps was in marching order; rest, rations, earth itself forgotten; one thought,—to be first on that Gettysburg road. The iron-faced veterans were transformed to boys. They insisted on starting out with colors flying, so that even the night might know what manner of men were coming to redeem the day.

All things, even the most common, were magnified and made mysterious by the strange spell of night. At a turn of the road a staff officer, with an air of authority, told each colonel as he came up, that McClellan was in command again, and riding ahead of us on the road. Then wild cheers rolled from the crowding column into the brooding sky, and the earth shook under the quickened tread. Now from a dark angle of the roadside came a whisper, whether from earthly or unearthly voice one cannot feel quite sure, that the august form of Washington had been seen that afternoon at sunset riding over the Gettysburg hills. Let no one smile at me! I half believed it myself,—so did the powers of the other world draw nigh!

But there were wayside greetings such as we had never met before. We were in a free state, and among friendly people. All along the road, citizens came out to contemplate this martial array with a certain awe, and greet us with hearty welcome. But, most of all, our dark way was illumined by groups of girls in sweet attire gathered on the embowered lawns of modest homes, with lights and banners and flowers, and stirring songs whose import and effect were quite other than impersonal. Those who were not sisters of the muse of song waved their welcome in the ripple of white handkerchiefs—which token the gallant young gentlemen of the staff were prompt to take as summons to parley, and boldly rode up to meet with soft, half-tone scenes under the summer night; those meetings looked much like proposals for exchange of prisoners, or unconditional surrender. And others still, not daring quite so much, but unable to repress the gracious impulse of giving, offered their silent benediction in a cup of water. And we remembered then with what sanction it was that water had been turned to wine in Cana of Galilee!

OUR BATTLEFIELD, ATHIRST FOR BLOOD

Snatching an hour's sleep by the roadside just before dawn, we reached at about seven o'clock in the morning the heights east of Gettysburg, confronting the ground over which the lost battle of the first day had ebbed. After a little, we were moved to the left, across Rock Creek and up the Baltimore Pike to an open field more nearly overlooking the town. On our front and left were the troops of the Eleventh and First Corps; on a commanding height to our right was strongly established the Twelfth Corps of our army. Told to rest awhile, we first resumed the homely repast so sharply interrupted the evening before. Next we stretched ourselves on the ground to make up lost sleep, and rest our feet after a twenty-four hours' scarcely broken march, and get our heads level for the coming test.

We knew that a great battle was soon to be fought, a desperate and momentous one. But what much more impressed my mind was the great calm, the uncertainty of overture, and seeming lack of tactical plan for the tremendous issue. We were aware that other troops were coming up, on one side and the other; but we had no means of knowing or judging which side would take the offensive and which the defensive, or where the battle would begin. All the forenoon we had no other intimation as to this, than an order given in an impressive tone to hold ourselves ready to take part in an attack on our right; but whether to be begun by us or the enemy, we neither knew, nor could guess.

We were on Cemetery Hill, the apex of the angle made by an extended ridge, on the right bending sharply back for a mile to end in a lofty wooded crest known as Culp's Hill, and on the left running southerly from the Cemetery, declining somewhat in its course till at the distance of two miles or more it makes an abrupt and rugged rise in a rocky spur 500 feet high, named Little Round Top. This was as now the outpost of a steep and craggy peak southward, one hundred and fifty feet higher, terminating the range, named Great Round Top. These landmarks for the whole region near and far, to the west and north especially, in a military point of view commanded the entire ground available for a great battle.

Within the wings of this sharp-beaked ridge there entered and met in the town two great thoroughfares, the Baltimore Pike and the Taneytown Road, perfectly commanded by the Little Round Top. The latter road opened the direct way to Washington, and in the aspect of affairs was our only practicable line of retreat in case of disaster. Our Second Corps, Hancock's, had taken position on the ridge, from the Cemetery, southerly; and on the extension on this line our Third Corps, Sickles', was forming—its left, we were told, resting on the northern slope of Little Round Top. This formation indicated a defensive attitude for us, and deepened our confidence in Meade.

Opposite Cemetery Ridge, occupied by us, westerly, something like a mile away, is another ridge, extending from behind the upper limits of the town to nearly opposite Great Round Top. This is known as Seminary Ridge, so named from the Lutheran Seminary on its northern slope. Between these two ridges comes another great thoroughfare, the Emmitsburg Road, entering the town close past the base of Cemetery Hill—thus all three thoroughfares mentioned converged. Along this ridge Hill's Confederate Corps had established itself, and up this Emmitsburg Road from Chambersburg, Longstreet's Corps were advancing. Ewell's Confederate Corps held the town, and Early's Division extended northerly and easterly around to the front of Culp's Hill. Their attack, it is curious to observe, was from the north and east—from the direction of York and Hanover—so quickly and completely had Lee turned from his first, and so far successful, attempt to occupy the northern cities, to face the army of the Potomac now threatening their rear.

Our orders and expectations still kept us looking anxiously to the right, where the yesterday's battle had left off, and the new one was to begin. But all was as yet uncertain. We were told that General Meade was now conferring with his Corps commanders as to the best point and part for the battle to open. But this symposium was cut short, and a plan of opening announced by a thunder burst of artillery from the rocks and woods away in front of the Round Tops, where we least of all expected it. A crash of musketry followed.

DOUBLE-QUICK TO THE HAVOC OF BATTLE

So the awakening bugle, sounded "To the left! At utmost speed!" Down to the left we pushed—the whole Fifth

Corps—our brigade nearest and leading; at the double-quick, straight for the strife; not seeking roads, nor minding roughness of the ground, thorn-hedges, stone-fences, or miry swamps mid-way, earth quaking, sky ablaze, and a deepening uproar as we drew near. We soon saw that our Third Corps was not where we thought—between the Second Corps and the Round Tops—but had been moved forward a mile, it seemed, almost to the Emmitsburg Road.

The fight was desperate already. We passed along its rear, first getting a glimpse of the Peach Orchard on the right, where our troops were caught between Hill's Corps on Seminary Ridge and Longstreet's Corps fast arriving on the Emmitsburg Road;—and the havoc was terrible. We passed on to the Wheat-field where heroic men standing bright as golden grain were ravaged by Death's wild reapers from the woods. Here we halted to be shown our places. We had a momentary glimpse of the Third Corps left in front of Round Top, and the fearful struggle at the Devil's Den, and Hood's out-flanking troops swarming beyond. Our halt was brief, but our senses alert. I saw our First and Second Brigades go on to the roaring woods, between the Peach Orchard and the Wheatfield.

THE RACE TO LITTLE ROUND TOP

In another instant, a staff officer from General Warren rushed up to find Sykes, our Corps Commander, to beg him to send a brigade at least, to seize Little Round Top before the enemy's surging waves should overwhelm it. Other supplications were in the air; calling for aid everywhere. Our Vincent, soldierly and self-reliant, hearing this entreaty for Round Top, waited word from no superior, but taking the responsibility ordered us to turn and push for Round Top at all possible speed, and dashed ahead to study how best to place us. We broke to the right and rear, found a rude log bridge over Plum Run, and a rough farm-road leading to the base of the mountain. Here, as we could, we took the double-quick.

Now we learned that Warren, chief engineer of our army, sent by Meade to see how things were going on the left, drawn to Little Round Top by its evident importance, found to his astonishment that it was unoccupied except by a little group of signal-men, earnestly observing the movements over in the region of the Emmitsburg Road beyond the Devil's Den. Warren, to test a surmise, sent word to a battery of ours in position below, to throw a solid shot into a mass of woods in that vicinity. The whir of the shot overhead brought out the glitter of many musket-barrels and bayonets in the slanting sunlight—the revelation of fact, the end of dreams! In a moment more, the fierce attack fell on our Third Corps' left, lashed the Devil's Den into a seething cauldron, leaving free a large Confederate force to sweep past for the base of the Round Tops. They would make short work in taking the height, and Warren did likewise in his call for the race.

Earnestly we scanned that rugged peak which was to be the touchstone of that day's battle. It bore a rough forbidding face, wrinkled with jagged edges, bearded with mighty boulders; even the smooth spots were strewn with fragments of rock like the play-ground or battle-ground of giants in the elemental storms of old. Straggling trees wrestled with the rocks for a foot-hold; some were in a rich vein of mould and shot up stark and grim. Altogether it was a strange and solemn place, looking forlorn and barren now, but to be made rich enough soon with precious blood and far-wept tears.

As we mounted its lower gradient, Longstreet's batteries across Plum Run had us in full view, and turned their whole force upon our path, to sweep the heights free of us till their gray line, now straining towards them, could take them by foot or hand. Shells burst overhead and brought down tree-tops as the hissing fragments fell; or glanced along the shelving ledges and launched splinters of rock to multiply their terrors; solid shot swept close above our heads, their compressed, burning breath driving the men's breath like lead to the bottom of their breasts.

At that fiery moment three brothers of us were riding abreast, and a solid shot driving close past our faces disturbed me. "Boys," I said, "I don't like this. Another such shot might make it hard for mother. Tom, go to the rear of the regiment, and see that it is well closed up! John, pass up ahead and look out a place for our wounded." Tom, the youngest Lieutenant of Company G, was serving as adjutant of the regiment; John, a little older, was sent out by the Christian Commission for this battle, and I had applied for him. We had no surgeon; the old ones were gone, and the new ones not come. So I pressed him into field hospital service, with Chaplain French and the ambulance men, under charge of Hospital Steward Baker.

"HOLD THE LINE AT ALL COSTS"

As we neared the summit of the mountain, the shot so raked the crest that we had to keep our men below it to save our heads, although this did not wholly avert the visits of tree-tops and splinters of rock and iron, while the boulders and clefts and pitfalls in our path made it seem like the replica of the evil "den" across the sweetly named Plum Run.

Reaching the southern face of Little Round Top, I found Vincent there, with intense poise and look. He said with a voice of awe, as if translating the tables of the eternal law, "I place you here! This is the left of the Union line. You understand. You are to hold this ground at all costs!" I did understand—full well; but had more to learn about costs.

The regiment coming up "right in front" was put in position by a quite uncommon order, "on the right by file into line;" both that we should thus be facing the enemy when we came to a front, and also be ready to commence firing as fast as each man arrived. This is a rather slow style of formation, but this time it was needful. Knowing that we had no supports on the left, I dispatched a stalwart company under the level-headed Captain Morrill in that direction, with orders to move along up the valley to our front and left, between us and the eastern base of the Great Round Top, to keep within supporting distance of us, and to act as exigencies of the battle should require.

DO DUTY OR BE SHOT

The Twentieth Maine Regiment had 358 men equipped for duty in the ranks with twenty-eight officers. They were all well-seasoned soldiers, and what is more, well-rounded men, body and brain. One somewhat important side-note must have place here, in order properly to appreciate the mental and moral attitude of the men before us. One hundred and twenty of these men from the Second Maine were recruits, whom some recruiting officer had led into the belief that they should be discharged with their regiment at the end of its term of service. In their enthusiasm they had not noticed that they were signing enlistment papers for "three years of the

war"; and when they had been held in the field after the
discharge of the regiment they had refused to do military duty,
and had been sequestrated in a prisoners' camp as mutineers,
waiting court-martial. The exigency of our movement the last
of May had not permitted this semi-civil treatment; and orders
from the Secretary of War had directed me to take these men
up on my rolls and put them to duty. This made it still harder
for them to accept, as they had never enlisted in this regiment.
However, they had been soon brought over to me under the
guard of the One Hundred and Eighteenth Pennsylvania, with
fixed bayonets; with orders to me to take them into my regiment and "make them do duty, or shoot them down the moment they refused;" these had been the very words of the
Corps Commander in person. The responsibility, I had thought,
gave me some discretionary power. So I had placed their
names on our rolls, distributed them by groups, to equalize
companies, and particularly to break up the "esprit de corps"
of banded mutineers. Then I had called them together and
pointed out to them the situation: that they could not be enter-
tained as civilian guests by me; that they were by authority of
the United States on my rolls as soldiers, and I should treat
them as soldiers should be treated; that they should lose no
rights by obeying orders, and I would see what could be done
for their claim. It is pleasant to record that all but one or two
had gone back manfully to duty, to become some of the best
soldiers in the regiment, as I was to prove this very day.

NOT A MAN WAVERS NOW

The exigency was great. I released the pioneers and
provost guards altogether, and sent them to their companies.
All but the drummer boys and hospital attendants went into
the ranks. Even the cooks and servants not liable to such
service, asked to go in. Others whom I knew to be sick or
footsore, and had given a pass to "fall out" on the forced
marches of the day and night before, came up, now that the
battle was on, dragging themselves along on lame and bleeding feet, finding their regiment with the sagacity of the brave,
and their places where need is greatest and hearts truest.
"Places?" Did any of these heroic men ever leave
them?—although for all too many we passed their names at
evening roll call thereafter, with only the heart's answer, "Here

forever!"

Our line looked towards the Great Round Top, frowning above us not a gunshot away, and raising grave thoughts of what might happen if the enemy should gain foothold there, even if impracticable for artillery. We had enough of that, as it was. For the tremendous cannonade from across the Plum Run gorge was still pounding the Little Round Top crests; happily, not as yet striking my line, which it would have enfiladed if it got the range.

The other regiments of the brigade were forming on our right; the Eighty-third Pennsylvania, the Forty-fourth New York and the Sixteenth Michigan. I was observing and meditating as to the impending and the possible, when something of the real was substituted by a visit from Colonel Rice. He thought it would be profitable for us to utilize these few minutes by going to the clearer space on the right of the regiment to take a look at the aspect of things in the Plum Run valley—the direction of the advance on our front. It was a fore-warning indeed. The enemy had already turned the Third Corps left, the Devil's Den was a smoking crater, the Plum Run gorge was a whirling maelstrom; one force was charging our advance batteries near the Wheat-field; the flanking force was pressing past the base of the Round Tops; all rolling towards us in tumultuous waves.

It was a stirring, not to say, appalling sight: here a whole battery of shot and shell cutting a ragged chasm through a serried mass, flinging men and horses like drift aside; there, a rifle volley at close range, with reeling shock, hands tossed in air, muskets dropped with death's quick relax, or clutched with last, convulsive energy, men falling like grass before the scythe—others with manhood's proud calm and rally; there, a little group kneeling above some favorite officer slain,—his intense spirit still animating the fiery steed pressing headlong with empty saddle to the van; here, a defiant regiment of ours, broken, slaughtered, captured; or survivors, of both sides crouching among the rocks for shelter from the terrible cross-fire where there is no rear! But all advancing—all the frenzied force, victors and vanquished, each scarcely knowing which—surging and foaming towards us; death around, behind, before, and madness everywhere!

Yes, brave Rice! It was well for us to see this; the better to see it through. A look into each other's eyes; without a word, we resumed our respective places.

A LULL, THEN THE CRASH OF HELL

Ten minutes had not passed. Suddenly, the thunder of artillery and the crash of iron that had all the while been roaring over the Round Top crests stopped short.

We understood this, too. The storming lines, that had swept past the Third Corps' flank, had got up the base of Little Round Top, and under the range and reach of their guns. They were close upon us among the rocks, we knew, unseen, because so near. In a minute more came the roll of musketry. It struck the exposed right center of our brigade.

Promptly answered, repulsed, and renewed again and again, it soon reached us, still extending. Two brigades of Hood's Division had attacked—Texas and Alabama. The Fourth Alabama reached our right, the Forty-seventh Alabama joined and crowded in, but gradually, owing to their echelon advance. Soon seven companies of this regiment were in our front. We had all we could stand. My attention was sharply called, now here, now there. In the thick and smoke, Lieutenant Nichols, a bright officer near our center, ran up to tell me something queer was going on in his front, behind those engaging us.

THE GRAY IS FLANKING US!

I sprang forward, mounted a great rock in the midst of his company line, and was soon able to resolve the "queer" impression into positive knowledge. Thick groups in gray were pushing up along the smooth dale between the Round Tops in a direction to gain our left flank. There was no mistaking this. If they could hold our attention by a hot fight in front while they got in force on that flank, it would be bad for us and our whole defence. How many were coming we could not know. We were rather too busy to send out a reconnaissance. If a strong force should gain our rear, our brigade would be caught as by a mighty shears-blade, and be cut and crushed. What would follow it was easy to foresee. This must not be. Our orders to hold that ground had to be liberally interpreted. That front had to be held, and that rear covered. Something must be done,—quickly and cooly. I called the captains and told them my tactics: to keep the front fire at the hottest, without special regard to its need or immediate effect, and at the same time, as they found opportunity, to take side steps to the left, coming gradually into one rank, file-closers and all. Then I took the colors with their guard and placed them at our extreme left, where a great boulder gave token and support; thence bending back at a right angle the whole body gained ground leftward and made twice our original front. And were not so long doing it. This was a difficult movement to execute under such a fire, requiring coolness as well as heat. Of rare quality were my officers and men. I shall never cease to admire and honor them for what they did in this desperate crisis.

TO THE RESCUE OR ALL IS LOST!

Now as an important element of the situation, let our thought turn to what was going on meanwhile to the right of us. When Warren saw us started for Little Round Top, looking still intently down, he saw Hood's two brigades breaking past the Third Corps' left and sweeping straight for Little Round Top. Then he flew down to bring reinforcement for this vital place and moment. He came upon the One Hundred and Fortieth New York, of Weed's Brigade of our Second Division, just going into Sickles' relief, and dispatched it headlong for Round Top. Weed was to follow, and Ayres' whole division—but not yet. Warren also laid hold of Hazlett, with his battery, D of the Fifth Regulars, and sent him to scale those heights—if in the power of man so to master nature. Meantime the tremendous blow of the Fourth and Fifth Texas struck the right of our brigade, and our Sixteenth Michigan reeled and staggered back under the shock. Confusion followed. Vincent felt that all was lost, unless the very gods should intervene. Sword aloft and face aflame, he rushed in among the broken companies in desperate effort to rally them, man by man. By sheer force of his superb personality he restored a portion of his line, and was urging up the rest. "Don't yield an inch now, men, or all is lost!" he cried, when an answering volley scorched the very faces of the men, and Vincent's soul went up in a chariot of fire. In that agonizing moment came tearing up the One Hundred and Fortieth New York, gallant O'Rorke at the head. Not waiting to load a musket or form a line, they sprang forward into that turmoil. Met by a withering volley that killed its fine young colonel and laid low many of his intrepid officers and a hundred of his men, this splendid regiment, as by a providence we may well call divine, saved us all in that moment of threatened doom.

To add a tragic splendor to this dark scene, in the midst of it all, the indomitable Hazlett was trying to get his guns—ten pounder rifled Parrotts—up to a working place on the summit close beyond. Finally he was obliged to take his horses entirely off, and lift his guns by hand and handspike up the craggy steep, whence he launched death and defiance wide and far around.

The roar of all this tumult reached us on the left, and heightened the intensity of our resolve. Meanwhile the flanking column worked around to our left and joined with those before us in a fierce assault, which lasted with increasing fury for an intense hour. The two lines met and broke and mingled in the shock. The crush of musketry gave way to cuts and thrusts, grapplings and wrestlings. The edge of conflict swayed to and fro, with wild whirlpools and eddies. At times I saw around me more of the enemy than of my own men; gaps opening, swallowing, closing again with sharp convulsive energy; squads of stalwart men who had cut their way through us, disappearing as if translated. All around, strange, mingled roar—shouts of defiance, rally, and desperation; and underneath, murmured entreaty and stifled moans; gasping prayers, snatches of Sabbath song, whispers of loved names; everywhere men torn and broken, staggering, creeping, quivering on the earth, and dead faces with strangely fixed eyes staring stark into the sky. Things which cannot be told—nor dreamed.

How men held on, each one knows—not I. But manhood commands admiration. There was one fine young fellow, who had been cut down early in the fight with a ghastly wound across his forehead, and who I had thought might possibly be saved with prompt attention. So I had sent him back to our little field hospital, at least to die in peace. Within a half-hour, in a desperate rally I saw that noble youth amidst the rolling smoke as an apparition from the dead, with bloody bandage for the only covering of his head, in the thick of the fight, high-borne and pressing on as they that shall see death no more. I shall know him when I see him again, on whatever shore!

THE COLORS STAND ALONE

So, too, another. In the very deepest of the struggle while our shattered line had pressed the enemy well below their first point of contact, and the struggle to regain it was fierce, I saw through a sudden rift in the thick smoke our colors standing alone. I first thought some optical illusion imposed upon me. But as forms emerged through the drifting smoke, the truth came to view. The cross-fire had cut keenly; the center had been almost shot away; only two of the color guard had been left, and they fighting to fill the whole space; and in the center, wreathed in battle smoke, stood the Color-Sergeant, Andrew Tozier. His color-staff planted in the ground at his side, the upper part clasped in his elbow, so holding the flag upright, with musket and cartridges seized from the fallen comrade at his side he was defending his sacred trust in the manner of the songs of chivalry. It was a stirring picture—its import still more stirring. That color must be saved, and that center too. I sent first to the regiment on our right for a dozen men to help us here, but they could not spare a man. I then called my young brother, Tom, the adjutant, and sent him forward to close that gap somehow; if no men could be drawn from neighboring companies, to draw back the salient angle and contract our center. The fire down there at this moment was so hot I thought it impossible for him to get there alive; and I dispatched immediately after him Sergeant Thomas whom I had made a special orderly, with the same instructions. It needed them both; and both came back with personal proofs of the perilous undertaking. It was strange that the enemy did not seize that moment and point of weakness. Perhaps they saw no weakness. Perhaps it was awe or admiration that held them back from breaking in upon that sublime scene.

When that mad carnival lulled,—from some strange instinct in human nature and without any reason in the situation that can be seen—when the battling edges drew asunder, there stood our little line, groups and gaps, notched like saw-teeth, but sharp as steel, tempered in infernal heats like a magic sword of the Goths. We were on the appointed and entrusted line. We had held ground—"at all costs!"

But sad surprise! It had seemed to us we were all the while holding our own, and had never left it. But now that the smoke dissolved, we saw our dead and wounded all out in front of us, mingled with more of the enemy. They were scattered all the way down to the very feet of the baffled hostile line now rallying in the low shrubbery for a new onset. We could not wait for this. They knew our weakness now. And they were gathering force. No place for tactics now! The appeal must be to primal instincts of human nature!

DOWN THE DEATH-STREWN SLOPE!

"Shall they die there, under the enemy's feet, and under your eyes?" Words like those brokenly uttered, from heart to heart, struck the stalwart groups holding together for a stand, and roused them to the front quicker than any voice or bugle of command. These true-hearted men but a little before buffeted back and forth by superior force, and now bracing for a dubious test, dashed down the death-strewn slope into the face of the rallied and recovering foe, and hurled them, tore them from above our fallen as the tiger avenges its young. Nor did they stop till they had cleared the farthest verge of the field, redeemed by the loving for the lost—the brave for the brave.

Now came a longer lull. But this meant, not rest, but thought and action. First, it was to gather our wounded, and bear them to the sheltered lawn for saving life, or peace in dying; the dead, too, that not even our feet should do them dishonor in the coming encounter. Then—such is heavenly human pity—the wounded of our Country's foes; brothers in blood for us now, so far from other caring; borne to like refuge and succor by the drummer-boys who had become angels of the field.

In this lull I took a turn over the dismal field to see what could be done for the living, in ranks or recumbent; and came upon a manly form and face I well remembered. He was a sergeant earlier in the field of Antietam and of Fredericksburg; and for refusing to perform some menial personal service for a bullying quartermaster in winter camp, was reduced to the ranks by a commander who had not carefully investigated the case. It was a degradation, and the injustice of it rankled in his high-born spirit. But his well-bred pride would not allow him to ask for justice as a favor. I had kept this in mind, for early action. Now he was lying there, stretched on an open front where a brave stand had been made, face to the sky, a

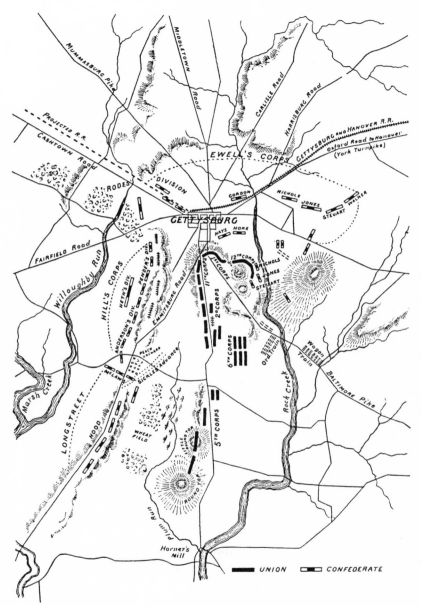

BATTLE-FIELD OF GETTYSBURG, PA., JULY 2, 1863.

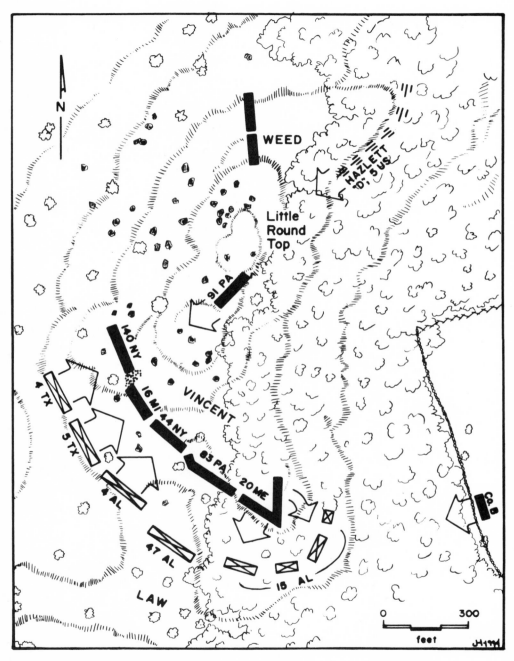

Position of Vincent's Brigade, Fifth Army Corps, on the extreme left flank of the Union Army on July 2, 1863.

great bullet-hole in the middle of his breast, from which he had loosened the clothing, to ease his breathing, and the rich blood was pouring in a stream. I bent down over him. His face lightened; his lips moved. But I spoke first, "My dear boy, it has gone hard with you. You shall be cared for!" He whispered, "Tell my mother I did not die a coward!" It was the prayer of home-bred manhood poured out with his life blood. I knew and answered him, "You die a sergeant. I promote you for faithful service and noble courage on the field of Gettysburg!" This was all he wanted. No word more. I had him borne from the field, but his high spirit had passed to its place. It is needless to add that as soon as a piece of parchment could be found after that battle, a warrant was made out promoting George Washington Buck to sergeant in the terms told him; and this evidence placed the sad, proud mother's name on the rolls of the Country's benefactors.

MY LIFE HANGS ON AN IMPULSE

As for myself, so far I had escaped. How close an escape I had had I did not know till afterwards. I think I may mention here, as a psychological incident, that some years after the war, I received a letter written in a homely but manly style by one subscribing himself "a member of the Fifteenth Alabama," in these words:

Dear Sir: I want to tell you of a little passage in the battle of Round Top, Gettysburg, concerning you and me, which I am now glad of. Twice in that fight I had your life in my hands. I got a safe place between two rocks, and drew bead fair and square on you. You were standing in the open behind the center of your line, full exposed. I knew your rank by your uniform and your actions, and I thought it a mighty good thing to put you out of the way. I rested my gun on the rock and took steady aim. I started to pull the trigger, but some queer notion stopped me. Then I got ashamed of my weakness and went through the same motions again. I had you, perfectly certain. But that same queer something shut right down on me. I couldn't pull the trigger, and, gave it up—that is, your life. I am glad of it now, and hope you are. Yours Truly.

I thought he was that, and answered him accordingly,

asking him to come up North and see whether I was worth what he missed. But my answer never found him, nor could I afterwards.

THE LAST CARTRIDGE AND BARE STEEL

The silence and the doubt of the momentary lull were quickly dispelled. The formidable Fifteenth Alabama, repulsed and as we hoped dispersed, now in solid and orderly array—still more than twice our numbers—came rolling through the fringe of chaparral on our left. No dash; no yells; no demonstration for effect; but settled purpose and determination! We opened on them as best we could. The fire was returned, cutting us to the quick.

The Forty-seventh Alabama had rallied on our right. We were enveloped in fire, and sure to be overwhelmed in fact when the great surge struck us. Whatever might be otherwhere, what was here before us was evident; these far-outnumbering, confident eyes, yet watching for a sign of weakness. Already I could see the bold flankers on their right darting out and creeping catlike under the smoke to gain our left, thrown back as it was. It was for us, then, once for all. Our thin line was broken, and the enemy were in rear of the whole Round Top defense—infantry, artillery, humanity itself—with the Round Top and the day theirs.

Now, too, our fire was slackening; our last rounds of shot had been fired; what I had sent for could not get to us. I saw the faces of my men, one after another, when they had fired their last cartridge, turn anxiously towards mine for a moment; then square to the front again. To the front for them lay death; to the rear what they would die to save. My thought was running deep. I was combining the elements of a "forlorn hope," and had just communicated this to Captain Spear of the wheeling flank, on which the initiative was to fall. Just then—so will a little incident fleck a brooding cloud of doom with a tint of human tenderness—brave, warm-hearted Lieutenant Melcher, of the Color Company, whose Captain and nearly half of his men were down, came up and asked if he might take his company and go forward and pick up one or two of his men left wounded on the field, and bring them in before the enemy got too near. This would be a most hazardous move in itself, and in this desperate moment, we could not break our line. But I admired him. With a glance, he understood, I answered, "Yes, sir, in a moment! I am about to order a charge!"

Not a moment was about to be lost! Five minutes more of such a defensive, and the last roll-call would sound for us! Desperate as the chances were, there was nothing for it, but to take the offensive. I stepped to the colors. The men turned towards me. One word was enough,—"BAYONET!"—It caught like fire, and swept along the ranks. The men took it up with a shout, one could not say, whether from the pit, or the song of the morning star! It was vain to order "Forward." No mortal could have heard it in the mighty hosanna that was winging the sky. Nor would he wait to hear. There are things still as of the first creation, "whose seed is in itself." The grating clash of steel in fixing bayonets told its own story; the color rose in front; the whole line quivered for the start; the edge of the left-wing rippled, swung, tossed among the rocks, straightened, changed curve from scimitar to sickle-shape; and the bristling archers swooped down upon the serried host—down into the face of half a thousand! Two hundred men!

It was a great right wheel. Our left swung first. The advancing foe stopped, tried to make a stand amidst the trees and boulders, but the frenzied bayonets pressing through every space forced a constant settling to the rear. Morrill with his detached company and the remnants of our valorous sharpshooters who had held the enemy so long in check on the slopes of the Great Round Top, now fell upon the flank of the retiring crowd, and it turned to full retreat—some amidst the crags of Great Round Top, but most down the smooth vale towards their own main line on Plum Run. This tended to mass them before our center. Here their stand was more stubborn. At the first dash the commanding officer I happened to confront, coming on fiercely, sword in one hand, and big navy revolver on the other, fires one barrel almost in my face; but seeing the quick saber-point at his throat, reverses arms, gives sword and pistol into my hands and yields himself prisoner. I took him at his word, but could not give him further attention. I passed him over into the custody of a brave sergeant at my side, to whom I gave the sword as emblem of his authority, but kept the pistol with its loaded barrels, which I thought might come handy soon, as indeed it did.

Ranks were broken; many retired before us somewhat hastily; some threw their muskets to the ground—even loaded;

sunk on their knees, threw up their hands, calling out, "We surrender. Don't kill us!" As if we wanted to do that! We kill only to resist killing. And these were manly men, whom we could befriend, and by no means kill, if they came our way in peace and good will. Charging right through and over these, we struck the second line of the Forty-seventh Alabama doing their best to stand, but offering little resistance. Their Lieutenant-Colonel as I passed—and a fine gentleman was Colonel Bulger—introduced himself as my prisoner, and as he was wounded, I had him cared for as best we could. Still swinging to the right as a great gate on its hinges, we swept the front clean of assailants. We were taking in prisoners by the scores—more than we could hold, or send to the rear, so that many made final escape up Great Round Top. Half way down to the throat of the vale I came upon Colonel Powell of the Fourth Alabama, a man of courtly bearing, who was badly wounded. I sent him to the Eighty-third Pennsylvania, nearest to us and better able to take care of him than we were.

TWO FOR EVERY MAN OF US

When we reached the front of the Forty-fourth New York, I thought it far enough. Beyond on the right the Texas Brigade had rallied or rendezvoused, I took thought of that. Most of the fugitives before us, rather than run the gauntlet of our whole brigade, had taken the shelter of the rocks of Great Round Top, on our left, as we now faced. It was hazardous to be so far out, in the very presence of so many baffled but far from beaten veterans of Hood's renowned division. A sudden rush on either flank might not only cut us off, but cut in behind us and seize that vital point which it was our orders and our trust to hold. But it was no light task to get our men to stop. They were under the momentum of their deed. They thought they were "on the road to Richmond." They had to be reasoned with, persuaded, but at last faced about and marched back to that dedicated crest with swelling hearts.

Not without sad interest and service was the return. For many of the wounded had to be gathered up. There was a burden, too, of the living. Nearly four hundred prisoners remained in our hands—two for every man of ours.

THE FAREWELL MESSENGERS

Shortly the twilight deepened, and we disposed ourselves to meet any new assault that might come from the courage of exasperation. But the attack was not renewed. Whether that cold steel had chilled the ardor, which flaming muzzles seem to enliven and sustain, or the revulsion of the retiring mood was not yet over, a wide silence brooded over the hostile line. Our worn-out men, bid at last to rest, fitted themselves to their environment or followed their souls' behest. Some bent as if senseless to the earth, some gazed up at the stars and sent wireless messages through them to dear ones far-away; some wandered dreamily away in a search for water to wash from their throats the nitrous fumes of battle; others too manly to seek a surgeon, looked even for a shred of cartridge paper to staunch a too free wound, or yet more deeply drawn sought the sheltered nook where our wounded had been borne to render such aid as they could, and take the farewell message home from lips of brave men to hearts that had to be more brave.

At nine o'clock the next morning we were withdrawn, being relieved by our First Brigade. But we were sent to anything but a place of rest. Our new position was in support of Hancock's troops near the left center of the Union line, which proved to be the point aimed at by Pickett's charge that afternoon.

This is the story of my participation in the action and the passion of the second day at Gettysburg.

It was certainly a narrow chance for us, and for the Round Tops. Had we not used up our ammunition, and had we continued to meet the enemy musket to musket, this "give and take" would soon have finished us by reason of the enemy's superior numbers. Or had the Fifteenth Alabama continued their onset not regarding our preposterous demonstrations, they would have walked over our bodies to their victory. Or, still again, if one more Confederate regiment had come upon our flank, we must have been rolled into a zero figure and swallowed up in the envelopment. It was a psychological success,—a miracle in the scheme of military science. Those brave Alabama fellows—none braver or better in either army—were victims of a surprise, of their quick and mobile imagination.

Return we now to our field and our parting. On the

Fourth of July we took part in a reconnaissance over the wreck-strewn field amidst scene of insupportable horror. Pushing out as far as Willoughby's Run, finding no enemy, we returned to our ground. We were now told to rest and be ready to move from the field the next day.

DEATH'S SOFT WHISPER

But there was neither removal nor rest for us, till we had gone up the Round Top slopes to bid farewell to our dead. We found them there on the sheltered lawn where we had laid them, on the velvet moss fringed by low cedars that veiled the place with peace and beauty. I rode up near, and flinging the rein upon my horse's neck, dismounted to bend over them for a soldier's farewell. There they lay, side by side, with touch of elbow still; brave, bronzed faces where the last thought was written: manly resolution, heroic self-giving, divine reconciliation; or where on some young face the sweet mother look had come out under death's soft whisper.

We buried them there, in a grave, alas, too wide, on the sunny side of a great rock, eternal witnesses of their worth—the rock and the sun. Rude head-boards, made of ammunition boxes, rudely carved under tear-dimmed eyes, marked and named each grave, and told each home.

I went—it is not long ago—to stand again upon that crest whose one day's crown of fire has passed into the blazoned coronet of fame; to look again upon the rocks whereon were laid as on the altar the lives of Vincent and O'Rorke, of Weed and Hazlett—all the chief commanders. And farther on, where my own young heroes mounted to fall no more—Billings, the valor of whose onward-looking eyes not death itself could quench; Kendall, almost maiden-sweet and fair, yet heeding not the bolts that dashed his life-blood on the rocks; Estes and Steele, and Noyes and Buck, lifted high above self, pure in heart as they that shall see God; and far up the rugged sides of Great Round Top, swept in darkness and silence like its own, where the impetuous Linscott halted at last before the morning star.

I thought of those other noble men of every type, commanders all, who bore their wounds so bravely—many to meet their end on later fields—and those on whose true hearts further high trusts were to be laid. Nor did I forget those others, whether their names are written on the scrolls of honor and fame, or their dust left on some far field and nameless here—nameless never to me, nor nameless, I trust in God, where they are to-night.

I sat there alone, on the storied crest, till the sun went down as it did before over the misty hills. and the darkness crept up the slopes, till from all earthly sight I was buried as with those before. But oh, what radiant companionship rose around, what steadfast ranks of power, what bearing of heroic souls. Oh, the glory that beamed through those nights and days. Nobody will ever know it here!—I am sorry most of all for that. The proud young valor that rose above the mortal, and then at last was mortal after all; the chivalry of hand and heart that in other days and other lands would have sent their names ringing down in song and story!

UNFORGOTTEN SONS OF GOD

They did not know it themselves—those boys of ours whose remembered faces in every home should be cherished symbols of the true, for life or death—what were their lofty deeds of body, mind, heart, soul, on that tremendous day.

Unknown—but kept! The earth itself shall be its treasurer. It holds something of ours besides graves. These strange influences of material nature, its mountains and seas, its sunset skies and nights of stars, its colors and tones and odors, carry something of the mutual, reciprocal. It is a sympathy. On that other side it is represented to us as suffering. The whole creation, travailing in pain together, in earnest expectation, waiting for the adoption—having right, then, to something which is to be its own.

And so these Gettysburg hills, which lifted up such splendid valor, and drank in such high heart's blood, shall hold the mighty secret in their bosom till the great day of revelation and recompense, when these heights shall flame again with transfigured light—they, too, have part in that adoption, which is the manifestation of the sons of God!

3

REMINISCENCES OF
PETERSBURG AND APPOMATTOX

I am honored that you think it of interest to hear the recital of some impressions made upon me by a recent visit to Petersburg and Appomattox Courthouse, Virginia, the first and the last battle-fields of the final campaign of the Army of the Potomac and the Army of Northern Virginia.

I have no reason to expect that what most drew my interest there will equally command, or deserve, yours. My motive was primarily personal; to assure myself as to two certain points on those fields, the last visions of which had left my memory somewhat clouded,—the one, with the sudden overcast of my own early down-going amidst storm and disaster; the other, with the thrilling phantasmagoria of the consummation. I am not trying to write history; nor, indeed, to write at all. I am yielding to the mood of the hour; letting these scenes review me as much as I them,—what is unchanged testing the changed. Pardon me if the personal element in this recital may seem a blemish upon the description.

I wished especially to revisit the ground of the first few days' fighting before Petersburg, in June, 1864. This embraced scarcely more than a tenth part of what afterwards became our entrenched line. But we do not quite realize what storied and bloody ground that first three days' fighting made. The Union losses within those days were a hundred and twenty-eight in a thousand. Compare this with other fields more famous; with our losses at Spotsylvania, for example, which in the whole struggle were in the ratio of a hundred and eight to a thousand; or with that at the slaughter-pen of Cold Harbor, which was a hundred and eleven in a thousand. This higher rate of a hundred and twenty-eight in a thousand shows sharp work for our first dash at Petersburg, and the casualty list of ten thousand men of those engaged in that overture gives this some rank among battles and battle-fields, without counting what followed in the long siege and sojourn there.

It may seem strange that on my return from a somewhat protracted removal, I should not have taken early occasion to visit this region in cool blood,—if there was any of that left,—in order to find justification of my former opinion as to the nature of that position, and that attack. The explanation is two-fold: first that immediately on my return I was sent to the extreme left of our ever leftward creeping line, and in that way was so closely occupied until the end of it all, that I could not get a day off for seeing old curiosities; and the other reason, quite as effective,—that during the whole feverish siege thereafter, the conditions were not encouraging; no man could show his head above the parapets or outside the bomb-proofs and keep it level a moment, unless with, and of the dead;—the two limits of my early operations having been appropriately named by those later domiciled there, Fort Hell and Fort Damnation, two places, or conditions, I desired to form the habit of avoiding.

The relations which your kindness has established for this occasion makes me desirous of bringing them still nearer, that our minds may take up this review from the same point of vision. In other words, I desire to recall to your minds the reason and manner in which we came to be here at all.

The movement on Petersburg, as you know, was intended to be a surprise, and a success. The old plan of operations,—across the Virginia rivers, Richmond the objective, with the perpetual side-issue of "not uncovering Washington," which made our successive steps of advance a zig-zag, like the knight's move on the chess-board, and our whole grand tactics a horizontal ricochet along the enemy's front from left to right, a series of operations of which Grant had said he would "fight it out on this line, if it took all summer,"—had been pretty thoroughly executed. A most memorable summer it made for us; and a casualty list of seventy thousand men indicated that it had been "fought out" pretty well by our army. Certainly some climax had been reached in Grant's mind; for he suddenly and courageously changed his plan altogether; swinging his army across the James River, for a bold dash to flank Richmond by way of Petersburg, cutting Lee's communications and forcing him from his base instead of consolidating him upon it. This was a masterly move, and ought to have been successful. Strikingly it was so at the first. The advance of our army got fairly in front of Petersburg before Lee knew we were across the James. Beauregard was then holding the defences of Petersburg, with only Wise's Legion, of twenty-four hundred men, and Dearing's cavalry and some picked-up men, about as many more. We could have walked right into the city at the first dash; and would have done it, as the desperate valor and direful cost two days afterwards proved.

But Grant expected Butler to do this, from his advantageous position on the James, near by. Indeed, the Eighteenth Corps under "Baldy" Smith did make a successful attack from this direction, carrying the enemy's works on the northeast side of the city, but then strangely stopped. Meade had not been told that his army was to take a direct part with Butler, but ordered Hancock, with our Second Corps, as soon as he got rations after crossing, to proceed to a designated spot, which proved to be incorrectly laid down on the maps, and if it had any existence at all was miles away from his proper direction and inside the enemy's lines. In this situation Hancock was overtaken by an order from Grant to go to the assistance of Smith, but arrived only after dark, when it was in Smith's opinion too late to follow up his advantage. Had Meade been informed of what might be expected, Hancock and the Second Corps would have been inside of Petersburg when the sunset gilded its spires, and the fate of that field and of many a man in our army would have been far different from what followed. This matter never has been understood. Grant, we knew, was much vexed at the turn of things this day; but was wonderfully patient, as if blaming nobody but himself.

Thus the golden moment was lost. Our several corps, meanwhile, crossing the James by pontoons and transports, marching day and night, coming up successively into position as "on the right into line," attacked as soon as each found the enemy's front. This was not difficult to find, for Lee was now rapidly reinforcing Beauregard, so that each corps as it came up had to meet at least an equal number of Lee's old army, on interior lines, well covered by strong entrenchments. The Second and the Ninth Corps worked in their own stalwart fashion, forcing the enemy's advanced positions. Our Fifth Corps came up on the next night, and passing in the rear of these, attacked on the left; but by that time all Lee's army were before us. So we had to take up the old game,—the eternal feeling to the left, with continuous, costly, fruitless engagements, in wearisome monotony. The conditions of the situation compelling us to throw up breastworks, our entrenched line came to extend more than sixteen miles, and we were forced to "sit down" as it is whimsically called,—and in this case most literally, and in rather hard-bottomed chairs,—to an irregular siege of more than nine months. And in all that time we got no nearer Petersburg than we were on the eighteenth of June, 1864, and not until Lee was flanked at Five Forks, April 1, 1865.

Quite different this from a "surprise." And with experiences not yet written in history, though grimly registered by nature herself in a thousand fantastic forms far outstrewn, making the dreary stretch seem like a haunted land. And truly indeed may it be so; when we remember that twenty-two thousand brave spirits of ours left their bodies there behind those tree-clumps and on the slopes before those rueful works of man.

Now thirty-nine years was time enough to cool one's blood, so as to gather the various data for mature judgment more reliable perhaps than confused recollections of personal experience. Reminding myself, too, that things, also as well as men, may change somewhat in that lapse of years, I deemed it expedient to take a guide, and one a little more calm and collected than those of previous occasions there, when the staff officers bringing orders scarcely dared to lift their chins from their breast-bones. So I got an intelligent citizen of Petersburg who had made a special study of this ground and its history, to take me in his much-enduring, gig-like vehicle along the strangely half-hidden lines, whose wonted tumult seemed to me only half-hushed, waiting the moment to burst into roar and flame.

We first drove out over the old Confederate ground to the vicinity of the "Hare house," the scene of repeated desperate struggle, begun and continued by our Second Corps. The thing that most took my attention was a shapely white monument shining in the midst of a grove of young oaks sombered with the tints of autumn. Seeking a nearer view, I was deeply moved to find it the monument of the 1st Maine Heavy Artillery, serving here then as infantry, and serving ever since, I

may say, as high example of heroic valor. It marks the scene
of a gallant fight,—or, in more exact statement, of superb
courage and sublime obedience in making a charge against
overwhelming odds under an order which should not have been
given. The regimental association, I was told, had bought five
acres of this storied ground, and set up this monument to the
immortal honor of more than six hundred of its men who fell in
that one onset, and were buried in the earth beneath, uptorn
by plunging shot and shell. This memorial is the more impressive for being the only monument erected as such,—with thoughtful purpose, and honoring remembrance, on the entire field.
The sight of it was a fitting overture for the tragic reminiscences of the day before me. This, indeed, was the
surprise,—that so broad a field of heroic devotion and costly
sacrifice should call for no monuments to perpetuate remembrance or consecrate ground. It seems to fall out of view, like
"patient continuance in well-doing."

The first broad aspect of this ground is not impressive;
there is so much of it, and of such sameness or repetition.
Large stretches of rolling surface; gently confronting slopes
descending to some branch or run draining the rain-wash and
underground springs towards the tributaries of the Appomattox.
Only rarely a house or hut, and scarcely a cultivated field, in
the entire extent. But the most striking feature is that the
whole ground looks strangely cut up with hedge-like lines of
shrubbery running in queer directions not suggested by the
natural lay of the land, nor its present uses; with rows of
rugged oaks and scattered tufts of evergreens; wild, uncut
grasses grave-yard like, in patches here and there; all giving to
the face of things a wrinkled and haggard look.

But coming nearer one sees that these hedges mark the
sites of old picket lines, rifle pits and breastworks; shallow
trench and low parapet grown over not only with native herb-
age, but with apple, pear, peach and plum, sprung from seeds
sown in the long days and nights when such luxuries found
their way to the men on the sharp-edged front, with not much
room between their faces and the bare earth; and that these
heavy clumps of trees, mostly evergreens, many as large as
cannon or nail-kegs, have sprung up by some hidden law of
nature from the deeper loosened earth around the batteries,
bomb-proofs, mortar-pits, and covered ways, wherein men used
to be put to their wit's end how not to be knocked out of their

five senses. As those old scenes rise before us, the contrast makes the picture more dramatic.

For here when last seen by me before, on the one side and the other, mighty masses and serried ranks of brave, true men stood, and struck, and went willingly to death for what they, strangely contrariwise, deemed the right; conflict of the deep-felt and the far-seen in principles, interests and ideals, out of which the new nation was to emerge. It was the travail of the people. This is not too strong a figure. For was not this undergone? Sorrow, suffering, sacrifice, surrender, devotion, death,—that something for the world's good should be born into being? Know you not that the tears of this were drawn up into the heavens to descend on these fields in the ever new-creating rains to consecrate this mingled blood to the building of "the house not made with hands," here upon the earth? But for such thought, how desolating would this vision be!

And of the thousands left buried there, not all forgotten! I saw all along the edge of the trenches, in the fringe of the grasses and thickets, little hillocks, sunken oblongs of earth, familiar, unmistakable to experienced eyes. Now and then, strange to see, a drooping flower placed lately at the head by far-remembering love, or a wild rose planted by some unknowing but caring heart, or nature's own sweet hand.

Passing amidst these relics and mementoes, where nature buries what she wishes to preserve, we wonder what it is that is most abiding. Here after Vesuvian convulsions, men are gone; things remain. The mighty actors are suddenly lifted from the scene and their works stand, silent, rugged, realistic, unadorned; truthful monitors of tremendous struggle. I should not say unadorned, for nature has touched them with her own adornment; hillocks which were walls of thundering, havoc-dealing cannon, now thickly overgrown with peaceful pines sighing in the soft winds; the shallow trenches far-stretching or queerly curved and angled, once breasted with brave hearts and fringed with fire, now fringed by soft embroidery of growing plants, with varied threads, rich in texture, form and color; the slopes and middle grounds which ran red with blood, now veiled with grasses strangely rank and vital; nature's subtle alchemy and ever-brooding spirit transmuting into new, calm life, the bodies of the thousands once battling for peace under law,—of which this multiform peace of nature is the ghost or adumbration.

There is a peculiar impressiveness about the forsaken. Some deep places in us are more moved by a forlorn field like this than by a glorified one like Gettysburg. At any rate, the contrast is wide and striking. There, action concentrated, intense, decisive; here, struggle long-drawn, persistent, indecisive; there, the mighty stake, the destinies of nations determined by the issue of an hour; here, stubborn patience, tireless fortitude, unflinching gaze at overwhelming death days and nights and months together, to test the merits of a tactical plan. Then as to material, visible elements; at Gettysburg, the constructive work of man uppermost; at Petersburg, the covering work of nature. That, made a magnificent mausoleum, a splendid spectacle; this, the bald fact, held fast, as cased in amber; there, highest art in head-stone, monument and statue; here, grim trees, wild grasses, clinging mosses; there, luxurious avenues laid out for artistic effect, or convenience of visitors, even though confusing the old battle-lines; here only the very lines themselves, laid out by daring courage or desperate need, and behind them the foot-worn paths carpeted now by fallen leaf and ripened cone; there, the remaining gathered in a noble cemetery consecrated with immortal eloquence, cherished in eternal honor; here, sleeping in their blood, canopied by swaying branches growing out of it, the last resting-place marked by the chance staying of some wild rose, named only by the birds singing love-notes above them. There, all remembered; here, all but forgotten! Which is the grandest, most magnificent, I am not asking. Which is most impressive, I claim not to decide. That depends on the man, or the mood. I have memories of both, but hold largely of the forgotten.

Except the trees and shrubbery that had grown up on the battle-lines, the face of things on our side seemed but little changed. In very few places field had replaced forest, or forest field. In some favored spots, then fallow, new fields had been laid out, chiefly where the ground had been furrowed and fertilized by the harrowings of nine months' siege and sortie. Going over some of these, the earth having been loosened or beaten down by recent heavy rains, I saw now and then a bullet or fragment of shell washed to the surface. This, even now,—although for years the neighboring residents had made it a business to gather such relics, at first in quantities to pay for carting away and selling for profit as metal. And still, in the few poor little homes set up here and there along the lines

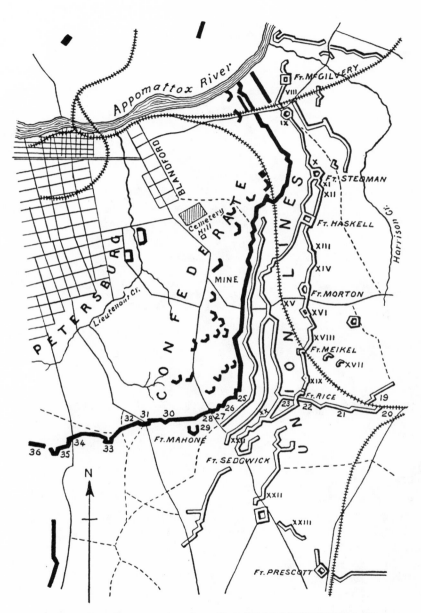

MAP OF FORTIFICATIONS E. AND S. E. OF PETERSBURG, VA.
The lines with Roman numerals were captured and turned.

Brigadier General Joshua L. Chamberlain, 1864
(Library of Congress)

by the cultivators of the grounds, the revenue from these now gathered sold as relics, helps materially in making up the margin of their little livelihood. I bought some of them, out of charity, or compliment, or compliance with evident expectation. The inhabitants of these houses are said to be Union men's families. But by what tenure or tolerance holding; whether relics of the war or products of later circumstances, I forbore to ascertain.

The principal crops on the old battle slopes are sweet potatoes, corn and peanuts,—there's monumental glory for you! I was told these were all very profitable, especially the latter, not requiring as yet replenishment of fertilizers since the old lavish top-dressing of human bodies and sharp cross-harrowing of cannon. Indeed, I saw many a bone that once helped make up a stalwart man, scattered, half-buried over these fields, yielding up its lime and phosphates for body and brain of people hardly the equals of those which these elements had braced for great things done and suffered. But this illustrates that strange law of exchange in human economics,—the greater given for the less. In certain spots specially and significantly fertile, which could bear the tasking, tobacco is the best paying crop. And smoke of this being solace for sorrows and substance of day-dreams has wide demands.

On the other side, as a general rule, the old Confederate fortifications, lying nearer town, are mostly obliterated. Here the ground lies for the most part better to the sun. It seems also to have a more substantial soil for cultivation. The proximity of the prosperous, growing city has naturally created a demand for these lands. Their soldier-dead are gathered in the conspicuous and beautiful cemetery. The battle mounds are mostly leveled, and the wounds healed. Farther out, where the two lines nearly met, are some stark relics still.

The hostile lines were, on the average, about a mile apart. But at certain important points they narrowed in to close range distance. In such places, after the daily experiences of being raked with shot and shell, pounded with mortars, and chopped up with canister and musketry, the men so close at hand could join in each others' psalm-singing, and perhaps more personal exhortations across the breastworks and rifle-pits until the grim guardians of the night took up their watch.

The batteries and mortars, of course, were not always

placed with a view to immediate effect, but occasionally to collateral or remote effect, being so disposed as best to keep down the fire of some annoying battery of the opponent, or effectually to enfilade any advance or sortie from a position otherwise advantageous for such movement, or perhaps to protect their own infantry front by a sweeping cross-fire. Such a battery, or mortar-pit, might be a mile away from any obvious need in its immediate front. So the pieces on this checkered board were curiously set for a wide play of arms.

What I especially wished to see was the part of the Confederate line called Rives' Salient, and the ground opposite, which was the point of the extreme advance of our army on June 18, 1864. This position, on the outskirts of the city, covered the approaches of the Norfolk Railroad and the Jerusalem Plank Road, two of the enemy's most important lines of communication towards the sea, and, of course, was very strongly fortified.

As you are kindly offering to share some of the emotions with which I revisited this scene, I may be justified in not omitting what I had recalled and recorded here, as to some points in the action of the day referred to, which by reason of the troubled ending of that day have not been brought out in official reports, or popular war sketches; relating, indeed, mostly to personal history of no great moment outside a very narrow circle, which you now do me the honor of broadening.

When, on the evening of June 17, under the sharp attack of our Second and Ninth Corps, the enemy drew in the outer line of their defenses, they left on an outlying crest near the "Deep Cut" of the Norfolk Railroad, an advanced artillery post, commanding the approaches from our side, to the fortifications at Rives' Salient. From this position early on the eighteenth, they opened a strong slant fire on our division then drawn up for an assault in our immediate front north of the railroad. Our attack was thus delayed while our own batteries were getting into position to support this assault. Our line, however, was held in place,—perhaps to take the enemy's attention from the movement of our guns. This raking fire along our ranks was very trying to the nerves, as well as to our judgment of the tactics which held us there, when we were not allowed to move forward nor to hit back,—I am not saying, to get back! Our men were going down fast, and for no good, that we could see. It was therefore a welcome piece of information when our corps commander came along with the euphemistic statement that this was "very annoying;" which remark prefaced the suave inquiry if I thought I could carry that position.

I understood the purport of the mild inquiry. "Thought," indeed, was required; but the meaning was action. The enemy's fire had an unobstructed range over a clear slope of ground, and the deep cut between us forbade a straight-away rush. By a pardonable ruse of occupying their attention, we crossed the railroad south of the cut, gained a clump of woods on the flank of their guns, and by a sharp and hot, but short, encounter, we realized our commander's wish. We carried everything. But we found it a more perilous place to hold than to carry, for we were greeted by a storm of shot and shell from the enemy's main works at the Salient, under which we should soon lose more men than we did in carrying the position. I therefore drew the men back to gain the shelter of the crest, and disposed my lines front and flank for the best defense against expected counter assault.

Reconnoitering the situation I could see no likelihood of being able to hold this place long, nor in my judgment was it of importance to hold, now that the batteries were dislodged which had annoyed our troops in the designed assault. Moreover, I discovered that the position was completely commanded by the enemy's main works at the Salient. Three or four hundred yards in our front were plainly seen several strong earthworks with twelve or fifteen guns so disposed as to deliver a smashing cross-fire over the ground between us, and just across the Plank Road was a large fort with heavy guns ready to sweep the crest we were occupying. Between these works was a solid, entrenched infantry line of at least three thousand men. We were a mile away from the rest of the army, and I prepared to "take care of myself." I hurried up three batteries entrusted to me, running the guns up under cover of the crest, leveling slight platforms, on the hither slope, so that the men could work their guns, taking advantage of their recoil at discharge to reload, and easily run them up again, the muzzles lying in the grass,—all as yet unperceived by the enemy,—and made ready for what might happen. This position would be of use in case of a general assault by our army, and this was what I looked for.

At this juncture what was my astonishment at receiv-

ing a verbal order through a staff officer personally unknown
to me, directing me in the name of "the general commanding"
to assault the enemy's main works in my front with my brigade.

This was certainly a compliment to my six splendid
regiments. But I think you will justify my astonishment, as
well as my back-handed courage and recklessness of personal
consequences in presuming to send back to the general a written statement of the situation with the opinion that that position could not be carried with a single brigade, even of Gettysburg
veterans.

Grant had lost all patience that morning, and his chief
subordinates were excited and flurried in a manner I had not
seen before. I received, however, a courteous answer saying
the whole army would join in on my right. But the single
brigade was to make the assault, and prove the prophecy. In
such an assault musketry was not to be thought of. It must be
a storm of cannonade, a rush of infantry with pieces at the
shoulder. Over the works and bayonet the enemy at their
guns! It was desperate, deadly business. The bugler sounded
the "charge." Under that storm of fire the earth flew into the
air, men went down like scythe-swept grain; a wall of smoke
veiled the front. I had thought it necessary to lead the charge,
with full staff following; but in ten minutes not a man was left
mounted. My staff were scattered; my flag-bearer shot dead,
my own horse down. To cheer and guide the men, where no
voice could be heard, nor rank distinguished, I picked up the
flag and bore it aloft, till, close upon the enemy's works, a
minie-ball cut me through, and the red cross came down to the
reddened, riddled earth. I saw my men rush past me to the
very muzzles of the guns, then torn in pieces and trickling
back,—the enemy rushing out beyond our left to flank our
batteries on the crest behind us. I had only strength to send
two broken regiments to support the batteries before I saw
that all else was lost. In the midst of this seething turmoil I
lay half-buried by clods of up-torn earth for an hour, when the
shrouding smoke lifting, I was borne from the field by some of
Major Bigelow's men of the Ninth Massachusetts Battery on
the crest.

When you picture that field, air and earth cross-cut
with thick-flying, hitting, plunging, burying, bursting missiles,
you will not wonder that we did not succeed in "bayonetting

the enemy at their guns inside their works." You will rather wonder that some of my men got near enough to fall within twenty feet of them.

I have given some detail to this description because this ground so taken and so fortified, was afterwards strongly entrenched, under that name "Fort Sedgwick," which together with the formidable work on my left front opposite, named Fort Mahone, became famous all through the siege as the hottest point of contact of the hostile lines. I have remarked to you that these places were rechristened with Bible names by the matter-of-fact men of both sides,—not from poetic inspiration, nor romantic fancy, but in the old-fashioned style, from the most striking characteristic of the object, or its principal occupation.

It was interesting to go over this ground again after so many eventful years. The strength of this Fort Hell of ours was as much in the earth as in its guns, so it was well preserved. We found its walls pierced for twenty-five guns,—fourteen four-and-one-half-inch Rodmans, thirty-pounders; two siege howitzers; eight field guns. This showed what was needed through the terrible siege; at long or short range,—half musket shot distant from the entrenched infantry in front, and with a long reach on both flanks answering the enemy's heavy batteries. Its embankments remain full formed,—high and steep; the interior cut up by ridges of traverses protecting from flank fire, and the bottom gashed with the cavernous bomb-proofs making thick cover from the terrific work of great guns and mortars all through the dreary siege,—looking now like the underground beast-dens of the old Roman Coliseum. Grown over now,—the whole of it,—with trees so thick and dark and somber, and casting so gloomy a shade down among the strange pits and dens, I almost shuddered even at the shadow of the scenes enacted here in that year of tragedy, and wondered deeply how the men kept their cheer, as the brave hearts did.

Out in the open front are the hedge-marked lines of low parapet and rifle-pits of our advanced infantry and out-lying pickets,—though some are close under the guns of the fort. The ditches are still so sharp we could not drive over them with safety to our carriage, but had to dismount and climb across, pushing our way through the dense hedge. On the smooth slopes between the two opposing lines, the rank broomsedge, leg-deep, softly waving; here and there little garden-beds of richer shrubbery, where the ever-living spirit has transfigured immortal blood.

Passing across the slight valley to the enemy's works, we found them also in good form. My guide assured me they were now little changed from their old appearance as on the day of our assault. He added that the Confederates regarded this as the strongest part of their lines. It was easy to trace the entrenchments of the infantry,—Kershaw's Mississippians, Georgians and South Carolinians, and on their right some of our old Alabama friends,—companions of the symposium at Round Top the year before, troops of Longstreet's Corps who had come up early in the evening before, and taken the place of Johnson's Division there;—not less than five thousand men behind those entrenchments. At close intervals are the heavier works, the places of their guns telling no uncertain story.

Consulting the worn Confederate war map of that date I had taken along, the old muniments were readily identified, and the record of their power applied to the justification of memory. At the redan in front, five guns; in the two lunettes right and left, seven guns each; behind the interval, in a retired work, four guns. Twenty-three guns, then, opposite our advance, where we were to pass through the cross-fire of the entrenched infantry, and carry the guns at the bayonet point. Moreover, four hundred yards to their right, (our left), across the Plank Road, Fort Mahone, its seven great guns enfilading every inch of our advance from beginning to end,—and the end so dark, foreordained, and to me, at least, foreknown. I could see now how well based that foreknowledge was.

Crossing the little run in front, which showed me where I fell, I came upon a little bunch of sassafras bushes, rather lavishly nourished, it seemed, and I cut one of them to serve, like pansies,—"for thoughts." Doing this, I saw a bullet point sticking up out of the ground, and stooping to pick this up, others came to view. Without moving more than a step, I picked up four more minie-balls, a pistol bullet, and a Union officer's vest-button.

Some good angel was near again, for a young girl came out from the Rives house a little behind the line of works, and not far from my last position picked up a fragment of shrapnel with two lead bullets still held fast in the iron band. This with native grace, or instinctive recognition, she handed me; and I was moved to give her in return a fair-sized piece of silver, in token of her ministry and of my thanksgiving that I did not get it otherwise,—the shell I mean,—when I was younger. But all that has passed;—let it pass now.

Regretting that my vision could not extend for five miles further leftward along the lines where so many engagements costly but fruitless had ensanguined the history of every corps and battery of our army, especially the ground of the splendid charge of our Sixth Corps, carrying the last defences of Petersburg, we returned towards the town, passing the somber grove which now covers the "crater" of so sad a story, where after the explosion of the mine, our assaulting columns instead of seizing the moment of the enemy's confusion to rush them through into the town, were led into the smoking crater itself, there to huddle under storms of shrapnel and canister, till forced to give up and get back,—those who could,—and let the enemy sit down there and count the hecatombs of dead. This monument also remains,—dark, deep-cut intaglio. To us it speaks only of gloom;—skilled plan, long toil, brave endeavor, made fruitless through lack of grip and grit on the part of intermediate commanders.

Then turning, we peacefully entered that once so longingly beheld, long waited for, long fought for city; now so prosperous, so bright, so beautiful. Now as then, city of churches and schools; the roofs and spires still as we saw then shining in morning or sunset light, so graceful, so sweet, so heaven-pointing,—so hell-surrounded!

Wrapped in these reflections, the shadow of that whole, dark campaign of 1864 came over me,—which up to that June day had cost our army seventy thousand men. Then I was nearing the crest of manhood, where life looks back and forward,—the middle-point of our allotted years,—but it seemed that experience was at the climax. I remember how often in those days stole over my spirit that mood of Dante, at the beginning of the "Inferno," which I give you in his own deep echoing words:

> Nel mezzo del camin di nostra vita,
> Mi retrovai per una selva oscura
> Che la diritta via era smaritta.

(Midway the path of life, I found myself in a gloomy wood,

where the right way out was perplexed.)

You were younger yet, I take it, my Companions,—in the flower of youth, or to change the figure, in the borderland of manhood, the testing ground of the knighthood which you won. By what crucial tests, through what ordeals of initiation, you passed to that high degree! Far deeper yours than those of the days of chivalry; the old investiture of knighthood,—the searching purifications, the fastings and prayer, the day and night prostrations before the altar whereon the sword was laid, all the self-renouncing symbols of the "vigil of arms." And then the consummate salutation,—the accolade, the crowning stroke on the shoulder; theirs, with the flat of the sword,—yours with the fiery edge!

The heroism of those earlier days was personal, it is said. Was it otherwise than personal,—yours? The story of that ancient chivalry lives ever in romantic song. Where is the minstrelsy of yours?

On my return to Petersburg, I found myself among friends. The old Confederate officers in the city were gathered in force to greet my coming. And strong, manly men they were. Nothing could exceed their heartiness and hospitality. They opened for the occasion their hall of war records and relics, where we talked over the feats and defeats of many an old field. In the evening there was a symposium, where our various experiences and different views of things gave spice to comradeship.

Perhaps the most striking attention received was that of an old Confederate from the ranks, who was at Rives' Salient on that dark June day of the bloody years, and who was as badly cut up with wounds as any man I ever saw alive. Our interview was both sharpened and deepened by our reciprocal experiences on that mortal day.

Of course I felt a strong desire to linger on the South Side Railroad,—along that Appomattox River we had made the dead-line for the brave men we had failed to overcome by battle, and at last were glad to prevent from getting away. But I had to make better time now, than even in that last pursuit. The rush of thoughts was greater than either. I recalled many stirring scenes at all those stations,—particularly at the crossing of the Cox Road, where on the morning after Five Forks my command pressing back Fitz-Hugh Lee's cavalry, caught the last train on the South Side Railroad out of

Petersburg, when Colonel Cunningham, of the 32d Massachusetts, on my skirmish line, leaped upon the engine and pulled a blast of the whistle that made everybody shiver,—with different emotions! This train had many officers and notables taking "French leave" of doomed Petersburg. How the scene all came back to me of that bright morning which rose out from the shadow of the sorrowful cost of our victory the evening before!

This was storied ground for me, not only because of that eventful last campaign, but also because after the surrender I had for some time a peculiar command of the region twenty miles out from Petersburg, embracing the old fields of Gravelly Run, Hatcher's Run, Sutherland Station, the Quaker Road, White Oak Ridge, Five Forks and Dinwiddie Courthouse. This was a military assignment, but circumstances necessitated something like a civil jurisdiction. The homes and people here had been run over time and again by one army and then the other, with gangs of lawless camp-followers unchecked by any authority, law or gospel, and there was scarcely left here happiness, peace or property in any homes. My efforts to restore a semblance of civil order, and respect for personal rights, and even to preserve the physical existence of these suffering people, and their grateful recognition of this, held me by something more than memory,—by an abiding and living interest.

I will not try your good nature by dwelling on points interesting perhaps only to me,—simply remarking that for the most part this country looks much as it did in 1865,—but will quickly pass over that hundred miles to Appomattox Courthouse.

Here I found everything in ruin and designed forsakenness. It is not to be expected that the survivors of a lost cause should cherish with much enthusiasm the scenes and tokens of the last days of their glory, and the ground of their surrender. Even the roads are changed. I could not find that by which Sheridan switched off my command from the main column a mile out from the station, to strike Gordon's left, then pressing back our cavalry. The fancy of marking field boundaries had wiped this out.

In the village, the former owners are said to have sold out and abandoned the place and everything about it. The new owners manifest little interest in it,—hardly enough to cultivate the ground. The county-seat is removed to Appomattox Station. Here, indeed, is a fine set of county buildings, well kept up. Three fairly good little hotels are here, and some appearance of life and thrift. But on the old ground the court-house is burned down; the jail standing,—over-tall, gaunt and lean, fit for no use except to intensify solitary confinement. The McLean house, where Grant and Lee first met for confer-ence before the surrender, is torn down and left a dismal heap of ruin. As to the hamlet itself, most of the old houses are still there,—no improvement, and no addition; all looking uncared for and forlorn.

I had followed the road from the station which was taken by Ord's troops on the left of the Fifth Corps on the morning of April 9, 1865, and specially examined the ground taken up by the left of our enveloping lines, but could find no mark nor token of its position. I knew the ground in general well enough, but wished to ascertain the respective positions in detail both of these troops and of our cavalry mainly operating on that flank, in order to understand some of the reports afterwards made concerning these positions on that day and the following. But here again, no sign, no marker, was to be found.

Following along the principal street easterly,—the old Richmond Road,—I recognized on the right the heights from which on clearing away Gordon's Stonewall Brigade, we came into full view of Lee's whole baffled column on the two slopes of the Appomattox,—Gordon already across on our side of it, and the head of Longstreet's command halted on the other side, caught now between us and Meade's Second and Sixth Corps pressing his rear, with the grotesque feature, for a middle point, made by the motley crowd of citizens around the ford below, fleeing in terror from the demons they had been told we were. I wished to look again on the theater of that thrilling scene, barren as it now is. Following still the street, to get as near as possible before venturing the trespass of setting foot again on that crest I once held by that possession which is said to be "nine points of the law,"—right near the ruins of the courthouse I saw by the road-side a bronze tablet, placed at such an angle as to be easily read by the passer-by. I knew this ground well, but was curious to see what the tablet said. It read thus:

Near this spot was established the left of the line of the First Division, Fifth Corps, formed to receive the surrender of the arms of the Army of Northern Virginia, on the eleventh day of April, 1865.

Three hundred yards further on stood another tablet with this inscription:

Near this spot rested the right of the First Division, Fifth Corps, to receive the surrender of the Army of Northern Virginia, on the eleventh day of April, 1865.

This was a pleasant surprise to me. It was the troops of my command alone that were formed in line of battle for that ceremony, on our side, and the tablets were official certification. They were placed there by government authority and supervision. I had not known of it. Part of the satisfaction I felt in this was that it restored my confidence in my personal identity. Some persons, not being present there themselves at this particular time, have indulged in the statement that I was not there; and some officials of the Army of the James seem to have had the impression that they did and received the last things there; whereas, this ceremony did not begin until that army had left for Lynchburg.

It is true that some of the Confederate cavalry, who were near at hand (W. H. F. Lee's command), gave their arms into the custody of Mackenzie's cavalry of the Army of the James, soon after the surrender was announced; and portions of the Confederate artillery, too, having their organization and papers in better shape than others, gave their arms and paroles in the presence of some of Turner's Division of that army.

But as for the main point, these tablets are authoritative historic records. I think I need not take advantage of the kind rule which permits the accused to testify in his own behalf. If necessary, I might call attention to the testimony of General Robert E. Lee and General John B. Gordon, as given in their autobiographies.

While on this matter it may be well to repeat the statement that the formal surrender of the arms and colors of Lee's army took place on the twelfth of April, 1865. But the record is also true. We did move up to this line for that ceremony from our position on the right at about noon of the eleventh; but while the officers of Lee's army were permitted to sign the paroles for their own men, yet they were so scattered that much time was required to make up the rolls with any completeness; and so the formal ceremony was delayed, and actually begun at sunrise of the twelfth and was completed only at sunset of that day.

Moving out towards my last fighting ground, in the door-yard of a house I did not remember to have seen before, although our last skirmishing was among the houses in that little hamlet, I came upon another tablet, on which was this inscription:

From this spot was fired the last cannon of the Confederate line on the ninth of April, 1865.

This shot undoubtedly it was that killed one of my gallant young officers, Lieutenant Clark, of the 185th New York, just as the first flag of truce had reached me, and had been sent on to our corps commander, General Griffin.

Still further along the crest, near the spot where this flag was received, the boy who was my driver for this excursion, jumped off to pick up a grape-shot half showing itself above ground, which, having been originally intended for me and now more effectually delivered, thus satisfying the essential conditions of the law of property, I felt authorized to take into personal possession.

Crossing the Richmond Road in front, we came to another tablet bearing this inscription:

Near this spot General Grant and General Robert E. Lee met to confer as to the details of the surrender, April 10, 1865.

This tablet is on the ground between my two lines as they stood at the moment of the final cessation of hostilities. Lee came in on the Richmond Road, from where the rear of Longstreet's command then was, three miles away, confronted by our Second and Sixth Corps. He passed close in rear of me, as I was in the saddle waiting the command to resume hostilities after the truce of three hours. Grant came a little later by another road,—a roundabout country road, leading into town near my center. Both rode past me to the courthouse. On the following morning they had a final meeting, on the elevated ground in front of my right. The tablets and roads refreshed my recollection.

Over the Appomattox,—now as then a stream not more than boot-leg deep in the road-crossing, trampled to deep mud then, now running swift and clear,—a mile, perhaps, up the opposite slope, in the edge of the wide woods, stands one more tablet. This says:

On this spot General Robert E. Lee wrote his last order taking leave of the Army of Northern Virginia, April 10, 1865.

This, you perceive, was written midway between the head and rear of his army,—between Gordon and Longstreet. On the next day Longstreet moved up to the bank of the Appomattox, and on the twelfth, followed Gordon in the column for the surrender.

So much for the neglected relics and far-away tablets, lonely markers of once thrilling scenes; and so much for old Appomattox Courthouse, where great things were ended, and greater things begun.

4

MILITARY OPERATIONS ON THE WHITE OAK ROAD

The operations of the Fifth Corps on the White Oak Road on the 31st of March, 1865, were more serious in purpose and action than has been generally understood; and with reference either to their intended and possible results, or to their actual effect upon the ensuing eventful campaign, they are entitled to better consideration than they have yet received. Moreover, the peculiar complications attending them, bearing upon the personal issues which made a memorable episode of the battle of Five Forks on the following day, give these incidents a picturesque interest as well as historic value. I have thought that a recital based on personal knowledge of these operations and intimate association with some of the chief actors in them, might tend to draw the facts from the obscurity in which they have been left in official reports and professed histories of the last campaign of the Army of the Potomac; and while necessarily exhibiting, might perhaps tend to clear up, some of the confusion in which they have been involved by the peculiar circumstances under which this record has been presented to the public judgment.

It had not been the habit in the Fifth Corps to invite or encourage detailed reports on the part of subordinates; and in the rush and pressure of this intense campaign there was less opportunity or care than ever for such matters, while the impressiveness of the momentous close left little disposition to multiply words upon subordinate parts or participants. The fact also of an early change in the grand tactics of the campaign confused the significance, and sometimes the identity, of important movements; and the change of commanders in the crisis of its chief battle induced consequences which, even in official reports and testimony, affected the motive for sharply defining actions where personal concern had come to be an embarrassing factor.

At all events, the immediate reports of those days are meager in the extreme; and very much of what has come out since has been under the disadvantage of being elicited as *ex parte* testimony before military courts where the highest military officers of the government were parties, and the attitudes of plaintiff and defendant almost inevitably biased expression.

It will be distinctly borne in mind that the view here presented is of things as they appeared to us who were concerned in them as subordinate commanders. This is a chapter of experiences,—including in this term not only what was done, but what was known and said and thought and felt, not to say suffered, and showing withal a steadfast purpose, patience and spirit of obedience deserving of record even if without recompense.

In order to throw all possible light on the otherwise inexplicable confusions of this day, I have incorporated with my original account some evidence not before available now brought out in recent volumes of the Records of the War. Such reference to what was not then within our knowledge I have endeavored to make perfectly distinct, so as not to disturb the essential unity of a picture seen from the interior of what may with literal appropriateness be called the *transactions* of that day.

Yet I find embarrassments in approaching this narration. These facts, however simple, cannot but have some bearing on points which have been drawn into controversy on the part of those who were dear to me as commanders and companions in arms, and who have grown still dearer in the intimacies of friendship since the war, and in the fact that they are no longer here to speak for themselves. I feel, therefore, under increased responsibility in presenting these matters, assuring myself that I know of no bias of personality or partisanship which should make me doubtful of my ability to tell the truth as I saw and knew it to be, or distrust my judgment in forming an opinion

Another embarrassment is in the fact that the operations of this day are closely related parts of a series of movements which, whether continuous or broken, were intended to be directed towards a distinct objective; so that no one portion can be fully understood without reference to the rest, both before and after, and to the great controlling motive of the whole.

Indulge me, therefore, with your patience while I gather up as shortly as possible, the main preliminaries necessary to a fair understanding of the operations on the White Oak Road. Lee's army during the previous winter had become much weakened by lack of supplies, desertions[1] and general demoralization of the Confederate cause, and Grant was determined to take decisive measures to break the whole Confederate hold on Virginia. He planned a vigorous movement to cut Lee's communications, and also those of Richmond; and at the same time to turn the right flank of Lee's entrenched line before Petersburg and break up his army. For the first of these objects he was to send Sheridan, now commanding "The Middle Military Division," with the cavalry of the Army of the Shenandoah, two divisions, under General Merritt, and the cavalry division now commanded by General Crook, formerly belonging to the Army of the Potomac. For the second purpose he was to send out, with Sheridan though not under his command, the Fifth and Second Corps of the Army of the Potomac,—General Meade, its commander, accompanying the movement. The former places of these corps on the left of our entrenchments before Petersburg, were to be taken by troops of the Army of the James. On the right of these our Sixth and Ninth Corps were to hold their old positions in front of Petersburg, ready to break through the enemy's works if they should be stripped somewhat of troops by the necessity of meeting our assault on their right.

The scope of Grant's intentions may be understood from an extract from his orders to Sheridan, March 28, 1865:—

"The Fifth Army Corps will move by the Vaughan Road at three A.M. tomorrow morning. The Second moves at about nine A.M....Move your cavalry at as early an hour as you can,....and passing to or through Dinwiddie, reach the right and rear of the enemy as soon as you can. It is not the inten-

---

[1]The desertions in Pickett's Division alone from March 9 to 18 were 512 men. Rebellion Records, Serial 97, p. 1332, 1353. And they were shooting deserters at that time. Ibid. p. 1367.

tion to attack the enemy in his entrenched position, but to force him out, if possible. Should he come out and attack us, or get himself where he can be attacked, move in with your entire force in your own way, and with full reliance that the army will engage or follow the enemy as circumstances will dictate. I shall be on the field, and will probably be able to communicate with you. Should I not do so, and you find that the enemy keeps within his main entrenched line, you may cut loose and push for the Danville Road. If you find it practicable, I would like you to cross the Southside Road between Petersburg and Burkesville, and destroy it to some extent....After having accomplished the destruction of the two railroads, which are now the only avenues of supply to Lee's Army, you may return to this army or go on into North Carolina and join General Sherman...."

General Grant evidently intended to rely more on tactics than strategy in this campaign. In his personal letter to General Sherman, of March 22, giving the details of his plans for Sheridan's movement, he adds: "I shall start out with no distinct view, further than holding Lee's forces from following Sheridan. But I shall be along myself, and will take advantage of anything that turns up."

The general plan was that Sherman should work his way up to Burkesville, and thus cut off Lee's communications, and force him to come out of his entrenchments and fight on equal terms. Sherman says he and General Grant expected that one of them would have to fight one more bloody battle. He also makes the characteristic remark that his army at Goldsboro was strong enough to fight Lee's army and Johnston's combined, if Grant would come up within a day or two.[1]

The ground about to be traversed by us is flat and swampy, and cut up by sluggish streams, which, after every rain, become nearly impassable. The soil is a mixture of clay and sand quite apt in wet weather to take the character of sticky mire or of quicksands. The principal roads for heavy

---

[1]Sherman's Memoirs, Vol. II, p. 325. This seems to imply a reflection on the fighting qualities of the Army of the Potomac, as at that time Sherman's army did not exceed in number the Army of the Potomac but by about six thousand men. But it must be remembered that the Army of the Potomac confronted an enemy covered by entrenched works for sixteen miles,—a circumstance which gave the Confederates the great advantage of three to one in effective numbers.

travel have to be corduroyed or overlaid with plank. The streams for the most part find their way southeasterly into the tributaries of the Chowan River. Some, however, flow northeasterly into the waters of the Appomattox. Our available route was along the divide of these waters.

The principal road leading out westerly from Petersburg is the Boydton Plank Road; for the first ten miles nearly parallel with the Appomattox, and distant from it from three to six miles. The Southside Railroad is between the Boydton Road and the river. South of the Boydton is the Vaughan Road; the first section lying in rear of our main entrenchments, but from our extreme left at Hatcher's Run, inclining towards the Boydton Road, being only two miles distant from it at Dinwiddie Courthouse. Five miles east of this place the Quaker Road, called by persons of another mood, the "Military Road," crosses the Vaughan and leads northerly into the Boydton Road midway between Hatcher's Run and Gravelly Run, which at their junction became Rowanty Creek.

A mile above the intersection of the Quaker Road with the Boydton is the White Oak Road, leading off from the Boydton at right angles westerly, following the ridges between the small streams and branches forming the headwaters of Hatcher's and Gravelly Runs, through and beyond the "Five Forks." This is a meeting-place of roads, the principal of which, called the Ford Road, crosses the White Oak at a right angle, leading from a station on the Southside Railroad, three miles north, to Dinwiddie Courthouse, six miles south.

The enemy's main line of entrenchments west from Petersburg covers, of course, the important Boydton Plank Road; but only so far as Hatcher's Run, where at Burgess' Mill, their entrenchments leave this and follow the White Oak Road for some two miles, and then cross it, turning to the north and following the Claiborne Road, which leads to Sutherland station on the Southside Railroad ten miles distant from Petersburg, covering this road till it strikes Hatcher's Run, about a mile higher up. This "return" northerly forms the extreme right of the enemy's entrenched line.

When the instructions for this campaign reached us, all were animated with confidence of quick success. If Lee's lines before Petersburg were held in place, it would be easy work to cut his communications, turn his right, and roll him back upon Petersburg or Richmond; if, on the other hand, his main lines were stripped to resist our attack, our comrades in the old lines would make short work of Lee's entrenchments and his army. We were all good friends,—those who were to constitute the turning column. Humphreys of the Second Corps had formerly commanded a division in the Fifth; Warren of the Fifth had commanded the Second; Miles in the Second had won his spurs in the Fifth; Meade, commanding the army, had been corps commander of the Fifth; the cavalry division of our army, now to go to Sheridan, had been our pet and pride; Sheridan was an object of admiration and awe.

At daylight on the twenty-ninth of March the Fifth Corps moved out toward the enemy's right. As the movement was intended to mask its destination by a considerable detour to the rear, our column first moved southward to Arthur's Swamp, crossing the Rowanty at Monk's Bridge, and thence by way of the Old Stage Road into and down the Vaughan. My brigade, being the advance of the First Division, reached the Chapple House, about two miles from Dinwiddie, early in the forenoon, encountering only a few cavalry pickets. Sheridan, with the cavalry, moving by a still exterior route, reached Dinwiddie Courthouse only at about five o'clock in the afternoon, pressing before him also the enemy's pickets.

Our whole division[1] had arrived at the Chapple House when at about noon my command was ordered to retrace its steps by the Vaughan to the Quaker Road, and push up towards the salient of the enemy's works near Burgess' Mill. We soon found this road better entitled to its military than its Quaker appellation. The enemy's skirmishers were pressed back upon their reserves in a fairly well fortified position on the north bank of Gravelly Run, where they had destroyed the bridge to check our advance. Fording the run and forcing the position, we soon developed a strong line which had entrenched itself as an advanced post to cover the important point at Burgess' Mill, consisting of Gracie's, Ransom's, Wallace's and Wise's Brigades, of Bushrod Johnson's Division,[2] under Lieutenant General R. H. Anderson. After stubborn fighting for over two hours, involving a loss to us of one hundred and sixty-

---

[1]Griffin's Division at the opening of the campaign numbered in all present for duty, of all kinds, 6,547 men. Of these the First Brigade numbered 1,750; the Second, about the same; the Third, upwards of 3,000.

[2]Reported to be about 6,000 strong. Rebellion Records, Serial 97, page 116.

seven killed and wounded, including some of our most valued officers, and a much heavier loss to the enemy of whom more than one hundred killed and fifty wounded, with one hundred and sixty prisoners taken by a sudden countercharge, fell into our hands, and aided late in the action by portions of Gregory's and Bartlett's Brigades, which had then just arrived, and by Battery B, 4th U.S. Artillery, we pushed the enemy quite back to the White Oak Road, and into their entrenchments behind it. The Second Corps now came up and formed on our right.

With customary cognizance of our purposes and plans, Lee had on the twenty-eighth, ordered General Fitz Hugh Lee, with his division of cavalry, from the extreme left of his lines to the extreme right in the vicinity of Five Forks, to oppose what he believed to be Sheridan's intention of cutting his communications by way of the Southside Railroad.[1] Such despatch had Fitz Lee made that on the evening of the twenty-ninth he had arrived at Sutherland Station, within six miles of Five Forks, and about that distance from our fight that afternoon on the Quaker Road. Pickett's Division, consisting of the brigades of Stuart, Hunton, Corse and Terry, about five thousand strong, was sent to the entrenchments along the Claiborne Road, and Roberts' Brigade of North Carolina cavalry, to picket the White Oak Road from the Claiborne to Five Forks.

On the thirtieth, the Fifth Corps, relieved by the Second, moved to the left along the Boydton Road, advancing its left towards the right of the enemy's entrenchments on the White Oak Road. Lee, also, apprehensive for his right, sent McGowan's South Carolina Brigade and McRae's North Carolina, of Hill's Corps, to strengthen Bushrod Johnson's Division in the entrenchments there; but took two of Johnson's brigades—Ransom's and Wallace's—with three brigades of Pickett's Division (leaving Hunton's in the entrenchments), to go with Pickett to reenforce Fitz Hugh Lee at Five Forks. W. H. F. Lee's Division of cavalry, about one thousand five hun-

[1]Longstreet had advised Lee (March 28) that Grant would try to take Richmond by raiding on his communications rather than by attacking his lines of works, and suggesting putting a sufficient force in the field to prevent this. He says "the greater danger is from keeping too close within our trenches." Rebellion Records, Serial 97, page 1360. This advice was exactly in the line of what Grant desired as his best opportunity. Longstreet's discussion of the situation is interesting as given in "Manassas to Appomattox," page 588.

dred men, and Rosser's, about one thousand,[1] were also ordered to Five Forks. These reenforcements did not reach Five Forks until the evening of the thirtieth.

The precise details of these orders and movements were, of course, not known to General Grant nor to any of his subordinates. But enough had been developed on the Quaker Road to lead Grant to change materially his original purpose of making the destruction of the railroads the principal objective of Sheridan's movements. At the close of our fight there, Grant had despatched Sheridan: "Our line is now unbroken from Appomattox to Dinwiddie. I now feel like ending the matter, if possible, before going back. I do not want you, therefore, to cut loose and go after the enemy's roads at present. In the morning push around the enemy, if you can, and get on to his right rear. The movements of the enemy's cavalry may, of course, modify your action. We will act together as one army here, until it is seen what can be done with the enemy."

The effect of this message reached to something more than a measure of tactics. It brought Sheridan at once to Grant. It will be borne in mind that he was not under the orders of Meade, but an independent commander, subject to Grant alone. His original orders contemplated his handling his command as a flying column, independently of others—all the responsibility and all the glory being his own. The new instructions would bring him to act in conjunction with the Army of the Potomac, and render quite probable under army regulations and usages his coming under temporary command of General Meade, his senior in rank,—a position we do not find him in during this campaign. The logic of the new situation involved some interesting corollaries beyond the direct issue of arms.

It was a dark and dismal night, that twenty-ninth of March, on the Quaker Road. The chilling rain poured down, soaking the fields and roads and drenching the men stretched

---

[1]I leave these figures as I had them from reports at the time. General Fitz Hugh Lee states in his testimony before the Warren Court of Inquiry that his division numbered about 1,300; W.H.F. Lee's, about 1,000; and Rosser's, 900. (Records, page 474.) But General W.H.F. Lee testifying before the same court gives his numbers as between 1,700 and 1,800 (Same, page 530.) His command in ordinary times seems to have been much larger. General Humphreys quotes the morning report of February 20, 1865, showing for W.H.F. Lee's command, 3,935 sabers, and Fitz Lee's, 1,825. (Virginia Campaign, page 434, Appendix L.)

on the ground, worn, wounded and dying, all alike shrouded in ghastly gloom. Here and there with strange, will-o'-the-wisp motion, some ministering lantern sailing and sinking low in its quest of flickering life, shone weirdly through the mist and mirk,—one knew not whether near or far. Before morning the roads were impassable for wagons or artillery, and nearly so for the ambulances that came up ghost-like in the shivering dawn.

Meanwhile, not far in the rear of this scene, at General Grant's headquarters, Sheridan was holding long and close conference with him, having ridden up through the rain and mud immediately on receiving the message announcing the change of plan. All that is known of this outside is that at the end Sheridan was directed to gain possession of Five Forks early in the morning. He could easily have taken possession of that before; for all the afternoon and night of the twenty-ninth, there was nothing to oppose him there but the right wing of Roberts' slender brigade, picketing the White Oak Road. But when he received a positive order to secure that point on the morning of the thirtieth, he seems to have moved so late and moderately that Fitz Hugh Lee had time to march from Sutherland Station to Five Forks, and thence half-way to Dinwiddie Courthouse to meet him; and even then, attacking with a single division, although this outnumbered the enemy by a thousand men,[1] he permitted his demonstration on Five Forks, to be turned into a reconnaissance half-way out,[2] his advance being checked at the forks of the Ford and Boisseau Roads, where it remained all night and until itself attacked the next morning.[3] It is true that the roads and fields were heavy with rain; but this did not prevent our two infantry corps from moving forward and establishing themselves in front of the White Oak Road, in face of considerable opposition; nor hinder Lee from zealously strengthening the right of his lines, and pressing forward his reenforcements of infantry and cavalry to Fitz Hugh Lee at Five Forks, where they arrived at

[1]General Devin's Division numbered, according to returns of March 30, 169 officers and 2,830 men, present for duty.

[2]General Merritt's despatch of March 30. Rebellion Records: Serial 97, page 326.

[3]General Fitz Hugh Lee's testimony. Warren Court Records, Vol. I, page 469.

about sunset. What we cannot understand is why previous to that time General Sheridan, with thirteen thousand cavalry,[1] had not found it practicable to make an effective demonstration on Five Forks, covered all the morning only by what few men Roberts had there picketing the White Oak Road, and after that time, all day, only by Fitz Hugh Lee with eighteen hundred cavalry.

Early on the morning of the thirty-first the Fifth Corps had all advanced northerly beyond the Boydton Road towards the enemy at the junction of the White Oak and Claiborne Roads: Ayres, with the Second Division, in advance, about six hundred yards from this junction; Crawford, with the Third Division, on Ayres' right rear in echelon with him, about six hundred yards distant; and Griffin, with the First Division, in position about thirteen hundred yards in rear of a prolongation of Crawford's line to the left, entirely out of sight of both, owing to woods and broken ground, but within what was thought to be supporting distance. This position was along the southeast bank of a swampy branch of Gravelly Run, half a mile north of the Boydton Road, and a mile and a half south of the White Oak Road. Miles' Division of the Second Corps had

---

[1]This figure is what was understood by us at the time. General Humphreys, noted for painstaking accuracy, says in his "Virginia Campaign of 1864 and '65" the numbers of Sheridan's cavalry present for duty March 31, 1865 were 611 officers and 13,200 enlisted men. (Appendix, p. 433.) The official returns for that month, as compiled from subordinate returns, show for Sheridan's cavalry, exclusive of artillery, present for duty.

Merritt's command,	373 officers;	7,138 men,	=	7,511
Crook's Division,	210 officers;	5,625 men,	=	5,835
Totals:	583 "	12,763 "		13,346

(Rebellion Records, Serial 9, p. 391.)

For the month of April 1865 the official returns show for the above:

Merritt's command,	400 officers,	7,894 men,	=	8,294
Crook's command,	220 officers,	2,715 men,	=	2,935
Totals:	620 "	10,609 "		11,729

(Rebellion Records, Serial 97, p. 1043.)

In a paper presented before the Warren Court of Inquiry, understood to be a copy of General Sheridan's official report, he states the number of his effective command at the opening of this campaign to be: Merritt's command 5,700, and Crook's command, 3,300; a total of 9,000. He may have had in mind the effective numbers when dismounted; a fourth of the men being kept back holding horses.

extended to the left on the Boydton Road to connect with Griffin.

My command was the extreme left of our lines; my own brigade along the difficult branch of Gravelly Run, facing towards Ayres, with Gregory's Brigade (which had reported to me for this campaign) "refused"—bent back at right angles so as to face westerly—along a country road leading from the Boydton to the Claiborne Road; a portion of the artillery of the division being placed also in my lines to strengthen the defense of that flank, where we had reason to believe the enemy, after their old fashion, were very likely to make a dash upon our left while we were maneuvering to turn their right.

General Grant, understanding from General Sheridan that he was on the White Oak Road, near Five Forks, on the afternoon of the thirtieth, had replied to him that his position on this road was of very great importance, and concluded this answer with these words: "Can you not push up towards Burgess' Mills on the White Oak Road?"[1]

General Grant's wishes, as now understood, were that we should gain possession of the White Oak Road in our front. This was indicated in a despatch from him March 30, to General Meade, the purport of which was known to us and had much to do with shaping our energies for action. The despatch was the following:

"As Warren and Humphreys advance, thus shortening their line, I think the former had better move by the left flank as far as he can stretch out with safety, and cover the White Oak Road if he can. This will enable Sheridan to reach the Southside Road by Ford's Road, and, it may be, double the enemy up, so as to drive him out of his works south of Hatcher's Run."

In accordance with this understanding, Ayres had made a careful examination of the situation in his front, upon the results of which General Warren had reported to Generals Meade and Grant that he believed he could, with his whole corps, gain possession of the White Oak Road. This proposition was made in face of the information of Grant's order of 7.40

---

[1]Sheridan's despatch to Grant, March 30, 2.45 P.M., and Grant's reply thereto; Records, Warren Court of Inquiry, Vol. II, page 1309. It afterwards transpired that Sheridan's cavalry did not long hold this position. Grant's despatch to Meade, March 31, Rebellion Records, Serial 97, p. 339.

this morning, that owing to the heavy rains the troops were to remain substantially as they were, but that three days' more rations should be issued to the Fifth Corps; an intimation of a possible cutting loose from our base of supplies for a time.

Griffin's Division, being entrusted with a double duty—that of guarding the exposed left flank of the Fifth and Second Corps, and that of being in readiness to render prompt assistance in case of trouble arising from the demonstrations against the White Oak Road front—our adjustments had to be made for what in familiar speech is termed a "ticklish situation." Vague rumors from the direction of Five Forks added to what we knew of the general probabilities, justified us in considerable anxiety. There was a queer expression on Griffin's face when he showed me a copy of a message from Grant to Sheridan, late the evening before, which gave us the comical satisfaction of knowing that our inward fears had good outside support. This was what we thus enjoyed: "From the information I have sent you of Warren's position, you will see that he is in danger of being attacked in the morning. If such occurs, be prepared to push up with all your force to assist him." The morning had now come. It is needless to remark that there was no lethargy in the minds of any on that left flank of ours, in a situation so critical, whether for attack or defense.

It may seem strange that in such a state of things Warren should have made the suggestion for a movement to his front. But he was anxious, as were all his subordinates, to strike a blow in the line of our main business; which was to turn Lee's right and break up his army. Wet and worn and famished as all were, we were alive to the thought that promptness and vigor of action would at all events determine the conditions and chances of the campaign. And if this movement did not involve the immediate turning of Lee's right in his entrenchments, it would secure the White Oak Road to the west of them, which Grant had assured Sheridan was of so much importance, and would enable us to hold Lee's right in check, so that Sheridan could either advance on the White Oak Road towards us and Burgess' Mill, as Grant had asked him to do, or make a dash on the Southside Railroad, and cut their communications and turn their right by a wider sweep as Grant had also suggested to him to do.

Late in the forenoon Warren received through General Webb, chief of staff, the following order: "General Meade di-

rects that should you determine by your reconnaissance that
you can gain possession of, and hold the White Oak Road, you
are to do so, notwithstanding the order to suspend operations
today." This gave a sudden turn to dreams. In that humiliation, fasting and prayer, visions arose like prophecy of old. We
felt the swing and sweep; we saw the enemy turned front and
flank across the White Oak Road; Sheridan flashing on our
wheeling flank, cutting communications, enfilading the Claiborne
entrenchments; our Second Corps over the main works, followed up by our troops in the old lines seizing the supreme
moment to smash in the Petersburg defenses, scatter or capture all that was left there of Lee's army, and sweep away
every menace to the old flag between us and the James River.
Mirage and glamor of boyish fancy, measuring things by its
heart! Daydreams of men familiar with disaster, drenched and
famished but building, as ever, castles of their souls above the
level river of death!

It was with mingled feelings of mortification, apprehen-
sion and desperation, that in the very ecstacy of these visions,
word came to us of Sheridan's latest despatch to Grant the
evening before, that Pickett's Division of infantry was deployed
along the White Oak Road, his right reaching to Five Forks;
and the whole rebel cavalry was massing at that place, so that
Sheridan would be held in check by them instead of dashing
up, as was his wont, to give a cyclone edge to our wheeling
flank. Grant's despatch to Meade, transmitting this, was a
dire disenchantment. The knell rang thus: "From this despatch
Warren will not have the cavalry support on his left flank that
I expected. He must watch closely his left flank."

Although Grant had given out word that there should
be no movement of troops that day, Lee seems not so to have
resolved. Driven to seize every advantage or desperate expedient, he had ordered four brigades, those of Wise, Gracie and
Hunton, with McGowan's South Carolina Brigade, to move out
from their entrenchments, get across the flank of the Fifth
Corps and smash it in. We did not know this, but it was the
very situation which Grant had made the occasion for attacking ourselves. It was a strange coincidence, but it was to both
parties a surprise.

This was the condition of things and of minds when the
advance ordered for the White Oak Road was put into execution. Ayres advanced, soldier-like, as was his nature; resolute,

Brigadier General Joshua L. Chamberlain, 1864
(Library of Congress)

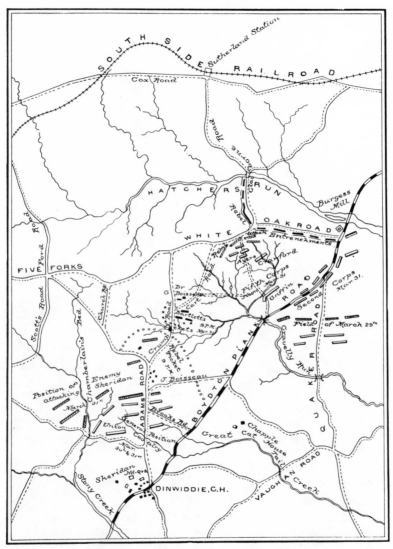

WHITE OAK ROAD, MARCH 31, 1865.

To avoid confusion, the position of the 5th Corps troops across the White Oak Road,
near the Claiborne, at 5 P. M., is not shown.

firm-hearted, fearing nothing; in truth not fearing quite enough. Although he believed his advance would bring on a battle, he moved without skirmishers, but in a wedge-like formation guarding both flanks. His First Brigade, commanded by the gallant Winthrop, had the lead in line of battle, his right and rear supported by the Third Brigade, that of Gwyn, who was accounted a good fighter; and Denison's Maryland Brigade formed in column on Winthrop's left and rear, ready to face outward by the left flank in case of need; while a brigade of Crawford's was held in reserve in rear of the center. This would seem to be a prudent and strong formation of Ayres' command. The enemy's onset was swift and the encounter sudden. The blow fell without warning, enveloping Ayres complete front. It appears that McGowan's Brigade struck squarely on Winthrop's left flank, with an oblique fire also on the Maryland Brigade, while the rest of the attacking forces struck on his front and right. General Hunton[1] says they were not expecting to strike our troops so soon and that the attack was not made by usual orders, but that on discovering our advance so close upon them, a gallant lieutenant in his brigade sprung in front of his line, waving his sword with the shout, "Follow me, boys!" whereupon all three brigades on their right dashed forward to the charge. Winthrop was overwhelmed and his supports demoralized. All he could hope for was to retire in good order. This he exerted himself to effect. But this is not an easy thing to do when once the retreat is started before a spirited foe superior in numbers, or in the flush and rush of success. In vain the gallant Denison strove to stem the torrent. A disabling wound struck down his brave example, and the effect of this shows how much the moral forces have to do in sustaining the physical. Brigade after brigade broke; that strange impulse termed a "panic" took effect and the retreat became a rout.

Ayres, like a roaring lion, endeavors to check the disorder, and make a stand on each favoring crest and wooded ravine. But in vain. His men stream past him. They come back on Crawford's veteran division and burst through it in spite of all the indignant Kellogg can do, involving this also in the demoralization; and the whole crowd comes back reckless of everything but to get behind the lines on the Boydton Road, plunging through the swampy run, breaking through Griffin's

[1]Records, Warren Court, p. 623.

right, where he and Bartlett reform them behind the Third
Brigade. The enemy pursuing, swarm down the bank opposite
us, and are met by a sharp fire of musketry and artillery
which we had made ready on hearing the noise of the retreat.
We were expecting them to fall in force on our left in Gregory's
front and I was riding along that line, anxious about this,
when General Warren and General Griffin came down at full
speed, both out of breath with their efforts to rally the panic-
stricken men whose honor was their own, and evidently under
great stress of feeling. Griffin breaks forth first, after his high-
proof fashion: "General Chamberlain, the Fifth Corps is eternally damned!" I essayed some pleasantry: "Not till you are in
heaven!" Griffin does not smile nor hear, but keeps right on: "I
tell Warren you will wipe out this disgrace, and that's what
we're here for." Then Warren breaks out, with stirring phrase,
but uttered as if in a delirium of fever: "General Chamberlain,
will you save the honor of the Fifth Corps? That's all there is
about it." That appeal demanded a chivalrous response. Honor
is a mighty sentiment, and the Fifth Corps was dear to me.
But my answer was not up to the key-note: I confess that. I
was expecting every moment an attack on my left flank now
that the enemy had disclosed our situation. And my little
brigade had taken the brunt of things thus far; but the day
before the last, winning a hard-fought field from which they
had come off grievously thinned and torn and worn, and whence
I had but hardly brought myself away. I mentioned Bartlett,
who had our largest and best brigade, which had been but
little engaged. "We have come to you; you know what that
means," was the only answer. "I'll try it, General; only don't
let anybody stop me except the enemy!" I had reason for that
protest as things had been going. "I will have a bridge ready
here in less than an hour. You can't get men through this
swamp in any kind of order," says Warren. "It may do to come
back on, General; it will not do to stop for that now. My men
will go straight through." So at a word the First Battalion of
the 198th Pennsylvania, Major Glenn, commanding, plunges
into the muddy branch, waist deep, and more,[1] with cartridge
boxes borne upon the bayonet sockets above the turbid waters;
the Second Battalion keeping the banks beyond clear of the

[1]General Warren states in his testimony before the Court of Inquiry that this
stream was sixty feet wide and four or five feet deep. Records, page 717.

enemy by their well-directed fire, until the First has formed in skirmishing order and pressed up the bank. I followed with the rest of the brigade in line of battle and Gregory's in column of regiments. The enemy fell back without much resistance until finding supports on broken strong ground, they made stand after stand. Griffin followed with Bartlett's Brigade, in reserve. In due time Ayres' troops got across and followed up on our left rear, while Crawford was somewhere to our right and rear, but out of sight or reach after we had once cleared the bank of the stream. It seems that General Warren sent to General Meade the following despatch: "I am going to send forward a brigade from my left, supported by all I can get of Crawford and Ayres, and attack....This will take place about 1.45, if the enemy does not attack sooner." This was the only recognition or record we were to have in official reports; it was not all we were to achieve in unwritten history.

At about this time Miles, of the Second Corps, had after the fashion of that corps gone in handsomely in his front, somewhat to the right of our division, and pressed so far out as to flank Wise's Brigade on the left of the troops that had attacked Ayres, and drove them back half-way to their starting-point. This had the effect to induce the enemy in my front to retire their line to a favorable position on the crest of a ravine where they made another determined stand. After sharp fighting here we drove them across an extensive field into some works they seemed to have had already prepared, of the usual sort in field operations,—logs and earth,—from which they delivered a severe fire which caused the right of my line to waver. Taking advantage of the slight shelter of a crest in the open field I was preparing for a final charge, when I received an order to halt my command and defend my position as best I could. I did not like this much. It was a hard place to stay in. The officer who brought me the order had his horse shot under him as he delivered it. I rode back to see what the order meant. I found General Griffin and General Warren in the edge of the woods overlooking the field, and reported my plans. We had already more than recovered the ground taken and lost by the Second and Third Divisions. The Fifth Corps had been rapidly and completely vindicated, and the question was now of taking the White Oak Road, which had been the object of so much wishing, and worrying. It was evident that things could not remain as they were. The enemy would soon attack and drive me back. And it would cost many men even to try to withdraw from such a position. The enemy's main works were directly on my right flank, and how the intervening woods might be utilized to cover an assault on that flank, none of us knew. I proposed to put Gregory's Brigade into those woods, by battalion in echelon by the left, by which formation he would take in flank and reverse in succession any attacks on my right. When Gregory should be well advanced I would charge the works across the field with my own brigade. My plan being approved, I instructed Gregory to keep in the woods, moving forward with an inclination towards his left to keep him closed in toward me, and at the same time to open the intervals in his echelons so that he would be free to deliver a strong fire on his own front if necessary; and the moment he struck any opposition to open at once with full volleys and make all the demonstration he could, and I would seize that moment to make a dash at the works in my front. Had I known of the fact that General Lee himself was personally directing affairs in our front,[1] I might not have been so rash, or thought myself so cool.

Riding forward I informed my officers of my purpose and had their warm support. Soon the roar of Gregory's guns rose in the woods like a whirlwind. We sounded bugles "Forward," and that way we go; mounted officers leading their commands; pieces at the right shoulder until at close quarters.

What we had to do could not be done by firing. This was foot-and-hand business. We went with a rush; not minding ranks nor alignments; but with open front to lessen loss from the long-range rifles. Within effective range,—about three hundred yards,—the sharp, cutting fire made us reel and shiver. Now, quick or never! On and over! The impetuous 185th New York rolls over the enemy's right, and seems to swallow it up; the 198th Pennsylvania, with its fourteen companies, half veterans, half soldiers "born so," swing in upon their left striking Hunton's Brigade in front; and for a few minutes there is a seething wave of countercurrents, then rolling back leaving a fringe of wrecks, and all is over. We pour over the works; on across the White Oak Road; swing to the right and drive the enemy into their entrenchments along the Claiborne Road, and

[1]Testimony of General Hunton and General McGowan; Warren Court Records, Vol. I, page 625 and 648.

then establish ourselves across the road facing northeast, and take breath.[1]

Major Woodward in his history of the 198th Pennsylvania giving a graphic outline of the last dash, closes with an incident I had not recorded. "Only for a moment," he says, "did the sudden and terrible blast of death cause the right of the line to waver. On they dashed, every color flying, officers leading, right in among the enemy, leaping the breastworks,— a confused struggle of firing, cutting, thrusting, a tremendous surge of force, both moral and physical, on the enemy's breaking lines,—and the works were carried. Private Augustus Zieber captured the flag of the 46th Virginia in mounting one of the parapets, and handed it to General Chamberlain in the midst of the mêlée, who immediately gave it back to him, telling him to keep it and take the credit that belonged to him. Almost that entire regiment was captured at the same time." It scarcely need be added that the man who captured that battle flag was sent with it in person to General Warren, and that he received a Medal of Honor from the Government.

In due time Gregory came up out of the woods his face beaming with satisfaction at the result to which his solid work, so faithfully performed, had been essential. His brigade was placed in line along the White Oak Road on our right, and a picket thrown out close up to the enemy's works. This movement had taken three hours, and was almost a continuous fight, with several crescendo passages, and a final cadence of wild, chromatic sweeps settling into the steady key-note, thrilling with the chords of its unwritten overtones and undertones. It had cost us a hundred men, but this was all too great, of men like these,—and for oblivion. It was to cost us something more,—a sense of fruitlessness and thanklessness.

It seems that in the black moment, when our two divisions were coming back in confusion, Meade had asked Grant to have Sheridan strike the attacking force on their right and rear, as he had been ordered to do in case Warren was attacked. For we have Grant's message to Meade, sent at 12.40, which is evidently a reply: "It will take so long to communicate with Sheridan that he cannot be brought to cooperation unless

---

[1]General Hunton, since Senator from Virginia, said in his testimony before the Warren Court, speaking of this charge, "I thought it was one of the most gallant things I had ever seen." Records, Part I, page 625.

he comes up in obedience to orders sent him last night. I understood General Forsyth to say that as soon as another division of cavalry got up, he would send it forward. It may be there now. I will send to him again, at once."

So far, to all appearance, all was well. The Fifth Corps was across the White Oak Road. General Grant's wish that we should extend our left across this road as near to the enemy as possible, so that Sheridan could double up the enemy and drive him north of Hatcher's Run, had been literally fulfilled. It had cost us three days' hard work and hard fighting, and more than two thousand men. It had disclosed vital points. General Grant's notice of all this as given in his memoirs (Vol. II, page 435), representing all these movements as subordinated to those of General Sheridan is the following: "There was considerable fighting in taking up these new positions for the Second and Fifth Corps, in which the Army of the James had also to participate somewhat, and the losses were quite severe. This is what was known as the battle of the White Oak Road."[1]

The understanding of this affair has been confused by the impression that it was the Second Corps troops which attacked and drove back the forces of the enemy that had driven in the Second and Third Divisions of the Fifth Corps. In the complicated rush and momentous consummation of the campaign, and particularly in the singular history of the Fifth Corps for those days, in which corps and division and brigade commanders were changed, there was no one specially charged with the care of seeing to it that the movements of this corps in relation to other corps were properly reported as to the important points of time as well as of place. General Miles, doubtless, supposed he was attacking the same troops that had repulsed part of the Fifth Corps. He moved promptly when Griffin, with infantry and artillery was checking the onrushing

[1]When the very assault we were in the act of making, or rather, of following up, on the enemy's right on the thirty-first of March, was triumphantly taken up by General Miles on the second of April, after the disaster at Five Forks had called away most of the defenders of the Claiborne entrenchments,—Generals Anderson and Johnson, with Hunton's, Wise's, Gracie's and Fulton's Brigades being of the number,—and the whole rebel army was demoralized, General Grant, now free to appreciate such action, despatches General Meade at once: "Miles has made a big thing of it, and deserves the highest praise for the pertinacity with which he stuck to the enemy until he wrung from him victory." Verily, something besides circumstances can "alter cases."

enemy now close upon our front; and attacking in his own front,—that of the Second Corps,—fought his way valiantly close up to the enemy's works in that part of their line. Miles reported to Humphreys that he was "ahead of the Fifth Corps," which subsequently bore off to the left of him and left a wide interval. This expression must not be understood as direction in a right line. It is used rather as related to the angular distance between the Boydton and the White Oak Roads,—this being less where Miles was, on the right, and widening by a large angle towards the left, where the Fifth Corps was. It is as one line is ahead of another when advanced in echelon; or as a ship tacking to windward with another is said to be "ahead " of the latter when she is on the weather beam of it. Miles did not come in contact with a single regiment that had attacked the Fifth Corps. He struck quite to the right of us all, attacking in his own front. But it got into the reports otherwise, and "went up." Grant accepted it as given; and so it has got into history, and never can be got out. General Miles did not get ahead of the Fifth Corps that day, but he came up gallantly on its flank and rendered it great assistance by turning the flank of General Wise and keeping the enemy from massing on our front. He reports the capture of the flag of the 47th Alabama, a regiment of Law's old brigade of Longstreet's Corps, which was nowhere near the front of the Fifth Corps on this day.

In the investigations before the Court of Inquiry, General Warren felt under the necessity of excusing himself from the responsibility of the disastrous results of Ayres' advance on the morning of the thirty-first. He is at pains to show that he did not intend an attack there, although he had suggested the probable success of such a movement.[1] What then was this advance? Surely not to create a diversion in favor of Sheridan before Dinwiddie. At all events, there was an endeavor to get possession of the White Oak Road. And that could not be done without bringing on a battle, as Ayres said he knew, beforehand,[2] and afterwards knew still better, and we also, unmistakably. Warren stated his intention correctly, no doubt; but then was he aware as he should be, of the condition of things

[1]Records, Warren Court, Part II, page 1525.

[2]Testimony, Warren Court, Part I, page 247.

in Ayres' front?

But, however this may have been, when Ayres' advance was repulsed, why was it felt necessary to recover that field and "the honor of the Fifth Corps?" Unless it was the intention to take forcible possession of the White Oak Road, the recovery of that field was not a tactical necessity, but only,—if I may so speak,—a sentimental necessity. And there was no more dishonor in this reconnaissance,—if it was only that,—being driven back than for Sheridan's reconnaissance toward Five Forks to be driven back upon Dinwiddie, for his conduct in which he received only praise. It is evident that General Grant thought an attack was somehow involved; for hearing of Ayres' repulse, he blames General Warren for not attacking with his whole corps, and asks General Meade, "What is to prevent him from pitching in with his whole corps and attacking before giving him time to entrench or retire in good order to his old entrenchments?" This is exactly what was done, before receiving this suggestion; but it did not elicit approval, or even notice, from Grant or Meade, or Warren. As things turned, Warren was put under a strong motive to ignore this episode; and as for Grant, he had other interests in mind.

In our innocence we thought we had gained a great advantage. We had the White Oak Road, and were across it, and as near to the enemy as possible, according to Grant's wish. Now we were ready for the consummate stroke, the achievement of the object for which all this toil and trial had been undergone. It needed but little more. The splendid Second Corps was on our right, close up to the enemy's works. We were more than ready. If only Sheridan with but a single division of our cavalry could disengage himself from his occupation before Dinwiddie, so far away to our rear, and now so far off from any strategic point where he had first been placed for the purpose of raiding upon the Danville and Southside Railroads,—which objective had been distinctly given up in orders by General Grant—if with his audacity and insistence Sheridan could have placed himself in position to obey Grant's order, and come to Warren's assistance when he was attacked, should dash up between us and Five Forks, we would have swiftly inaugurated the beginning of the end,—Grant's main wish and purpose latest expressed to Sheridan, of ending matters here, before he went back. But another, and by far minor objective interposed. Instead of the cavalry coming to help us complete our victories at the front, we were to go to the rescue of Sheridan at the rear.

Little did we dream that on the evening of the thirtieth Grant had formed the intention of detaching the Fifth Corps to operate with Sheridan in turning the enemy's right. This was consistent, however, with the understanding in the midnight conference on the twenty-ninth. The proposition to Sheridan was this: "If your situation in the morning is such as to justify the belief that you can turn the enemy's right with the assistance of a corps of infantry entirely detached from the balance of the army, I will so detach the Fifth Corps and place the whole under your command for the operation. Let me know early in the morning as you can your judgment in the matter, and I will make the necessary orders...." Precisely what Warren had proposed to do at that very time on Gravelly Run, only Sheridan would not have been in chief command. His assistance had however been promised to Warren in case he was attacked. Sheridan replies to this on the morning of the thirty-first. "....If the ground would permit, I believe I could with the Sixth Corps, turn the enemy's left, or break through his lines; but I would not like the Fifth Corps to make such an attempt." By "turning the enemy's right," and "breaking through his lines," he meant only the isolated position at Five Forks, where for the two days past there was nothing to prevent his handling them alone, and easily cutting the Southside Railroad. Fortunately for our cause, Lee was so little like himself as to allow the detachment of a considerable portion of his infantry from the entrenchments on the evening of the thirtieth to reenforce this position,—for the sake, probably of covering the Southside Road; to which however, this was not the only key.

Asking for the Sixth Corps shows a characteristic concentration of self-consciousness and disregard of the material elements of the situation wholly unlike the habits of our commanders in the Army of the Potomac. The Sixth Corps was away on the right center of our lines,—even beyond Ord with the Army of the James, and the roads were impracticable for a rapid movement like that demanded. Grant's predilection for his forceful and brilliant cavalry commander could not overcome the material difficulty of moving the Sixth Corps from its place in the main line before Petersburg: he could only offer him the Fifth. And Meade, with meekness quite suggestive of a newly regenerate nature, seems to have offered no objection to this distraction from the main objective, and this inauguration of proceedings which repeatedly broke his army into detachments serving under other commanders, and whereby in the popular prestige and final honors of the campaign, the commander of the Army of the Potomac found himself subordinated to the cavalry commander of the newly made "Middle Military Division."

So while Warren was begging to be permitted to take his corps through fields sodden saddle-girt deep with rain and mire, and get across the right of Lee's entrenched position, the purpose had already been formed of sending him and his corps to try to force the enemy from the position where they were gathering for a stand after having forced his cavalry back upon its base at the Boisseau Cross Road, and holding his main body inactive at Dinwiddie a whole day through. And after Warren had accomplished all that he had undertaken in accordance with the expressed wishes of his superiors, this purpose was to be put into execution.

I do not know that Warren was then aware of General Grant's loss of interest in this movement for the White Oak Road since the new plan for Sheridan and the Fifth Corps. Let us recall: at eight o'clock on the evening before, Meade had sent Grant a despatch from Warren, suggesting this movement. Meade forwarded it to Grant, with the remark: "I think his suggestion the best thing we can do under existing circumstances;—that is, let Humphreys relieve Griffin, and let Warren move on to the White Oak Road, and endeavor to turn the enemy's right." To this Grant replied at 8.35, "It will just suit what I intended to propose; to let Humphreys relieve Griffin's Division, and let that move further to the left. Warren should get himself strong to-night." Orders being sent out accordingly, and reported by Meade, General Grant replies late that evening: "Your orders to Warren are right. I do not expect him to advance in the morning. I supposed, however, that he was now up to the White Oak Road. If he is not, I do not want him to move up without further orders."[1] Meade replies: "He will not be allowed to advance unless you so direct."[2]

[1] Records, Warren Court, Vol. II. p. 1242.

[2] This is to be compared with Meade's order of 10.30 A. M., March 31, through General Webb.

It is impossible to think that Warren knew of this last word of Grant on the subject of the White Oak Road; but as we read it now, it throws light on many things then "dark." It was consistent with Grant's new purpose; but it must have perplexed Meade. And at the turn things took,—and men also,—during the next forenoon and midday, what must have been the vexation in Grant's imperturbable mind, and the ebullition of the few unsanctified remnants in Meade's strained and restrained spirit, those who knew them can freely imagine.

And as for Warren, when all this light broke upon him, in the midst of his own hardly corrected reverses, into what sullen depths his spirit must have been cast, to find himself liable to a suit for breach of promise for going out to a clandestine meeting with Robert Lee, when he was already engaged to Philip Sheridan!

A new anxiety now arose. Just as we had got settled in our position on the White Oak Road, heavy firing was heard from the direction of Sheridan's supposed position. This attracted eager attention on our part; as with that open flank, Sheridan's movements were all important to us. At my headquarters we had dismounted, but had not ventured yet to slacken girths. I was standing on a little eminence, wrapped in thoughts of the declining day and of these heavy waves of sound, which doubtless had some message for us, soon or sometime, when Warren came up with anxious earnestness of manner, and asked me what I thought of this firing,—whether it was nearing or receding. I believed it was receding towards Dinwiddie; that was what had deepened my thoughts. Testing the opinion by all tokens known to us, Warren came to the same conclusion. He then for a few minutes discussed the situation and the question of possible duty for us in the absence of orders. I expressed the opinion that Grant was looking out for Sheridan, and if help were needed, he would be more likely to send Miles than us, as he well knew we were at a critical point, and one important for his further plans as we understood them, especially as Lee was known to be personally directing affairs in our front. However, I thought it quite probable that we should be blamed for not going to the support of Sheridan even without orders, when we believed the enemy had got the advantage of him. "Well, will you go?" Warren asked. "Certainly, General, if you think it best; but surely you do not want to abandon this position." At this point, General Griffin came up and Warren asked him to send Bartlett's Brigade at once to threaten the rear of the enemy then pressuring upon Sheridan. That took away our best brigade. Bartlett was an experienced and capable officer, and the hazardous and trying task he had in hand would be well done.

Just after sunset Warren came out again, and we crept on our hands and knees out to our extreme picket within two hundred yards of the enemy's works, near the angle of the Claiborne Road. There was some stir on our picket line, and the enemy opened with musketry and artillery, which gave us all the information we wanted. That salient was well fortified. The artillery was protected by embrasures and little lunettes, so that they could get a slant and cross-fire on any movement we should make within their range.

I then began to put my troops into bivouac for the night, and extended my picket around my left and rear to the White Oak Road, where it joined the right of Ayres' picket line. It was an anxious night along that front. The darkness that deepened around and over us was not much heavier than that which shrouded our minds, and to some degree shadowed our spirits. We did not know what was to come, or go. We were alert—Gregory and I,—on the picket line nearly all the night through. Griffin came up to us at frequent intervals, wide awake as we were.

In the meantime many things had been going on, and going back. It came to us now, in the middle of the night, that Sheridan had been attacked by Fitz Hugh Lee and Pickett's infantry, and driven pell-mell into Dinwiddie. He could hardly hold himself there. The polarities of things were reversed. Instead of admitting the Fifth Corps to the contemplated honor of turning Lee's right, or breaking through his lines, between Dinwiddie and Five Forks, orders and entreaties came fast and thick, in every sense of these terms, for the Fifth Corps to leave the White Oak Road, Lee's company, and everything else, and rush back five miles to the rear, floundering through the mire and dark, to help Sheridan stay where Pickett and Fitz Hugh Lee had put him. Indeed, the suggestive information had leaked out from Grant's headquarters that Sheridan might be expected to retreat by way of the Vaughan Road, quite to the rear of our entire left. This would leave all the forces that had routed Sheridan at perfect liberty to fall upon our exposed flank, and catch the Fifth Corps to be bandied to and fro between them and the enemy in their fortifications, near at hand. By the time the Fifth Corps began to be picked to pieces by divisions and brigades, and finally made a shuttle-cock as an entire organization, the situation of things and of persons had very much changed.

At 6.30 P. M. General Warren received an order to send a brigade to Sheridan's relief by threatening the rear of the enemy then in his front. Soon other orders followed,—the last of these being to send the brigade by the Boydton Road. This would have been quite a different matter. But Bartlett had already been gone an hour when this order came, and to the Crump Road, reaching this by aid of a cart track through woods and mire. Of course, Warren could not recall Bartlett. But to comply as nearly as possible with the order, he at once directed General Pearson, who with three of Bartlett's regiments was guarding the trains on the Boydton Road, to move immediately down towards Dinwiddie. Pearson got to the crossing of the main stream of Gravelly Run, and finding that the bridge was gone, and the stream not fordable, halted for orders. But things were crowding thick and fast. Pearson's orders were countermanded, and orders came from army head-quarters for Griffin's Division to go.

On the news of Sheridan's discomfiture, Grant seems first to have thought of Warren's predicament. In a despatch to Meade early in the evening he says: "I would much rather have Warren back on the Plank Road than to be attacked front and rear where he is. He should entrench, front and rear of his left, at least, and be ready to make a good fight of it if he is attacked in the morning. We will make no offensive movement ourselves to-morrow."

That was on the evening before the battle of Five Forks!

This was a significant despatch; showing among other things Grant's intention of holding on, if possible, for the present at least, to the White Oak Road, at the Claiborne salient; for that was where our two advanced brigades of the Fifth Corps were holding. This evidence has not been well appreciated by those who have formed their judgment, or written the history, of those three days' battles. And Meade had been trying all day to get up entrenching tools and implements for making the roads passable for wheels. A thousand men had been working at this for the two days past.

At 8.30 came the notice,—communicated confidentially, I remember,—that the whole army was going to contract its lines. At nine o'clock came an order from Grant to Meade: "Let Warren draw back at once to his position on the Boydton Road, and send a division of infantry to Sheridan's relief. The troops to Sheridan should start at once, and go down the Boydton Road." Meade promptly sent orders for the corps to retire, and for Griffin to go to Sheridan, and go at once.

Apparently nobody at general headquarters seems to have remembered two incidents concerning the selection of Griffin's Division for this movement; first, that Bartlett of this division was already by this time down upon the enemy's rear, by another, more direct, though more difficult road, and in a far more effective position for the main purpose than could be reached by the Boydton; and secondly, that the two remaining brigades of this division were with me on and across the White Oak Road,—the farthest off from the Boydton Road, and most impeded by difficult ground, of any troops remaining on our lines. Another circumstance, forgotten or ignored, was that the bridge at the Plank Road crossing of Gravelly Run was gone,[1] and that the stream was not fordable for infantry. Warren, in reporting his proceeding to comply with the order, reported also the destruction of the bridge and his intention to repair it; but this seems somehow from first to last, to have added to the impatience felt towards him at those headquarters.

Grant had experienced a sudden change of mind,—a complete and decided one. His imperative order now received meant giving up entirely the position we had just been ordered to entrench, across the hard-won White Oak Road. Within ten minutes from the receipt of this order, Warren directed his division commanders to gather up their pickets and all outlying troops, and take their position on the Boydton Road. Griffin was directed to recall Bartlett and then move down the Plank Road and report to Sheridan. But as it would take time for Griffin to get his scattered division together and draw back through the mud and darkness to the Boydton Road, ready to

---

[1]Colonel Theodore Lyman, aid-de-camp on the staff of General Meade, wrote in his diary on the night of March 30, "Roads reduced to a hopeless pudding. Gravelly Run swollen to treble its usual size, and Hatcher's Run swept away its bridges and required pontoons." Records, Warren Court of Inquiry, Vol I, p. 519.

start for Sheridan, Warren, anxious to fulfil the spirit and object of the order, rather than render a mechanical obedience to the letter of it, sends his nearest division, under Ayres, the strong, stern old soldier of the Mexican war, to start at once for Sheridan. Meantime, the divisions of Griffin and Crawford were taking steps to obey the order to mass on the Boydton Road. For my own part, I did not move a man; wishing to give my men all possible time for rest, until Bartlett should arrive, who must come past my rear.

This was the situation when at half past ten in the evening came an order throwing everything into a complete muddle. It was from Meade to Warren: "Send Griffin promptly as ordered by the Boydton Plank Road, but move the balance of your command by the road Bartlett is on, and strike the enemy in rear, who is between him and Dinwiddie. Should the enemy turn on you, your line of retreat will be by J. M. Brooks' and R. Boisseau's on Boydton Road. You must be very prompt in this movement, and get the forks of the road at Brooks' so as to open to Boisseau's. Don't encumber yourself with anything that will impede your progress, or prevent your moving in any direction across the country." The grim humor of the last suggestion was probably lost on Warren, in his present distraction. "Moving in any direction" in the blackness of darkness across that country of swamps and sloughs and quicksands, would be a comedy with the savage forces of nature and of man in pantomime, and a spectacle for the laughter of the gods. Nor was there much left to encumber ourselves with,—more especially in the incident of food. Grant had been very anxious about rations for us ever since early morning, when he had said that although there were to be no movements that day, the Fifth Corps must be supplied with three days' rations more. But all the day no rations had been got up. Indeed, I do not know how they could have found us, or got to us if they had. Grant had repeated imperative orders to Meade to spare no exertions in getting rations forward to the Fifth Corps; whereupon Meade, who had himself eaten salt with his old Fifth Corps, gave orders to get rations to us anyway;—if not possible for trains, then by pack-mules. The fortunate and picturesque conjuncture was that some few rations were thus got up by the flexible and fitting donkey-train, while we were floundering and plunging from every direction for our rendezvous on the Boydton Road or elsewhere, just at that witching hour of the night when the flying cross-shuttle of oscillating military orders was weaving such a web of movements between the unsubstantial footing of earth and the more substantial blackness of the midnight sky, matched only by the benighted mind.

By this order the Corps was to be turned end for end, and inside out. Poor Warren might be forgiven if at such an order his head swam and his wits collapsed. He responds thus,—and has been much blamed for it by those under canvas, then and since;—"I issued my orders on General Webb's first despatch to fall back; which made the divisions retire in the order of Ayres, Crawford, and Griffin, which was the order they could most rapidly move in. I cannot change them to-night without producing confusion that will render all my operations nugatory. I will now send General Ayres to General Sheridan, and take General Griffin and General Crawford to move against the enemy, as this last despatch directs I should. I cannot accomplish the object of the orders I have received."[1]

But what inconceivable addition to the confusion came in the following despatch from General Meade to Warren at one o'clock at night: "Would not time be gained by sending troops by the Quaker Road? Sheridan cannot maintain himself at Dinwiddie without reenforcements, and yours are the only ones that can be sent. Use every exertion to get the troops to him as soon as possible. If necessary, send troops by both roads, and give up the rear attack."

Rapidly changing plans and movements in effecting the single purpose for which battle is delivered are what a soldier must expect; and the ability to form them wisely and promptly illustrates and tests military capacity. But the conditions in this case rendered the execution of these peculiarly perplexing. Orders had to pass through many hands; and in the difficulties of delivery, owing to distance and the nature of the ground, the situation which called for them had often entirely changed. Hence some discretion as to details in executing a definite purpose must be accorded to subordinate commanders.

Look for a moment at a summary of the orders Warren

---

[1]See this despatch of 10.55 P.M. March 31st. War Records, Serial 97, p. 367, General Warren in his testimony before the Court of Inquiry, claimed that the word "Otherwise" should be prefixed to the last sentence of this order, as it was dictated. Records, page 730, note.

received that evening, after we had reached the White Oak Road, affecting his command in detail.

1. To send a brigade to menace the enemy's rear before Sheridan.

But he had already of his own accord sent Bartlett's Brigade, of Griffin's Division, the nearest troops, by the nearest way.

2. To send this brigade by the Boydton Road instead of the Crump.

This was a very different direction, and of different tactical effect. But impossible to recall Bartlett, Warren sent Pearson, already on the Boydton Road, with a detachment of Bartlett's Brigade.

3. To send Griffin's Division by the Boydton Road to Sheridan, and draw back the whole corps to that road.

Griffin's Division being widely and far scattered, and impossible to be collected for hours, Warren sends Ayres' Division, nearest, and most disengaged.

4. To send Ayres and Crawford by the way Bartlett had gone, and insisting on Griffin's going by Boydton Road.

This would cause Ayres and Bartlett to exchange places, crossing each other in a long, difficult and needless march.

5. Ayres having gone, according to Warren's orders, Griffin and Crawford to go by Bartlett's way.

But Griffin had sent for Bartlett to withdraw from his position and join the division ready to mass on the Boydton Road.

It is difficult to keep a clear head in trying to see into this muddle now: we can imagine the state of Warren's mind. But this was not all. Within the space of two hours, Warren received orders involving important movements for his entire corps, in four different directions. These came in rapid succession, and in the following order:

1. To entrench where he was (on the White Oak Road), and be ready for a fight in the morning. (This from Grant.)

2. To fall back with the whole corps from the White Oak Road to the Boydton, and send a division by this road to relieve Sheridan. (This from Grant.)

3. Griffin to be pushed down the Boydton Road, but the rest of the corps—Ayres and Crawford,—to go across the fields to the Crump Road, the way Bartlett had gone, and attack the enemy in rear who were opposing Sheridan. (This from Meade.)

This required a movement in precisely the opposite direction from that indicated in the preceding order,—which was now partly executed. Ayres had already started.

4. Meade's advice to send these troops by the Quaker Road, (ten miles around), and give up the rear attack.

5. To these may be added the actual final movement, which was that Ayres went down the Boydton Road, and Griffin and Crawford went by the "dirt" road across the country to the Crump Road as indicated in Meade's previous orders.

There is one thing more. General Grant thought it necessary, in order to make sure that Sheridan should have complete and absolute command of these troops,—to send a special message asking Meade to make that distinct announcement to Sheridan. (Despatch of 10.34 P.M., March 31.) To this Meade replies that he had ordered the Fifth Corps to Sheridan, and adds, "The messenger to Sheridan has gone now, so that I cannot add what you desire about his taking command, but I take it for granted he will do so, as he is senior. I will instruct Warren to report to him."

So General Grant's solicitude lest Sheridan should forget to assume command, as the regulations clearly provided, was faithfully ministered to by that expert in nervous diseases,—Meade.

The orders which came to General Warren that night were to an amazing degree confused and conflicting. This is charging no blame on any particular person. We will call it, if you please, the fault of circumstances. But of course, the responsibility for the evil effects of such conditions must naturally, in military usage and ethics, rest upon the officer receiving them. And when he is not allowed to use his judgment as to the details of his own command, it makes it very hard for him, sometimes. Indeed it is not very pleasant to be a subordinate officer; especially if one is also at the same time, a commanding officer.

But in this case I think the trouble was the result of other recognizable contributory circumstances,—if I might not say, causes.

1. The awkwardness of having in the field so many superior, or rather coordinate commanders: Grant, commanding the United States Armies, with his headquarters immediately with those of the commander of the Army of the Potomac; unintentionally but necessarily detracting from the dig-

nity and independence of this subordinate; Meade, commanding the Army of the Potomac, only two corps of which were
with him,—the two others being on the extreme right of our
entrenched lines, with Ord and the Army of the James between them; Sheridan, with an independent cavalry command,
guaranteed so to remain, yet in such touch with the Fifth
Corps that there was danger of more friction than support
between the commanders.[1]

2. A double objective: one point being Sheridan's independent operations to cut the enemy's communications; the
other, the turning of Lee's right and breaking up his army by
our infantry. It is true this double objective was in terms
given up when Sheridan was informed all were to "act together
as one army;" but the trouble is, this precept was never strictly
carried into effect; inasmuch as General Sheridan was not
inclined to serve under any other commander but Grant, and it
became difficult to humor him in this without embarrassing
other operations. And, as matter of fact, the communications
were not cut, either on the Southside or the Danville Roads,
until our infantry struck them,—Sheridan, however, contribut-
ing in his own way to this result.

3. These supreme commanders being at such distance
from the fields of operation on the thirty-first of March, that
it was impossible to have a complete mutual understanding
when orders were to be put into effect. Nor could they make
themselves alike familiar with material conditions, such as
grounds and bridges, or with the existing state of things at
important junctures, owing to rapid, unforeseen changes.

[1]How serious the practical effect was of having orders or despatches on the
same point from several superior or coequal commanders, is brought out by General
Sheridan's answers under close and almost "cross" examination at the Warren Court of
Inquiry. See Records, pages 64-73. As to the embarrassments experienced by General
Meade in giving orders to his subordinates, and by General Warren in handling his own
corps, an example is seen in the following note to General Sheridan by General Webb,
chief of Meade's staff, on the evening of March 31. Consider especially the last sentence.

"Gen. Meade has directed all the spare ambulances he can get hold of to go
down to Dinwiddie. Bartlett's Brigade is at Crump's house on Gravelly Run. Griffin,
with three brigades, is ordered down Boydton Plank, to attack in rear of force menacing
you. Gen. Grant is requested to authorize the sending of Warren's two other divisions
down the dirt road past Crump's, to hold and cover that road, and to attack at daylight."

Thus the Fifth Corps had three immediate commanders to order its divisions.

4. Time lost, and sequence confused, by the difficulty of getting over the ground to carry orders, or to obey them; owing to the condition of the roads, or lack of them, and the extreme darkness of the night.

We had very able officers of the general staff, at each headquarters; otherwise things might have been worse. The responsibilities, labors, tests and perils,—physical and moral,—that often fall upon staff officers in the field, are great and trying. Upon their intelligence, alertness, accuracy of observation and report, their promptitude, energy and endurance, the fate of a corps or a field, may depend.

The frictions, mischances and misunderstandings of all these circumstances falling across Warren's path, might well have bewildered the brightest mind, and rendered nugatory the most faithful intentions.

Meantime, it may well be conceived we who held that extreme front line had an anxious night. Griffin was with me most of the time, and in investigating the state of things in front of our picket lines some time after midnight, we discovered that the enemy were carefully putting out their fires all along their own visible front. Griffin regards this as evidence of a contemplated attack on us, and he sends this information and suggestion to headquarters, and thus adds a new element to the already well-shaken mixture of uncertainty and seeming cross-purposes. But with us, the chief result was an anxiety that forbade a moment's relaxation from intense vigilance.

Meantime Ayres had kept on, according to Warren's first orders to him, getting a small instalment of rations on the way, and arriving at Warren's "Bridge of Sighs" on the Gravelly Run, just as it was ready, at about two o'clock in the morning, whence he pushed down the Plank Road and reported to Sheridan before Dinwiddie just as the day was dawning. Whereupon he was informed that he advanced two miles further than General Sheridan desired, and he had to face about his exhausted men and go back to a cross road which he had passed for the very sufficient reason that Sheridan had no staff-officer there to guide him where he was wanted.

At three o'clock I had got in my pickets, which were replaced by Crawford's, and let my men rest as quietly as possible, knowing there would be heavy burdens laid on them in the morning. For, while dividing the sporadic mule-rations, word came to us that the Fifth Corps, as an organization, was to report to Sheridan at once and be placed under his orders. We kept our heads and hearts as well as we could; for we thought both would be needed. It was near daylight when my command,—all there was of Griffin's Division then left on the front,—drew out from the White Oak Road; Crawford's Division replacing us to be brought off carefully under Warren's eye. We shortly picked up Bartlett's returning brigade, halted, way-worn and jaded with marching and countermarching, and struck off in the direction of the Boisseau houses and the Crump Road, following their heavy tracks in the mud and mire marking a way where before there was none; one of those recommended "directions across the country," which this veteran brigade found itself thus compelled to travel for the third time in lieu of rest or rations, churning the sloughs and quicksands with emotions and expressions that could be conjectured only by a veteran of the Old Testament dispensation.

I moved with much caution in approaching doubtful vicinities, throwing forward an advance-guard, which as we expected to encounter the enemy in force, I held immediately in my own hand. Griffin followed at the head of my leading brigade, ready for whatever should happen. Arrived at the banks of the south branch of Gravelly Run, where Bartlett had made his dispositions the night before, from a mile in our front the glitter of advancing cavalry caught my eye, saber-scabbards and belt-brasses flashing back the level rays of the rising sun. Believing this to be nothing else than the rebel cavalry we expected to find somewhere before us, we made dispositions for instant attack. But the steady on-coming soon revealed the blue of our own cavalry, with Sheridan's weird battle-flag in the van. I reduce my front, get into the road again, and hardly less anxious than before move forward to meet Sheridan.

We come face to face. The sunlight helps out the expression of each a little. I salute: "I report to you, General, with the head of Griffin's Division." The courteous recognition is given. Then, the stern word, more charge than question: "Why did you not come before? Where is Warren?" "He is at the rear of the column, sir." "That is where I expected to find him. What is he doing there?" "General, we are withdrawing from the White Oak Road, where we fought all day. General Warren is bringing off his last division, expecting an attack." Griffin comes up. My responsibility is at an end. I feel better.

I am directed to mass my troops by the roadside. We are not sorry for that. Ayres soon comes up on the Brooks Road. Crawford arrives at length, and masses his troops also, near the J. Boisseau house, at the junction of the Five Forks Road. We were on the ground the enemy had occupied the evening before. It was Bartlett's outstretched line in their rear, magnified by the magic lens of night into the semblance of the whole Fifth Corps right upon them, which induced them to withdraw from Sheridan's front and fall back upon Five Forks.[1] So after all Bartlett had as good as fought a successful battle, by a movement which might have been praised as Napoleonic had other fortunes favored.

We cannot wonder that Sheridan might not be in the best of humor that morning. It is not pleasant for a temperament like his to experience the contradiction of having the ardent expectations of himself and his superior turned into disaster and retreat. It was but natural that he should be incensed against Warren. For not deeply impressed with the recollection that he had found himself unable to go to the assistance of Warren as he had been ordered to do, his mind retained the irritation of vainly expecting assistance from Warren the moment he desired it, without considering what Warren might have on hand at the same time. Nor could Warren be expected to be in a very exuberant mood after such a day and night. Hence the auguries for the cup of loving-kindness on this crowning day of Five Forks were not favorable. Each of them was under the shadow of yesterday: one, of a mortifying repulse; the other, of thankless success. Were Warren a mind-reader he would have known it was a time to put on a warmer manner towards Sheridan. For a voice of doom was in the air.

That morning, two hours after the head of the Fifth Corps column had reported to General Sheridan, an officer of the artillery staff had occasion to find where the Fifth Corps was,—evidently not knowing that under orders from superiors it had been like "all Gaul" divided into three parts, if not four quarters,—and went for that purpose to the point where Warren had had his headquarters the night before. Warren, in leaving at daybreak, had not removed his headquarters' material; but in consideration for his staff, who had been on severe duty all night, told Colonel Locke, Captain Melcher and a few

---

[1]Testimony of Gen. Fitz Hugh Lee, Warren Court, Vol. I, p. 481.

others to stay and take a little rest before resuming the tasking duties of the coming day. It was about nine o'clock in the
morning when the artillery officer reached Warren's old headquarters, and suddenly rousing Colonel Locke asked where the
Fifth Corps was. Locke, so abruptly wakened, his sound sleep
bridging the break of his last night's consciousness, rubbed his
eyes, and with dazed simplicity answered that when he went
to sleep the Fifth Corps was halted to build a bridge at Gravelly Run on the Plank Road. No time was lost in reporting this
at headquarters, without making further inquiries as to the
whereabouts of the Fifth Corps,—now for three hours with
Sheridan on the Five Forks Road. Thereupon General Grant
forthwith sends General Babcock to tell General Sheridan that
"if he had any reason to be dissatisfied with General Warren,"
or as it has since been put, "if in his opinion the interests of
the service gave occasion for it," he might relieve him from
command of his corps.[1]

"So do we walk amidst the precipices of our fate."

All was left to Sheridan's judgment and feeling. The
power was his. Still one must justify himself in the exercise of
rights and powers. We too must realize the situation. Sheridan,
with his habit of intense, concentrated purpose, and indomitable, virile will, was indispensable to Grant in the field. None
other of the commanders reminded us of Attila, king of the
Huns. Warren, with his bright mind, analytic rather than syn-
thetic, seeing things in their details, quick to seize a situation,
yet lacking that tornado force that sweeps only the path before
it, was scarcely suited to wield the thunderbolt of Sheridan.
He was a good fighter; but he thought of too many things.
   General Warren has been blamed, and perhaps justly,

---

[1]Records, Warren Court; testimony of Capt. Warner, page 38; of General
Babcock, page 901; also of General Sheridan, page 93; and General Grant, page 1028.
   General Grant afterwards stated that although this information about the
bridge was the occasion, it was not the reason, of his authorization of General Sheridan
to depose General Warren from his command. Ibid, page 1030.
   That bridge,—for a non-existent one,—had a strange potency. Considering
how various were the tests of which it was made the instrument, it well rivals that
other *pons asinorum* of Euclid; and certainly the associated triangle was of surpassing
attributes; for the squares described on the two "legs" of it were far more than equal to
that so laboriously executed on its hypothenuse.

for attacking with a single division on the White Oak Road. As he denies that he intended this for an attack, we will put it that he is blamed for not sufficiently supporting a reconnaissance; so that the repulse of it involved the disorderly retreat of two divisions of his corps. It is to be said to this that he very shortly more than recovered this ground, driving the enemy with serious loss into his works. But at the worst, was that a fault hitherto unknown among corps or army commanders? Sheridan attacked with a single division when he was ordered to take Five Forks on the day before, and was driven back by a very inferior force to that he had in hand. He was not blamed, although the result of this failure was the next day's dire misfortunes. And on this very day, driven back discomfited into Dinwiddie, he was not blamed; he was praised,—and in this high fashion. General Grant in his official report and subsequent histories speaking of this repulse says: "Here General Sheridan displayed great generalship. Instead of retreating with his whole command on the main army, to tell the story of superior forces encountered, he deployed his cavalry on foot, leaving only mounted men enough to take charge of the horses. This compelled the enemy to deploy over a vast extent of wooded and broken country and made his progress slow."

If Warren had the benefit of this definition of great generalship, he might have known better what to do on the White Oak Road. Perhaps also Pickett and Fitz Hugh Lee might have profited by this implied rebuke for allowing themselves to be so "bluffed," and "compelled to deploy," instead of following their old fashion of concentrating on a vulnerable point and launching javelin-like through their enemy's lines. Perhaps, however, they had a wise diffidence of so exhibiting themselves before our stalwart dismounted cavalry, having a well grounded opinion also that our cavalry breech-loaders, Spencers and repeaters were quite a match for the unwieldy muzzle-loading Richmond or Springfield rifles, and that for all purposes except running, a man on two legs is better than a man on four.

Warren was deposed from his command at Five Forks mainly, I have no doubt, under the irritation at his being slow in getting up to Sheridan the night before from the White Oak Road. But he was working and fighting all day to hold the advanced left flank of Grant's chosen position, and harassed all night with conflicting and stultifying orders, while held between two threatening forces; his left with nothing to prevent Lee's choice troops disengaged from Sheridan from striking it a crushing blow; and on the other hand, Lee himself in person, evidently regarding this the vital point, with all the troops he could gather there, ready to deliver on that little front a mortal stroke. For it is not true as has been stated by high authority that any troops that had fought us on the White Oak Road had gone to Pickett's support at Five Forks that day. And when in the gray of morning he moved out to receive Sheridan's not over-gracious welcome to the Fifth Corps, Warren withdrew from under the very eyes of Lee, his rear division faced by the rear rank, ready for the not-improbable attack, himself the last to leave the field that might have been so glorious,—now fated to be forgotten.

It may be presumption to offer opinions on the operations of that day under such commanders. But having ventured some statements of fact that seem like criticism, it may be required of me to suggest what better could have been done, or to show reason why what was done was not the best. I submit therefore, the following remarks:

1. Five Forks should have been occupied on the thirtieth as Grant had ordered, and when there was nothing formidable to oppose. The cavalry could then easily strike the Southside Railroad, and the Fifth and Second Corps be extended to envelope the entire right of the enemy's position, and at the opportune moment the general assault could be successfully made, as Grant had contemplated when he formed his purpose of acting as one army with all his forces in the field.

2. This plan failing, there were two openings promising good results; one, to let the cavalry linger about Dinwiddie and threaten Lee's communications, so as to draw out a large body of his troops from the entrenchments into the open where they could be attacked on equal ground, and his army be at least materially crippled; the other, to direct the assault immediately on the right of Lee's entrenched lines on the Fifth Corps front,—the cavalry, of course, sweeping around their flank so as to take them in reverse, while the infantry concentrated on their weakest point.

A third thing was to do a little of both;—and this is what we seem to have adopted, playing from one to the other, fitfully and indecisively, more than one day and night.

Beyond doubt it was Grant's plan when he formed his new purpose on the night of the twenty-ninth, to turn the enemy on their Claiborne flank, and follow this up sharply by vigorous assault on the weakest point of their main line in front of Petersburg. The positions taken up by the Fifth and Second Corps are explained by such a purpose, and the trying tasks and hard fighting required of them for the first three days are therein justified. The evidence of this purpose is ample.[1]

Everything was made ready, but the attack was suspended. I am not upon the inquiry whether this was postponed until Sheridan should have done something; my point is that if, or when, this purpose was abandoned for another line of action, other dispositions should have been promptly made, and information given to officers charged with responsibilities and environed with difficulties as Warren was, so that they could catch the change of key. Grant had set the machinery in motion for the White Oak Road, and it was hard and slow work to reverse it when he suddenly changed his tactics, and resolved to concentrate on Sheridan. Why was the Fifth Corps advanced after Ayres' repulse? The "reconnaissance" had been made; the enemy's position and strength ascertained, and our party had returned to the main line. There was no justification in pressing so hard on that point of the White Oak Road, at such costs, unless we meant to follow up this attack to distinct and final results. This may possibly be laid to Warren's charge in his anxiety and agony to "save the honor of the Fifth Corps." But this was not essential to the grander tactics of the field. I sometimes blame myself,—if I may presume to exalt myself into such high company,—for going beyond the actual

---

[1]As evidence that a general attack was intended, we may cite the order suspending it. It is from Grant to Meade, received by the latter at about one o'clock in the morning of the thirty-first. "I think it has now got to be so late for getting out orders, that it would be doubtful whether Wright could be fully cooperated with by all parts of the army if he was to assault as he proposes....You might notify him to arrange his preliminaries and see if Parke can get ready also; and if so, give him definite orders as soon as it is known. I will telegraph to Ord and ascertain if he can get ready. Warren and Humphreys would have nothing to do but to push forward where they are..." But a later order to Meade reads: "You may notify Parke and Wright that they need not assault in the morning....I have pretty much made up my mind what to do and will inform you in the morning what it is." Rebellion Records, Serial 97, pages 285, 286, and following. But the understanding of these orders is made difficult by their not being arranged in the order of their delivery.

recovery of Ayres' lost field, and pressing on for the White Oak Road, when it was not readily permitted me to do so. It may be that my too youthful impetuosity about the White Oak Road got Warren into this false position across this road, where all night, possessed with seven devils, we tried to get down to Sheridan and Five Forks. But I verily believed that what we wanted was the enemy's right, on the White Oak Road. How could we then know Grant's change of purpose? However, it was all a mistake if we were going to abandon everything before morning. We should have been withdrawn at once, and put in position for the new demonstration. That order to mass on the Boydton Road, received at about ten o'clock at night, should have been given much earlier,—as soon as we could safely move away from the presence of the enemy,—if we were to reenforce Sheridan on his own lines.

3. But better than this, as things were, it would have been to leave a small force on the White Oak Road to occupy the enemy's attention, and move the whole Fifth Corps to attack the rear of the enemy then confronting Sheridan, as Meade suggested to Grant at ten o'clock at night.[1] It would have been as easy for us all to go, as for Bartlett. With such force we would not have stopped on Gravelly Run, but would have struck Pickett's and Fitz Hugh Lee's rear, and compelled them to make a bivouac under our supervision, on that ground where they had "deployed." They would not have been able to retire in the morning, as they were constrained to do by Bartlett's demonstration.

4. No doubt it was right to save the honor of the cavalry before Dinwiddie, as of the Fifth Corps before the White Oak Road; and Sheridan's withdrawal to that place having lured out so large a force,—six thousand infantry and four thousand cavalry,—from a good military position to the exposed one at Five Forks, it was good tactics to fall upon them and smash them up. Lee, strangely enough, did not think we would do this; for he held himself in his main lines on his right, as the point requiring his presence; and sent reenforcements from there for his imperiled detachment only so late that they did not report until after the struggle at Five Forks was all over.

But we owe much to fortune. Had the enemy on the thirty-first let Fitz Hugh Lee with his cavalry reenforcements

[1]Records, Warren Court, p. 1251.

occupy Sheridan, and rushed Pickett's Division with the two
brigades of Johnson's down the White Oak Road upon the
flank of the momentarily demoralized Fifth Corps, while Hunton
and Gracie and Wallace and Wise were on its front, we should
have had trouble. Or had they, after repulsing Sheridan towards evening, left the cavalry deployed across his front to
baffle his observation, while Pickett should make the converse
movement on us to ours on him with Bartlett's Brigade, and
come across from that Crump Road to fall upon our untenable
flank position, it would have opened all eyes to the weakness
and error of our whole situation. What would have become of
us, some higher power than any there only could say.

The battle of Five Forks was also the battle of the
White Oak Road, on an extended front, in an accidental and
isolated position, and at a delayed hour. It was successful,
owing to the character of the troops, and the skill and vigor of
the commander. Appomattox was a glorious result of strong
pushing and hard marching. But both could have been fore-
stalled, and all that fighting, together with that at Sailor's
Creek, High Bridge and Farmville have been concentrated in
one grand assault, of which the sharp-edged line along the
White Oak Road would have been one blade of the shears, and
Ord and Wright and Parke on the main line the other, and the
hard and costly ten days' chase and struggle would have been
spared so many noble men. Lee would not have got a day's
start of us in the desperate race. Sheridan cutting the enemy's
communications and rolling up their scattering fugitives would
have shown his great qualities, and won conspicuous, though
not supreme honors. Warren would have shared the glories of
his corps. Humphreys and Wright with their veterans of the
Second and Sixth, whose superb action compelled the first flag
of truce contemplating Lee's surrender, would not have stood
idly around the headquarters' flag of the Army of the Potomac,
with Longstreet's right wing brought to bay before them, waiting till Lee's final answer to Grant should come through Sheridan
to the Fifth Corps front, where Ord, of the Army of the James,
commanded. And Meade, the high-born gentleman and high-
borne soldier, would have been spared the slight of being held
back with the main body of his army, while the laurels were
bestowed by chance or choice, which had been so fairly won by
that old army in long years of heroic patience in well-doing
and suffering;—might have been spared the after humiliation

of experiencing in his own person how fortune and favor preside in the final distribution of honors in a Country's recognition.

So we leave again,—the Fifth Corps and the White Oak Road. But it was by one of those strange overrulings of Providence, or what some might call poetic justice, and some the irony of history, that it befell Sheridan to have with him at Five Forks and at Appomattox Courthouse,—not slow nor inconspicuous,—the rejected old Fifth Corps.

5

FIVE FORKS

I present some reminiscences of things which fell under my observation on the first day of April, 1865, the day of Five Forks. This paper is the outcome of notes made within a few days of the occurrences, and written out soon after the stress of that campaign was over, and while the images of its experiences were vivid in the mind. It will be understood, therefore, that this is a description of facts as they occurred and appeared to me.

Since that was written, an unusual amount of light has been cast, through various atmospheres, on the proceedings of that day; first in official reports of prominent participants, then in published brochures of actors, claimants or advocates, and especially in the remarkable disclosures before the Court of Inquiry called to investigate the conduct of General Warren.

It seems best not to disturb the singleness of the point of view and simple unity of this sketch by incorporating corroborative or qualifying material; but to let it stand for what it may be worth in itself. I shall permit myself, however, to pay passing notice,—as it were, in parenthesis,—to certain collateral testimony or relevant remark of others, which may assist in setting facts in their true lines and light.[1]

Comparison and study of this later material give occasion for the reminder that even official reports, made often under first impressions,—from personal observation, indeed, but therein limited or partial,—are quite liable to disturb the true balance and perspective of the whole field of action. This

[1]In printing this, these added collateral references are thrown into footnotes, or into a separate discussion at the close.

liability is greater as the individual impression or experience is stronger. Such testimony is valuable as giving what was done, or seen at particular points or believed at the time; and is to be weighed by the credibility of the narrator, as to character, temperament, or state of mind. It is only by gathering, sifting and comparing these that the truth in detail or in the whole can be comprehended.

I present this paper, subject perhaps to the criticism I have just indicated, as being mainly a contribution of the partial kind, and standing on the general credibility of the narrator; but claiming also as to certain specific conclusions to rise to the more comprehensive view afforded by enlarged opportunities for judgment.

The vicissitudes of that day, and the grave and whimsical experiences out of which we emerged into it, exhibited the play of that curious law of the universe seen in tides, reactions, or reversals of polarities at certain points of tension or extremes of pressure, and which appears also in the mixed relations of men and things. There are pressure-points of experience at which the unsupportably disagreeable becomes "a jolly good time." When you cannot move in the line of least resistance, you take a very peculiar pleasure in crowding the point of greatest resistance. No doubt there is in the ultimate reasons of human probation special place for that quality of manhood called perseverance, patience, pluck, push, persistence, pertinacity,—or whatever other name beginning with this "explosive mute,"—the excess of which, exhibited by persons or things, is somewhat profanely referred to as "pure cussedness."

After such a day and night as that of the thirty-first of March, 1865, the morning of April 1 found the men of the Fifth Corps strangely glad they were alive. They had experienced a kaleidoscopic regeneration. They were ready for the next new turn,—whether of Fortunatus or Torquemada. The tests of ordinary probation had been passed. All the effects of "humiliation, fasting and prayer," believed to sink the body and exalt the spirit, had been fully wrought in them. At the weird midnight trumpet-call they rose from their sepulchral fields as those over whom death no longer has any power. Their pulling out for the march in the ghostly mists of dawn looked like a passage in the transmigration of souls—not sent back to work out the remnant of their sins as animals, but lifted to the "third plane" by that three days of the underworld,—eliminating sense,—incorporating soul.

The pleasantries associated with April 1 were not much put in play: none of those men were going to be "fooled" that day.

When we joined the cavalry, some of us were aware of a little shadow cast between the two chief luminaries,—him of the cavalry and him of the infantry; but that by no means darkened our disks. If not "hale fellows," we were "well met." The two arms of the service embraced each other heartily, glad to share fortunes. Particularly we; for the cavalry had the habit of being a little ahead, and so got all the chickens,—as we knew by the kind of bones we found when we came after them. And we thought the cavalry, though a little piqued at our not going down and picking up what they had left at Dinwiddie the night before, were quite willing we should share whatever they should get to-day. Sheridan had also come to the opinion that infantry was "a good thing to have around,"—however by some queer break in the hierarchy of honor subordinated to the chevaliers,—the biped to the quadruped, and by some freak of etymology named infantry—the "speechless"—whether because they couldn't talk, or because they mustn't tell. We were glad to be united to Sheridan, too, after the broken engagements of the day before, perhaps renewed reluctantly by him; glad to fight under him, instead of away from him, hoping that when he really struck, the enemy would get hurt more than friends.

Griffin's and Crawford's Divisions were massed near the house of J. Boisseau, on the road leading from Dinwiddie Courthouse to Five Forks. Ayres was halted a mile back at the junction of the Brooks Road, which he had reached by his roundabout, forced march during the night. We were waiting for Sheridan, at last. And he was waiting until the cavalry should complete one more "reconnaissance," to determine the enemy's position and disposition at Five Forks, three miles northward.

Although the trains which had got up were chiefly ammunition wagons, a considerable halt was indicated and the men seized the occasion to eat, to rest, to sleep,—exercises they had not much indulged in for the last three days,—and to make their toilets, which means to wring the water out of their few articles of clothing, *seriatim*, and let the sun shine into the bottom of their shoes; and also,—those who could—to make their three days' vital equation of rations,—hard-tack, pork, coffee and sugar,—concluding by stuffing their haversacks and pockets with twenty rounds extra ammunition for dessert.

Meantime those of us who were likely to have some special responsibilities during the approaching battle, had anxious thoughts. We had drawn away from the doubly confused conflict of yesterday; we were now fairly with Sheridan, cut off from reach of other wills, absolved from the task of obeying commands that made our action seem like truants driving hoops,—resulting mostly in tripping up dignitaries, and having a pretty hard time ourselves, without paternal consolations when we got home. We knew there would be some fighting of no common order now. General Griffin came and sat by me on the bank-side and talked quite freely. He said Sheridan was much disturbed at the operations of the day before, as Grant's language to him about this had been unwontedly severe,[1] and that all of us would have to help make up for that day's damage. He told me also that Grant had given Sheridan authority to remove Warren from command of the corps, when he found occasion, and that we should see lively times before the day was over. We remarked how these things must affect Sheridan: Grant's censure of his failures the day before; the obligation to win a decisive battle to-day; and the power put in his hands to remove Warren. We could not but sympathize with Sheridan in his present perplexities, and, anxious for Warren, were resolved to do our part to make things go right.[2] (Footnote 2 appears on page 104.)

The troops had enjoyed about four hours of this unwonted rest, when, the cavalry having completed its reconnaissance, we were ordered forward. We turned off on a narrow road said to lead pretty nearly to the left of the enemy's defences at Five Forks on the White Oak Road. Crawford led, followed by Griffin and Ayres,—the natural order for prompt

[1]Griffin knew of the dispatch sent by Grant to Sheridan from the Butler house on the Boydton Plank Road at about 2 P.M. of the thirty-first of March, just as I was advancing, after Ayres' repulse. This read: "Warren and Miles' Division are now advancing. I hope your cavalry is up, where it will be of assistance. Let me know how matters stand now with the cavalry; where they are; what their orders, etc. If it had been possible to have had a division or two of them well up on the right hand road taken by Merritt yesterday, they could have fallen on the enemy's rear as they were pursuing Ayres and Crawford." Records, Warren Court, p. 1313.

and free movement.   The road had been much cut up by
repeated scurries of both the contending parties, and was even
yet obstructed by cavalry led horses, and other obstacles,—which
it would seem strange had not been got off the track during all
this halt.   We who were trying to follow closely were brought
to frequent stand-still.   This was vexatious;—our men being
hurried to their feet in heavy marching order, carrying on their
backs perhaps three days' life for themselves and a pretty
heavy instalment of death for their antagonists, and now compelled every few minutes to come to a huddled halt in the
muddy road, "marking time" and marking place also with deep
discontent.   In about two hours we get up where Sheridan
wants us, in some open ground and thin woods near the Gravelly Run Church, and form as we arrive, by brigades in column
of regiments.   The men's good nature seems a little ruffled on
account of their manner of marching, or being marched.   They
have their own way of expressing their wonder why we could
not have taken a shorter road to this cavalry rendezvous,
rather than to be dragged around the two long sides of an
acute-angled triangle to get to it,—why the two-legged and
four-legged elements of animal geometry had not been bal-

[2]Much after-light is thrown on the elements of the situation by observing, as
we are now able to do in the published records of the war, the tenor of the Hon. Charles
A. Dana's dispatches to the War Office of May 9 and 12, 1864, referring to Warren's
movements as slow and piece-meal, so as to fail of the desired effect in the plans of the
general commanding the army.   He accuses him of not handling his corps in a mass, and
even implies a positive disobedience of orders on his part in attacking with a division
when ordered by Grant to attack with his whole corps. (Serial No. 67, pp. 64, 68.)

   Still the Fifth Corps "got in" enough to lose ten thousand six hundred and
eighty-six men in the first two fights. (Dana's report, War Records Serial 64, p. 71.)

   Even more light is turned on.   For no dispatch of Dana's concerning Warren
compares in severity with Dana's to the Secretary or War, July 7, 1864, denouncing
General Meade, and advising that he be removed from the command of the army.
(Serial No. 80, p. 35.)

   It now appears that Warren was in great disfavor with Meade also, after
arriving before Petersburg.   Meade called upon Warren to ask to be relieved from
command of his corps on the alternative that charges would be preferred against him.
(Dana's dispatch, June 20, 1864, War Records, Serial No. 80, p. 26.)

   Meade was much displeased too with Warren for his characteristic remark to
the effect that no proper superior commanding officer was present at the time of the
Mine explosion, to take control of the whole affair.

   And now, with Sheridan against him, poor Warren may well have wished at
least for David's faculty of putting his grievances into song, with variations on the
theme: "Many bulls have compassed me about; yea, many strong bulls of Bashan."

anced by a better equation,—in short, what magic relics there were about "J. Boisseau's," that we should be obliged to make a painful pilgrimage there before we were purified enough to finish dying at Five Forks.

It is now about four o'clock. Near the church is a group of restless forms and grim visages, expressing their different tempers and temperaments in full tone. First of all, the chiefs: Sheridan, dark and tense, walking up and down the earth, seeking,—well, we will say, some adequate vehicle or projectile of expression at the prospect of the sun's going down on nothing but his wrath; evidently having availed himself of some incidental instrumentalities to this end, more or less explicit or expletive,—for Warren is sitting there like an eagle brought to bay in forced restraint,—all his moral energies compressed into the nerve-centers somewhere behind his eyes, and masked by his sallow, sunken cheeks; Griffin, alert and independent, sincere to the core, at his ease, ready for anything,—for a dash at the enemy with battery front, or his best friend with a bit of satire when his keen sense of the incongruous or pretentious is struck; Bartlett, with drawn face, like a Turkish cimetar, sharp, springy, curved outward, damascened by various experience and various emotion; Crawford, a conscious gentleman, having the *entrée* at all headquarters, somewhat lofty of manner; not of the iron fibre, nor spring of steel, but punctilious in a way, obeying orders in a certain literal fashion that saved him the censure of superiors; a pet of his State, and likewise, we thought, of Meade and Warren, judging from the attention they always gave him; possibly not quite fairly estimated by his colleagues as a military man,—but the ranking division commander of the corps. Ayres comes up after a little, ahead of his troops, bluff and gruff at questions about the lateness of his column; twitching his moustache in lieu of words, the sniff of his nostrils smelling the battle not very much afar; sound of heart, solid of force, all the manly and military qualities ready in reserve;—the typical old soldier.

During this impatient waiting for the seemingly slow preparatory formation, our spiritual wheels were lubricated by the flow of discussion and explanation about the plan of attack. Sheridan took a saber or scabbard and described it graphically on the light earth. The plan in general was for the cavalry to occupy the enemy's attention by a brisk demonstration along the right front of their works, while the Fifth Corps should fall upon their left and rear, by a sort of surprise if possible, and scoop them out of their works along the White Oak Road, and capture or disorganize them. The report of the cavalry reconnaissance, as it came to us, was that the enemy had fortified this road for nearly a mile westward, and about three-quarters of a mile eastward from Five Forks, and at the extreme left made a return northerly for perhaps one hundred and fifty yards, to cover that flank. As I understood it, the formation and advance were to be such that Ayres should strike the angle of the "return," and Crawford and Griffin sweep around Ayres' right, flanking their "return" and enfilading their main line. This was perfectly clear, and struck us all as a splendid piece of tactics, cyclone and Sheridan-like, promising that our success was to be quick and certain. Our somewhat jaded faculties were roused to their full force.

As Ayres' troops were forming, officers of the other two divisions were taking their respective stations. I was in my place but had not yet mounted, when General Fred Winthrop of Ayres' leading brigade came over and said: "Dear old fellow, have you managed to bring up anything to eat? We moved so suddenly I had to leave everything. I have had scarcely a mouthful to-day." I sent back an orderly and hurried up whatever we had. The best was poor, and there was not much of it. We sat there on a log, close behind the lines, and acted host and guest, while he opened his heart to me as men sometimes will quite differently from their common custom, under the shadow of a forecasting presence. It was a homely scene and humblest fare; but ever to be held in memory as the last supper of high companionship, and vision of the higher. Half an hour afterwards, in the flame and whirl of battle, leading his brigade like a demigod, as in a chariot of fire he was lifted to his like.

The corps formation was: Ayres on the left, west of the Church Road, the division in double brigade front in two lines, and Winthrop with the First Brigade in reserve, in rear of his center; Crawford on the right, east of the road, in similar formation; Griffin in rear of Crawford, with Bartlett's Brigade in double column of regiments, three lines deep; my own brigade next, somewhat in echelon to the right, with three battalion lines in close order, while Gregory at first was held massed in my rear. General Mackenzie's cavalry, of the Army of the James, had been ordered up from Dinwiddie, to cross the White

Brevet Major General Joshua L. Chamberlain, 1865
(Courtesy Pejepscot Historical Society)

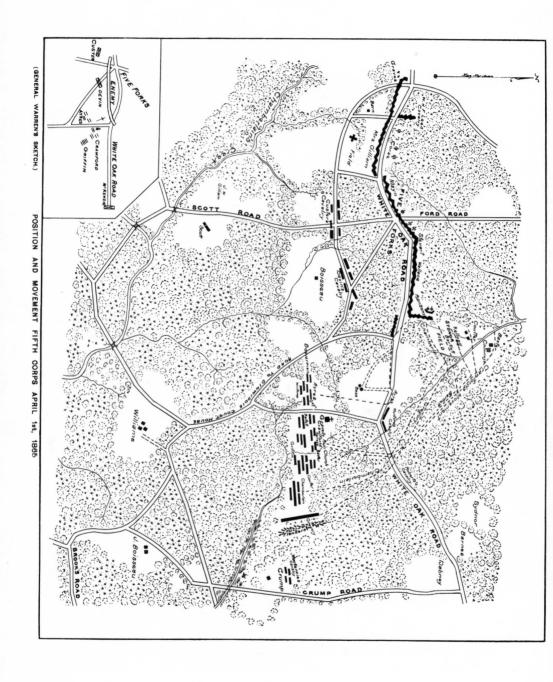

(GENERAL WARREN'S SKETCH.)

POSITION AND MOVEMENT FIFTH CORPS APRIL 1st, 1865

Oak Road and move forward with us covering our right flank. Nevertheless, just as we were moving, General Griffin cautioned me: "Don't be too sure about Mackenzie; keep a sharp look-out for your own right." Accordingly I had Gregory throw out a small battalion as skirmishers and flankers, and march another regiment by the flank on our right, ready to face outwards, and let his other regiment follow in my brigade column.

At four o'clock we moved down the Gravelly Run Church Road, our lines as we supposed nearly parallel to the White Oak Road, with Ayres directed on the angle of the enemy's works. Just as we started there came from General Warren a copy of a diagram of the proposed movement. I was surprised at this. It showed our front of movement to be quite oblique to the White Oak Road,—as much as half a right angle,—with the center of Crawford's Division directed upon the angle, and Ayres, of course, thrown far to the left, so as to strike the enemy's works half way to Five Forks. Griffin was shown as following Crawford; but the whole direction was such that all of us would strike the enemy's main line before any of us could touch the White Oak Road. The diagram, far from clearing my mind, added confusion to surprise. The order read: "The line will move forward as formed till it reaches the White Oak Road, when it will swing around to the left, perpendicular to the White Oak Road. General Merritt's and General Custer's cavalry will charge the enemy's line as soon as the infantry get engaged." This was perfectly clear. The whole corps was to reach the White Oak Road before any portion of it should change direction to the left; Ayres was to attack the angle, and the rest of us swing round and sweep down the entrenchments along the White Oak Road.

The diagram showed the Gravelly Run Church Road as leading directly to and past the angle of the enemy's works. The formation shown led us across the Church Road and not across the White Oak Road at all, which at the point of direction was behind the enemy's entrenched lines. Advancing to the White Oak Road over the enemy's breastworks, and then changing front to flank in a hand-to-hand mêlée was a thing absurd to conceive, and could not be intended to command.

Ill at ease at such confusion of mind, I rode over to General Griffin, who with General Warren was close on my left at this early stage of the movement, and asked for an

explanation. Griffin answers quickly: "We will not worry ourselves about diagrams. We are to follow Crawford. Circumstances will soon develop our duty." In the meantime we were
moving right square down the Church Road, and not oblique to
it as the diagram indicated. However, I quieted my mind with
the reflection that the earth certainly was a known quantity,
and the enemy susceptible to discovery, whatever might be
true of roads, diagrams or understandings.

Crawford crossed the White Oak Road, his line nearly
parallel to it, without encountering the expected angle. This
road, it is to be remarked, made a considerable bend northerly
at the crossing of the Church Road, so that Ayres had not
reached it when Crawford and even Griffin were across. We
naturally supposed the angle was still ahead. Crawford immediately ran into a sharp fire on his right front, which might
mean the crisis. I had been riding with Griffin on the left of
my front line, but now hastened over to the right, where I
found Gregory earnestly carrying out my instructions to guard
that flank. I caught a glimpse of some cavalry in the woods on
our right, which I judged to be Roberts' North Carolina Brigade, that had been picketing the White Oak Road, and so
kept Gregory on the alert. The influence of the sharp skirmish
fire on Crawford's right tended to draw the men towards it;
but I used all my efforts to shorten step on the pivot and press
the wheeling flank, in order to be ready for the "swing" to the
left. Still, the firing ahead kept me dubious. It might mean
Fitzhugh Lee's cavalry making a demonstration there; but
from the persistence of it was more likely to mean infantry
reinforcements sent the enemy from the Claiborne entrenchments where we had left them the day before. It was afterwards seen how near it came to being that.[1]

I had managed, however, to gain towards the left until
we had fairly got past Crawford's left rear. Some firing we
had heard in the supposed direction of our cavalry, but it did
not seem heavier than that in Crawford's front. We were
moving rapidly, and had been out about twenty minutes from

---

[1]Wise's, Grace's and Hunton's Brigades had been ordered out of the Claiborne
entrenchments that afternoon to attack the right flank of the Fifth Corps; but being
obliged to take a roundabout way and getting entangled among the streams and marshes
north of the White Oak Road, they were too late to reach the scene of action until all
was over. Records, Warren Court: Lee's testimony, p. 473: McGowan's, p. 651: Hunton's,
p. 626.

the Church, and perhaps nearly a mile distant, when a sudden burst of fire exactly on our left roused very definite thoughts. This could only be from Ayres' attack. I halted my line and rode ahead through the woods to some high, cleared ground, the southeastern corner of a large field, known as the "Sydnor field," along the opposite edge of which I could see strong skirmishing along Crawford's front; and turning southerly, looking across broken, scrubby ground, could see Ayres' troops engaged in a confused whirl of struggling groups, with fitful firing. This was about as far away, I judged, as Crawford's skirmishing,—about six hundred yards. The great gap between these engagements made me feel that something was "all wrong." I was anxious about my duty. My superiors were not in sight. Bartlett had closely followed Crawford, away to my right. But I could see the corps flag in the Sydnor field, moving towards Crawford, and on the other side, in a ravine half way to Ayres, I saw the division flag. There was Ayres fighting alone, and that was not in the program. There was Griffin down there; that was order enough for me, and I took the responsibility of looking out for the left instead of the right, where my last orders committed me. I pulled my brigade out of the woods by the left flank, telling Gregory to follow; and, sending to Bartlett to let him know what I was doing, pushed across a muddy stream and up a rough ravine towards Ayres. Half way up, Griffin came to meet me,—never more welcome. He gave the look I wanted, and without coming near enough for words waved me to follow up to the head of the ravine and to attack on my right, along the bank where, hidden by brush and scrub, the enemy had a line perpendicular to their main one on the White Oak Road, and were commencing a slant fire in Ayres' direction. Griffin rode past me towards Warren and Bartlett.

At the head of the gully all we had to do was to front into line of battle, and scramble up the rough, brambly steep. The moment we showed our heads, we were at close quarters with the enemy. We exchanged volleys with good will, and then came the rush. Our lines struck each other obliquely, like shutting jaws. It was rather an awkward movement; for we had to make a series of right half wheels by battalion to meet the fire, and all the while gain to the left. Thus we stopped that cross-fire on Ayres, who was now lost from sight by intervening scrubby woods. The brunt of this first fell on my stalwart 185th New York, Colonel Sniper; but Gregory[1] soon coming in by echelon on their right took the edge off that enfilading fire.

Ayres' fitful fire was approaching, and I rode over towards it. Somewhere near the angle of the works I met Sheridan. He had probably seen me putting my men in, and hence I escaped censure for appearing. Indeed his criticism seemed to be that there was not more of me, rather than less. "By G—, that's what I want to see!" was his greeting, "general officers at the front. Where are your general officers?" I replied that I had seen General Warren's flag in the big field north of us, and that seeing Ayres in a tight place I had come to help him, and by General Griffin's order. "Then," cried he, with a vigor of utterance worthy of the "army in Flanders," "you take command of all the infantry round here, and break this dam—" I didn't wait to hear any more. That made good grammar as it stood. I didn't stand for anything, but spurred back to some scattered groups of men, demoralized by being so far in the rear, and not far enough to do them any good, yet too brave to go back. Captain Brinton of Griffin's staff came along, and I took him with me down among these men to get them up.[2] I found one stalwart fellow on his hands and knees behind a stump, answering with whimsical grimaces to the bullets coming pretty thick and near. "Look here, my good fellow," I called down to him, "don't you know you'll be killed here in less than two minutes? That would be a shame. This is no place for you. Go forward!" "But what can I do?" he cried; "I can't stand up against all this alone!" "No, that's just it," I replied. "We're forming here. I want you for guide center. Up, and forward!" Up and out he came like a hero. I formed those "reserves" on him as guide, and the whole queer line,—two hundred of them,—went in right up to the front and the thick of it. My poor fellow only wanted a token of confidence and appreciation to get possession of himself. He was proud of what he did, and so I was for him.

I let the staff officers take these men in, for I had

---

[1]His regiments were the 187th, 188th and 189th New York: thus the four New York regiments constituted the right of my command.

[2]Captain Laughlin of Griffin's staff, says he also joined in this. Records, Warren Court, p. 542.

caught sight of Ayres' Third Brigade coming out of the woods right behind me, and standing in the further edge of the scrubby field. The men were much excited, but were making a good line. General Gwyn was riding up and down their front in a demonstrative manner, but giving no sign of forward movement. I thought this strange for him and bad for us all, in the pinch things then were at, and with the warrant Sheridan had given me galloped down to him and asked him if he was acting under any particular orders from General Ayres. "No, General," he replied with an air of relief, "I have lost Ayres. I have no orders. I don't know what to do." "Then come with me," I said, "I will take the responsibility. You shall have all credit. Let me take your brigade for a moment!" His men gave me good greeting as I rode down their front and gave the order, "Forward, right oblique!" On they came, and in they went, gallantly, gladly, just when and where they were needed, with my own brigade fighting the "return," and ready to take touch with Ayres. His fire was advancing rapidly on my left, and I rode over to meet him. Sheridan was by my side in a moment, very angry. "You are firing into my cavalry!" he exclaims,—his face darkening with a checked expletive. I was under a little pressure, too, and put on a bold air. "Then the cavalry have got into the rebels' place. One of us will have to get out of the way. What will you have us do, General?" "Don't you fire into my cavalry, I tell you!" was the fierce rejoinder. I felt a little left out in the cold by General Sheridan's calling them "my cavalry," as if we were aliens and did not belong to him also; but, whosesoever they were, I could not see what business they had up here at the "angle." This was our part of the field. The plan of the battle put them at the enemy's right and center, a mile away on the Dinwiddie Road and beyond.

Fortunately for me, Ayres comes up, his troops right upon the angle,—the right, the Maryland Brigade, on the "return,"—brave Bowerman down—and Winthrop's Brigade,—gallant Winthrop gone,—reaching beyond, across the White Oak Road, driving a crowd before them. I have only time to say to Ayres, "Gwyn is in on the right;" for Sheridan takes him in hand. "I tell you again, General Ayres, you are firing into my cavalry!"

"We are firing at the people who are firing at us!" is the quick reply. "These are not carbine shot. They are minie balls.

I ought to know."

But I felt the point of Sheridan's rebuke. As my oblique fire across the "return" was now so near the enemy's main line on the White Oak Road, it was not unlikely that if any of the cavalry were up here on their front, I might be firing into them and they into me. There was a worse thing yet: if we continued advancing in that direction, in another minute we should be catching Ayres' fire on our left flank. He was already in, with his men. Griffin coming up, detains me a moment. Sheridan greets him well. "We flanked them gloriously!" he exclaims with a full-charged smile implying that all was not over yet. After a minute's crisp remark, Griffin wheels away to the right, and I am left with Sheridan. He was sitting right in the focus of the fire, on his horse "Rienzi,"—both about the color of the atmosphere,—his demon pennon, good or ill, as it might bode, red and white, two-starred, aloft just behind him. The stream of bullets was pouring so thick it crossed my mind that what had been to me a poet's phrase,—"darkening the air,"—was founded on dead-level fact. I was troubled for Sheridan. We could not afford to lose him. I made bold to tell him so, and begged him not to stay there;—the rest of us would try to take care of things, and from that place he could be spared. He gave me a comical look, and answered with a peculiar twist in the toss of his head, that seemed to say he didn't care much for himself, or perhaps for me,—"Yes, I think I'll go!" and away he dashed, right down through Ayres' left, down the White Oak Road, into that triple cross-fire we had been quarreling about.

I plunged into my business, to make up for this minute's lost time. My men were still facing too much across Ayres' front, and getting into the range of his fire. We had got to change that, and swing to the right, down the rear of the enemy's main works. It was a whirl. Every way was front, and every way was flank. The fighting was hand to hand. I was trying to get the three angles of the triangle into something like two right angles, and had swung my left well forward, opening quite a gap in that direction, when a large body of the enemy came rushing in upon that flank and rear. They were in line formation, with arms at something like a "ready," which looked like "business." I thought it was our turn to be caught between two fires, and that these men were likely to cut their way through us. Rushing into the ranks of my left battalion I shouted the order, "Prepare to fire by the rear rank!" My men faced about at once, disregarding the enemy in front; but at this juncture our portentous visitors threw down their muskets, and with hands and faces up cried out, "We surrender," running right in upon us and almost over us. I was very glad of it, though more astonished, for they outnumbered us largely. I was a little afraid of them, too, lest they might find occasion to take arms again and revoke the "consent of the governed." They were pretty solid commodities, but I was very willing to exchange them for paper token of indebtedness in the form of a provost marshal's receipt. So getting my own line into shape again, I took these well-mannered men, who had been standing us so stiff a fight a few minutes before, with a small escort out over the "return," into the open field in rear, and turned them over to one of Sheridan's staff, with a request for a receipt when they were counted.[1]

In the field I find Ayres, who is turning over a great lot of prisoners. The "angle" and the whole "return" are now carried, but beyond them the routed enemy are stubbornly resisting. I have time for a word with Ayres now, and to explain my taking up Gwyn so sharply. He is not in the mood to blame me for anything. He explains also. He had been suddenly attacked on his left, and had been obliged to change front instantly with two of his brigades. Their two commanders, Winthrop and Bowerman, falling almost at the first stroke, he had taken these brigades in person, and put them in, without sending any word to Gwyn on his right. I could see how it was. Losing connection, Gwyn was at a loss what to do, and in the brief time Ayres was routing the enemy who had attacked him, I had come upon Gwyn and had put him in, really ahead of the main line of Ayres, who soon came up to him. So it all came about right for Ayres[2] (Footnote appears on page 114).

---

[1]The receipt sent me bore the whole number of prisoners turned over by me during the battle; but most of them were taken in this encounter. This acknowledges from my command two colonels, six captains, eleven lieutenants, and a thousand and fifty men sent in by my own brigade; and four hundred and seventy men by Gregory's. It is not impossible that some of these prisoners turned over to General Sheridan's provost marshal, may have been counted twice,—with the cavalry captures as well as my own. It should be said that the prisoners taken by us were due to the efficiency and admirable behavior of all the troops in our part of the field near the "angle," and not alone to that of my immediate command.

General Bartlett now came appealing for assistance. Two of his regiments had gone off with Crawford, and Bartlett had more than he could do to make head against a stout resistance the enemy were making on a second line turned back near the Ford Road.   I helped him pick up a lot of stragglers and asked Gregory to give him the 188th New York for assistance.

Meanwhile Warren, searching for Crawford, had come upon his First Brigade, Kellogg's, and had faced it southerly towards the White Oak Road, as a guide for a new point of direction for that division, and had then gone off in search of the rest of these troops to bring them in on the line.   Thereupon one of Sheridan's staff officers came across Kellogg standing there, and naturally ordered him to go forward into the "fight." Kellogg questioned his authority, and warm words took the place of other action, till at length Kellogg concluded it best to obey Sheridan's representative, and moved promptly forward, striking somewhere beyond the left of the enemy's refused new flank.   It seems also that Crawford's Third Brigade, Coulter's, which was in his rear line, had anticipated orders or got Warren's, and moved by the shortest line in the direction Kellogg was taking.   So Crawford himself was on the extreme wheeling flank, with only Baxter's Brigade and two regiments of Bartlett's of the First Division immediately in hand.   His brigades were now moving in echelon by the left, which was in fact about the order of movement originally prescribed, and that which the whole corps actually took up, automatically as it were, or by force of the situation.   Our commands were queerly mixed; men of every division of the corps came within my jurisdiction, and something like this was probably the case with several other commanders.   But that made no difference; men and officers were good friends.   There was no jealousy among us subordinate commanders.   We had eaten salt to-

[2]To complete this reference, I will mention that Brevet Brigadier-General Gwyn was colonel of the 118th Pennsylvania Volunteers, in Griffin's Division, and had been assigned to command one of Ayres' Brigades.   Not long afterwards I came in command of the division, and, a general court martial being convened, charges were preferred against Gwyn by some who did not understand the facts of this occurrence as well as I did.   When the papers reached me, I disapproved them and sent them back with the endorsement that General Gwyn had done his best under peculiarly perplexing circumstances, and had gone in with his brigade handsomely, under my own eye at a critical moment of the battle.   I believed this to be justice to a brave officer.

gether when we had not much else. This liveliness of mutual
interest and support, I may remark, is sometimes of great
importance in the developments of a battle.

The hardest hold-up was in front of my left center, the
First Battalion of the 198th Pennsylvania. I rode up to the
gallant Glenn, commanding it and said, "Major Glenn, if you
will break that line you shall have a colonel's commission!" It
was a hasty utterance, and the promise unmilitary, perhaps;
but my every energy was focussed on that moment's issue.
Nor did that earnest soldier need a personal inducement; he
was already carrying out the general order to press the enemy
before him, with as much effect as we could reasonably expect.
But it was deep in my mind how richly he already deserved
this promotion, and I resolved that he should get it now. It
was this thought and purpose which no doubt shaped my phrase,
and pardoned it. Glenn sprung among his men, calling out,
"Boys, will you follow me?" wheeled his horse and dashed
forward, without turning to see who followed. Nor did he
need. His words were a question; his act an order. On the
brave fellows go with a cheer into the hurricane of fire. Their
beautiful flag sways gracefully aloft with the spring of the
brave youth bearing it, lighting the battle-smoke; three times
it goes down to earth covered in darkening eddies, but rises
ever again passing from hand to hand of dauntless young
heroes. Then bullet-torn and blood-blazoned it hovers for a
moment above a breast-work, while the regiment goes over
like a wave. This I saw from my position to the left of them
where I was pressing on the rest of my command. The sight so
wrought upon me that I snatched time to ride over and con-
gratulate Glenn and his regiment. As I passed into a deeper
shadow of the woods, I met two men bearing his body,—the
dripping blood marking their path. They stopped to tell me. I
saw it all too well. He had snatched a battle flag from a
broken regiment trying to rally on its colors, when a brute
bullet of the earth once pronounced good, but since cursed for
man's sin, struck him down to its level. I could stop but a
moment, for still on my front was rush and turmoil and tragedy. I could only bend down over him from the saddle and
murmur unavailing words. "General, I have carried out your
wishes!"—this was his only utterance. It was as if another
bullet had cut me through. I almost fell across my saddle bow.
My wish? God in heaven, no more my wish than thine, that

this fair body, still part of the unfallen "good," should be smitten to the sod,—that this spirit born of thine should be quenched by the accursed!

What dark misgivings searched me as I took the import of these words! What sharp sense of responsibility for those who have committed to them the issues of life and death! Why should I not have let this onset take its general course and men their natural chances? Why choose out him for his death, and so take on myself the awful decision into what home irreparable loss and measureless desolation should cast their unlifted burden? The crowding thought choked utterance. I could only bend my face low to his and answer: "*Colonel*, I will remember my promise; I will remember *you!*" and press forward to my place, where the crash and crush and agony of struggle summoned me to more of the same. War!—nothing but the final, infinite good, for man and God, can accept and justify human work like that!

I feared most of all, I well remember,—such hold had this voice on me,—that it might not be given me to be found among the living, so that I could fulfill my word to him. But divine grace and pity granted me this. As soon as the battle was over, I sent forward by special messenger my recommendation for two brevets for him, in recognition of his conspicuous gallantry and great service in every battle of this campaign, up to this last hour. These were granted at once, and Glenn passed from us to other recognition, "Brevet-Colonel of United States Volunteers,"—and that phrase, so costly won, so honorable then, made common since, has seemed to me ever after, tame and something like travesty.[1]

By this time Warren had found Crawford, who with Baxter's Brigade had been pursuing Munford's dismounted cavalry all the way from where we had crossed the White Oak

---

[1] I sought for him from the Governor of Pennsylvania lineal promotion in his regiment, though he had but few hours to live. But that grade was held by an accomplished gentleman detached from his regiment on office duties in the cities, and there was no place for Glenn. The colonel, dear old Sickel, was in hospital with an amputated arm, shattered at the Quaker Road three days before. Within that time this regiment had now lost in battle colonel, major and adjutant, and all we could secure for the rest of the service, that great regiment of fourteen companies, was a major's rank. This, indeed, was worthily bestowed. It came to Captain John Stanton, who after the fall of Sickel and Macuen, had acted as a field officer with fidelity and honor, and had distinguished himself in the struggle for the flag snatched by Glenn with more than mortal energy and at mortal cost.

Road, by a wide detour reaching almost to Hatcher's Run, until he had crossed the Ford Road, quite in rear of the breaking lines which Ransom and Wallace and Wood were trying to hold together.[1] Hence he was in position to do them much damage, both by cutting off their retreat by the Ford Road and taking many prisoners, and also by completing the enemy's envelopment. To meet this, the enemy, instead of giving up the battle as they would have been justified in doing stripped still more their main works in front of our cavalry by detaching nearly the entire brigade of General Terry, now commanded by Colonel Mayo, and facing it quite to its rear pushed it down the Ford Road and across the fields to resist the advance of Warren with Crawford.

We, too, were pressing hard on the Ford Road from the east, so that all were crowded into that whirlpool of the fight. Just as I reached it, Captain Brinton of Griffin's staff dashed up at head-long speed and asked if I knew that Griffin was in command of the corps. I was astonished at first, and incredulous afterwards. I had heard nothing from General Warren since I saw his flag away in the Sydnor field when I was breaking out from the column of march to go to Ayres' support. My first thought was that he was killed. I asked Brinton what he meant. He told me the story. General Warren when he got to the rear of the Ford Road sent an enthusiastic message by Colonel Locke, his chief of staff, to Sheridan saying that he was in the enemy's rear, cutting off his retreat, and had many prisoners. This message met scant courtesy. Sheridan's patience was exhausted. "By G—, sir, tell General Warren he wasn't in the fight!" Colonel Locke was thunderstruck. "Must I tell General Warren that, sir?" asked he. "Tell him that, sir;" came back the words like hammer-blows. "I would not like to take a verbal message like that to General Warren. May I take it down in writing?" "Take it down, sir; tell him, by G—, he was not at the front!" This was done. Locke, the old and only adjutant-general of the Fifth Corps, himself just back from a severe wound in the face on some desperate front with Warren, never felt a blow like that.

[1]To my grief over the costs of this struggle was added now another, when borne past me on the right came the form of Colonel Farnham of the 16th Maine, now on Crawford's staff, who, sent to bear an order into this thickening whirl, was shot through the breast and fell as we thought mortally wounded; but the courage and fortitude, which never forsook him, carried him through this also.

Soon thereafter Sheridan came upon General Griffin, and without preface or index, told the astonished Griffin, "I put you in command of the Fifth Corps!" This was Brinton's story; dramatic enough, surely; pathetic, too. I hardly knew how to take it. I thought it possible Sheridan had told every general officer he met, as he had told me, to take command of all the men he could find on the field and push them in. I could not think of Warren being so wide-off an exception.

Pressing down towards the Forks, some of Ayres' men mingled with my own, on emerging into a little clearing I saw Sheridan riding beside me like an apparition. Yet he was pretty certain flesh and blood. I felt a little nervous;—not in the region of my conscience, nor with any misgiving of the day's business; but because I was alone with Sheridan. His expression was at its utmost bent; intent and content, incarnate will. But he greeted me kindly, and spoke freely of the way things had been going. We were riding down inside the works in the woods covering the Forks and Ford Road, now the new focus of the fight. Just then an officer rode flightily up from that direction, exclaiming to General Sheridan, "We are on the enemy's rear, and have got three of their guns." "I don't care a d— for their guns, or you either, sir. What are you here for? Go back to your business, where you belong! What I want is that Southside Road." The officer seemed to appreciate the force of the suggestion, and the distant attraction of the Southside Road. I looked to see what would happen to me. There were many men gathered round, or rather we had ridden into the midst of them, as they stood amazed at the episode. The sun was just in the tree-tops;—it might be the evening chill that was creeping over us. Then Sheridan, rising in his stirrups, hat in hand waving aloft at full arm's length, face black as his horse, and both like a storm-king, roared out: "I want you men to understand we have a record to make before that sun goes down that will make hell tremble!—I want you there!" I guess they were ready to go; to that place or any other where death would find them quickest; and the sooner they got there, the safer for them.

Griffin came down now from the right, dashed ahead of me and jumped his horse over the works. I thought myself a pretty good rider, but preferred a lower place in the breast-works. My horse saw one and made for it. Just as he neared the leap, a bullet struck him in the leg, and gave him more impetus than I had counted on. But I gave him free rein and held myself easy, and over we went, and down we came, luckily feet-foremost, almost on top of one of the enemy's guns, which we were fortunate enough not to "take." In truth, there was a queer "parliament of religions" just then and there, at this Five Forks focus. And it came in this wise. As Ransom's and Wallace's and Wood's reinforced but wasting lines had fallen back before us along the north and east side of their works, our cavalry kept up sharp attacks upon their right across the works, which by masterly courage and skill they managed to repel, replacing as best they could the great gaps made in their defences by the withdrawal of so many of Steuart's and Terry's Brigades, to form the other sides of their retreating "hollow square." Driven in upon themselves, and over much "concentrated," they were so penned in there was not a fair chance to fight. Seizing the favorable moment Fitzhugh's and Pennington's Brigades of Devins' and Custer's cavalry made a magnificent dash right over the works each side the Forks, just an instant before Ayres' and Griffin's lines had reached that focus. Bartlett also, with some of Crawford's men following, came down nearly at the same time from the north on the Ford Road. All, therefore, centered on the three guns there; so that for a moment there was a queer colloquy over the silent guns. The cavalry officers say, and perhaps with good reason, that they captured the guns, but Griffin would not let them "take" them. Crawford and Bartlett also both report the capture of the guns; but as the enemy had abandoned them before these troops struck them, the claimants of the capture should be content to rank their merits in the order of their coming. There were, however, some guns further up the Ford Road,—whether those at first under Ransom on the "refused" flank, or those hurried from Pegram's command on the White Oak Road to the support of the breaking lines vainly essaying to cover the Ford Road. Of the capture of these there is no doubt. These Major West Funk,—a strange misnomer, but a better name in German than in English, showing there is some "sparkle" in his blood,—actually "took," by personal touch,—both ways. First dodging behind trees before their canister, then shooting down the horses and mules attached to the limbers, as well as the gunners who stood by them, his two little regiments made a rush for the battery, overwhelmed it, unmanned it, and then swept on, leaving the guns behind them, making no fuss about it, and so very likely to get no credit for it. This little episode, however, was not unobserved by me; for these two regiments—the 121st and 142d Pennsylvania, now attached to Crawford's Division, were all that was left to us of the dear lost old First Corps, and of my splendid brigade from it in Griffin's Division, in the ever memorable charge of "Fort Hell," June 18, 1864.

"Taking guns" is a phrase associated with very stirring action. But words have a greater range than even guns. There is the literal, the legal, the moral, the figurative, the poetic, the florid, the transcendental. All these atmospheres may give meaning and color to a word. But dealing with solid fact, there is no more picturesque and thrilling sight, no more telling, testing deed, than to "take a battery" in front. Ploughed through by booming shot; torn by ragged bursts of shell; riddled by blasts of whistling canister;—straight ahead to the guns hidden in their own smoke; straight on to the red, scorching flame of the muzzles,—the giant grains of cannon-powder beating, burning, sizzling into the cheek; then in upon them!—pistol to rifle-shot; saber to bayonet; musket-butt to handspike and rammer; the brief frenzy of passion; the wild "hurrah"; then the sudden, unearthly silence; the ghastly scene; the shadow of death; the aureole of glory;—much that is telling here, but more that cannot be told. Surely it were much better if guns must be taken, to take them by flank attack, by skilful maneuver, by moral suasion, by figure of speech, or even by proxy.

But this is digression, or reminiscence. For the matter in hand, the guns taken at the Forks and on the Ford Road, with due acknowledgements of individual valor, were taken by all the troops who closed in around them, front, flank and rear; by the whole movement, indeed, from the brain of the brilliant commander who planned, to the least man who pressed forward to fulfil his high resolve.

We had pushed the enemy a mile from the left of their works,—the angle, their tactical center,—and were now past the Forks. Something remained to be done, according to Sheridan's biblical intimation. But the enemy made no more resolute, general stand. Only little groups, held back and held together by individual character, or the magnetism of some superior officer, made front, and gave check. For a moment, after the deafening din and roar, the woods seemed almost given back to nature, save for the clinging smoke and broken bodies and breaking moans which betokened man's intervention.

Our commands were much mixed, but the men well moving on, when in this slackening of the strain, Griffin and Ayres, who were now riding with me, spoke regretfully, sympathizingly of Warren. They thought he had sacrificed himself for Crawford, who had not proved equal to the demands of the situation. "Poor Warren, how he will suffer for this!" they said with many variations of the theme. Griffin did not say a word about his being placed in command of the corps. He was a keen observer, a sharp critic, able and prompt to use a tactical advantage; but he was not the man to take pleasure which cost another's pain, or profit from another's loss. It was high promotion, gratifying to a soldier's ambition; it was special preferment, for he was junior to Crawford. But he took it all modestly, like the soldier and man he was, thinking more of duty and service than of self.

Sheridan came upon us again, bent to his purpose. "Get together all the men you can," he says, "and drive on while you can see your hand before you!" The men were widely scattered from their proper commanders. Griffin told me to gather the men of the First Division and bring them to the White Oak Road. I rode in along the ground of the wide pursuit, and kept my bugler sounding all the brigade calls of the division. This brought our officers and men to the left. Among others General Warren came riding slowly from the right. I took pains to greet him cheerfully, and explained to him why I was sounding all the bugle calls. "You are doing just right," he replies, "but I am not in command of the corps." That was the first authoritative word I had heard spoken to this effect. I told him I had heard so, but that General Sheridan had been putting us all in command of everything we could get in hand, and perhaps after the battle was over we would all get back where we belonged. I told him I was now moving forward under Sheridan's and Griffin's order, and rode away from him towards the left with my gathered troops, shadowed in spirit for Warren's sake. I could not be sorry for the corps, nor that Griffin was in command of it: he had the confidence of the whole corps. And however sharp was Griffin's satire, he had the generosity which enables one to be truly just, and never made his subordinates vicarious victims of his own interior irritations.

We had now come to the edge of a wide field across the road and the works on the enemy's right, known as the Gilliam field. Here I came to Sheridan and Griffin, my troops all up, and well in hand. A sharp cavalry fight was going on, in which some of Ayres' men and my own had taken part. On the right, along the White Oak Road were portions of Crawford's infantry that had swung around so quickly as to get ahead of us and they were the ones now principally engaged.

Here Warren took his leave of the corps, himself under a shadow as somber as the scene and with a flash as lurid as the red light of the battle-edge rolling away into the darkness and distance of the deep woods. When our line was checked at this last angle, Griffin had ordered one of Crawford's colonels to advance. The colonel, a brave and well-balanced man, replied that where soldiers as good as Griffin's men had failed, he did not feel warranted in going in without proper orders. "Very well I order you in!" says Griffin, without adding that he did it as commander of the corps. The gallant colonel bows,—it is Richardson, of the 7th Wisconsin,—grasps his regimental colors in his own hand, significant of the need and his resolution in face of it, and rides forward in advance of his men. What can they do but follow such example? General Warren, with intensity of feeling that is now desperation, snatches his corps flag from the hands of its bearer, and dashes to Richardson's side. And so the two leaders ride, the corps commander and his last visible colonel,—colors aloft, reckless of the growing distance between them and their followers, straight for the smoking line—straight for the flaming edge; not hesitating at the breastworks, over they go; one with swelling tumult of soul, where the passion of suffering craves outburst in action; the other with obedience and self-devotion, love-like, stronger than death. Over the breastworks, down among the astonished foe; one of whom, instinct overmastering admiration, aims at the foremost a deadly blow, which the noble youth rushes forward to parry, and shielding with his own the breast of his uncaring commander, falls to earth, bathing his colors with his blood. Need more be told? Do men tarry at such a point? One crested wave sweeps on; another, broken, rolls away. All is lost; and all is won. Slowly Warren returns over the somber field. At its forsaken edge a staff officer hands him a crude field order. Partly by the lurid flashes of the last guns, partly by light of the dying day, he reads: "Major-General Warren, commanding the Fifth Army Corps, is relieved from duty and will at once report for orders to Lieutenant-General Grant, commanding Armies of the United States. By command of Major-General Sheridan."

With almost the agony of death upon his face, Warren approaches Sheridan and asks him if he cannot reconsider the order. "Reconsider. Hell! I don't reconsider my decisions. Obey the order!" fell the last thunder-bolt on Warren's heart.

The battle has done its worst for him. The iron has entered his soul. With bowed head and without a word, he turns from the spectral groups of friend and foe mingled in the dark, forbidding cloud of night, to report to the one man on earth who held power over what to him was dearer than life,—and takes his lonely way over that eventful field, along that fateful White Oak Road, which for him had no end on earth.

After nightfall the corps was drawn in around Five Forks, for a brief respite. We were all so worn out that our sinking bodies took our spirits with them. We had reasons to rejoice so far as victory gives reasons; but there was a strange weight on the hearts of us all. Of things within? or things without? We could not tell. It was not wholly because Warren had gone; although in the sundering of old ties there is always a strain, and Warren had been part of the best history of the Fifth Corps from the beginning. And even about victory,—it is not for itself; it looks to a cause and an end. And we thought of this; pondering on the worth and the cost, and to what that end might unfold to which this was the beginning. There were other emotions, too, which will arise when night draws over a scene like that, and with it the thoughts come home.

We grouped ourselves around Griffin at the Forks, center of the whirling struggle,—we who were left of those once accustomed to gather about him in field or bivouac,—alas for those who came no more!—half-reclining against the gloomy tree-trunks and rudely piled defences so gallantly lost and won, torn by splintering shot and rush of men; half-stretched on the ground moistened by the dews of night and the blood of the mingled brave; hushed at heart, speaking but in murmurs answering to the whispers of the night; with a tremulous sensitiveness, an awe that was not fear. Few things we said; but they were not of the history that is told.

Suddenly emerged from the shadows a compact form,

with vigorous stride unlike the measure and mood of ours and a voice that would itself have thrilled us had not the import of it thrilled us more. "Gentlemen," says Sheridan, as we half started to our feet, "I have come over to see you. I may have spoken harshly to some of you to-day; but I would not have it hurt you. You know how it is: we had to carry this place, and I was fretted all day till it was done. You must forgive me. I know it is hard for the men, too; but we must push. There is more for us to do together. I appreciate and thank you all."

And this is Phil Sheridan! A new view of him surely, and amazingly. All the repressed feeling of our hearts sprung out towards him. We were ready to blame ourselves if we had been in any way the cause of his trouble. But we thought we had borne a better part than that.

We had had a taste of his style of fighting, and we liked it. In some respects it was different from ours; although this was not a case to test all qualities. We had formed some habits of fighting too. Most of us there had been through Antietam, Fredericksburg, Chancellorsville, Gettysburg, Mine Run, The Wilderness, Spotsylvania, Cold Harbor, Bethesda Church, The North Anna, Petersburg;—we had formed habits. We went into a fight with knowledge of what it meant and what was to be done. We went at things with dogged resolution;—not much show; not much flare; not much accompaniment of brass instruments. But we could give credit to more brilliant things. We could see how this voice and vision, this swing and color, this vivid impression on the senses, carry the pulse and will of men. This served as the old "fife and drum," and "Hail Columbia," that used to stir men's souls. We had a habit, perhaps, drawn from dire experience, and for which we had also Grant's quite recent sanction[1], when we had carried a vital point or had to hold one, to entrench. But Sheridan does not entrench. He pushes on; carrying his flank and rear with him,—rushing, flashing, smashing. He transfuses into his subordinates the vitality and energy of his purpose; transforms them into part of his own mind and will. He shows the power of a commander,—inspiring both confidence and fear.

As a rule, our corps and army commanders were men of

---

[1]The order to entrench on the White Oak Road, March 31. See War Papers, Vol. I, p. 235.

brains rather than of magnetism. They relied on brains in others. Warren was one of these. He was well capable of organizing an entire plan of battle on a great field. He would have been an admirable chief of staff of the army. There brains outweigh temperament. He could see the whole comprehensively and adjust the parts subordinate to it. But he had a certain ardor of temperament which, although it brought him distinction as a subordinate commander, seemed to work against him as corps commander. It led him to go in personally with a single division or brigade, when a sharp fight came on. Doing this when having a larger command, one takes the risk of losing grasp of the whole. That was what he did in trying to change front with Crawford's Division under fire. It was a difficult thing. He put his personality into it; just as Sheridan would do and did in this very fight. It was the cruelest thing to say of him that he "was not in the fight." This blamed him for the very opposite of what had been complained of as his chief fault; and this time the accusation was not true. He was in the fight; and that in fact was his fault; at any rate it was his evil fate. That he felt this accusation keenly was manifest in that last reckless onset in the charge in the Gilliam field: he would let Sheridan see whether he was in the fight or not. But this did no good. It was too late. If he had so brought Crawford in where Griffin came, it might have saved him. But that long labor of his out of Sheridan's sight missed the moment. It was too late. The day was done. So he rode through into the night.

In the later dispositions of the corps the several divisions were moved out in directions which would best guard against sudden attack, not unexpected: Crawford, down the Ford Road, half way to the Run; Ayres out the White Oak Road on the right, and Bartlett on the left, facing towards the enemy supposed to be gathered in their last stronghold where we had left their main body the day before,—the Claiborne entrenchments. It fell to me to be held in reserve, and by midnight my command was left alone on the field over which the sweeping vision of power had passed. The thunder and tumult of the day had died with it. Now only the sighing of the night winds through the pine tops took up the ghostly refrain; and moans from the darkened earth beneath told where we also belonged. So the night was not for sleep; but given to solemn and tender duties, and to thoughts that passed beyond that field.

This is the story of Five Forks within my knowledge of what was done and suffered there. It shows confusions and struggles besides those of the contending lines. It shows extent and complexity quite beyond what would appear from an outside view of the movement or the orders concerning it. The story that went out early, and has taken lodgment in the public mind, is more simple. Taking its rise and keynote from Sheridan's report, somewhat intensified by his staff officers, and adopted by Grant without feeling necessity of further investigation, this story is that Sheridan and his cavalry, with the assistance of a part of Ayres' Division, carried Five Forks with all its works, angles and returns, its captives, guns and glory.[1]

The widely drawn and all-embracing testimony before the Warren Court of Inquiry in 1879 and 1880, although in some instances confused and even contradictory,—the result, however, in no small degree of the preoccupation in the witnesses' minds by the accounts so early and abundantly put forth, and without rectification for so long a time,—yet reveals for all some spreading of the plan of battle, a steadfast, well-connected and well-executed conformity to the ideas under which the battle was ordered. It also affords ample means of understanding the confusions and frictions which were actual passages in the battle, and not artificial and intensified in statement under the necessity of sustaining a thesis or vindicating an act of authority. The light shed by these records and the official War Records lately published enables us now, by some effort of attention it is true, to see in proper perspective, sequence and comprehension, the complex details of that battle.

The whole trouble and disturbance of Sheridan's pre-

---

[1]See for instance, Sheridan's statement before the Warren Court, Records, p. 118, and those of his officers all through this investigation. Also Grant's account of this battle: Memoirs, Vol. II, pp. 443-446; the details of which, however, are so erroneous as to movements, their time and place and bearing on the result, that they would not be recognized as pertaining to that battle by anyone who was there;—an observation which adds to our sorrow at the distressing circumstances under which the distinguished writer was compelled to conclude his last volume without opportunity for examining the then existing evidence in that case.

conceived image of the battle arose from a wide misunderstanding of the relative positions of the Fifth Corps formation and that of the enemy. We took the latter to be an entrenched line, which was to be turned by a flank and rear attack. The general plan as given to us verbally was well understood by all. The specific written orders were in accordance with the idea in our minds. "The line will move forward as formed till it reaches the White Oak Road, when it will swing around to the left, perpendicular to the White Oak Road. General Merritt's and General Custer's cavalry will charge the enemy's line as soon as the infantry get engaged." The intention evidently was that the left of the Fifth Corps (Ayres) should strike the left of the enemy's entrenched line on the White Oak Road, and on this pivot the corps should make a great left turn, and flank and envelop the rebel position; the cavalry in the meantime engaging the enemy's attention by vigorous demonstrations on their right and center. It was a brilliant piece of tactics, and if properly carried out its success was as certainly predicted as anything in warfare can be. There was no lack of loyalty and earnestness. The importance of the battle was felt, and Sheridan's impatience shared by all.

It will seem strange that at the very start the diagram furnished for our guidance was the cause of serious confusion in our minds by the disagreement of figure and fact, and of more serious confusion of movement attending.

1. The diagram showed Crawford,—the extreme right of the corps, directed on the angle, instead of Ayres,—the extreme left. By this, not a man of the Fifth Corps could reach the White Oak Road without doing so on top of the enemy entrenched upon it. Swinging to the left on reaching it, would have to be done inside the enemy's lines, or in front of them at close touch, presenting the right flank of each subdivision to their raking fire.

2. The diagram placed the angle of the enemy's works at the crossing of the White Oak Road and the road we were formed on,—the Gravelly Run Church Road; while as matter of fact, the angle was twelve hundred yards west of this crossing. So that "the line as formed" moving forward, instead of its right striking the angle, as the diagram indicated, the left of the line would pass it at the distance of nearly five hundred yards.

3. The line as formed was not so oblique to the Church

Road as represented in the diagram. In fact, for our whole right,—Crawford's and Griffin's Divisions,—it was nearly parallel to the White Oak Road. But we soon discovered that at the crossing of these roads the course of the latter bends northerly at an angle of nearly forty-five degrees. This shows how it was that Crawford and Griffin struck the White Oak Road squarely; and how it was that Ayres' right crossed it some time before his left, and was struck, as was Crawford, by the enemy's dismounted cavalry posted there.

4. It is now perfectly shown, although not clearly held in mind by all, even at the Warren investigation, that the celebrated "angle" and "return" were not the extreme left of the enemy's lines, nor of his fortified position, as would appear by the diagram.[1] East of the angle as given there, was an extended work of similar character on the White Oak Road, but across it,—south of it,—running at least one hundred and sixty yards. It was this from which Ayres was struck on the left, when he had to change front. A thousand yards still east of this, near the Church Road crossing, was also a considerable breastwork thrown up by Munford's dismounted cavalry early in the afternoon. It was from this that the center of our advance, Ayres and Crawford, was first struck.[2]

5. Nor were the troops in the main works and about the "angle" and the "return," as both the orders and the diagram indicated, by any means all the force we had to contend with that day. Fitzhugh Lee's cavalry, dismounted, now commanded by Munford,—among them Stuart's old brigade,—and as their

[1]The confusing effect of this diagram was manifest in much of the testimony from remembrance given at the Warren Court of Inquiry. The "diagram" as impressed upon all, gave only the "return" and the "angle" at it, as the easternmost extent of the Confederate works. Judging from this, whatever force should be encountered would be assumed to be at the angle and the return: whereas, it is now the certain result of somewhat rapid and confused experience at the time, and of very careful examination and measurements made since, that the main works extended one hundred and sixty yards still east of the angle, on the south side of the White Oak Road. But the witnesses before the court frequently spoke of this advanced work, from which Ayres was struck, the "angle" and even the "return." This explains Sheridan's remark to Griffin: "We flanked them gloriously." A remark which would not apply to an assault on a solid angle like that at the "return." It is pretty hard to flank a right angle,—especially when manned by such men as were there.

[2]Testimony of General Munford, Warren Court Records, p. 442.

officers said, "as good marksmen as ever fired a gun,"[1] were confronting our advance with the solid resistance of twelve hundred to fifteen hundred men[2] west of the Church Road, and Roberts' North Carolina cavalry, six or eight hundred men, on the east side of it.[3] Thus all our way around was contested by not less than two thousand skilled and veteran soldiers,—no sort of people to be ignored by us, nor by those reporting the battle to be wholly on the angle and on our cavalry front.

Now who is responsible for this misapprehension? Warren made the diagram from information received from Sheridan. It is to be presumed that the staff-officer who reported the situation to General Sheridan was carefully cross-examined. It is, indeed, quite possible that as the enemy were busily at work every moment after they were aware of the approach of the Fifth Corps by the Church Road, these extended works were not thrown up at the time of the staff-officer's reconnaissance. Nor perhaps had Munford's cavalry then reached that portion of the field. But a discrepancy of one thousand yards for a vital point like that, is a pretty wide error. Warren is perhaps responsible for accepting and acquiescing in the information so given, and for not assuring himself more perfectly of the conditions in his front of attack. But Sheridan saw and approved the diagram; and if anybody is to be blamed, he must be considered ultimately, and in a military sense, responsible for these misapprehensions. We are not demanding perfection for General Sheridan. His objective was the enemy. If he cared less for diagrams or graphic sketches, it must be pardoned. To err is human; but the whole of that characteristic of humanity should not be charged to the Fifth Corps or its commander.

But the case against Warren seems to be labored. Small matters are accentuated and accumulated as if to make weight for some special conclusion.

First there is the accusation of a manner of indifference on Warren's part previous to the action. As to this, opinions would differ as different minds or tempers might take it. There

---

[1]Testimony of General Munford, Warren Court Records, pp. 448, 453.

[2]Same, p. 459; and Fitzhugh Lee's testimony, p. 478, putting the whole cavalry at three thousand two hundred.

[3]Testimony of General Munford, Records Warren Court Records, p. 443.

is no doubt this feeling on General Sheridan's part was very deep and disturbing. That must be considered. Those who knew Warren best saw no indifference. He was not in his usual spirits,—and we cannot wonder at it,—but he was intense rather than expressive. He knew what was depending, and what was called for, and put his energies into the case more mentally than muscularly. His subordinates understood his earnestness.

It was charged by General Sheridan and some of his staff that the right of Ayres' line, which they call skirmishers, behaved badly on receiving the first fire,—that they threw themselves on the ground and fired into the air; that they even broke and ran; and that General Warren did not exert himself to correct the confusion. As if the corps commander's duty was to be on a brigade skirmish line in a great wide-sweeping movement of his entire corps! Sheridan and Ayres would seem to be assistance enough for Gwyn in handling his little skirmish line. But Sheridan says more deliberately and explicitly before the Warren Court: "Our skirmish line lay down; the fire of the enemy was very slight. The line became confused, and commenced firing straight in the air." A somewhat difficult operation, it may be remarked parenthetically, for men lying down,—unless the resultant of two such compound forces as the enemy in front and Sheridan behind made them roll over flat on their backs, calling on heaven for aid. "The poor fellows," he continues, "had been fighting behind breastworks for a long period, and when they got out to attack breastworks, they seem to have been a little timid."[1] They were attacking breastworks then, out at the Church Road crossing! But this is perhaps a fling at the Army of the Potomac in the soft places of "Grant's Campaign," in which they lost more men than Lee had in his entire army, and saved the other quarter by now and then entrenching when put momentarily on the defensive. Ayres does not relish this remark, whether intended for excuse or sarcasm. He answers that his troops, most of them, had fought at Gettysburg, and through the Wilderness, Spotsylvania, Cold Harbor, Petersburg and the Weldon Railroad, and none of them had ever but once fought behind breastworks.[2]

[1]Testimony, Warren Court Records, p. 254.

[2]Testimony, Warren Court Records, p. 450.

The unsteadiness of Ayres' skirmishers was no vital matter. It was a trifling circumstance, hardly relevant to the charge of indifference and incompetency on Warren's part. It was not cause enough to set thunderbolts flying over the whole Fifth Corps. At the worst, the commander of the skirmish line might have been reprimanded and "relieved," but hardly the commander of the corps.

I am pained on more accounts than one to find that General Grant in his notice of our action that afternoon, as given in his Memoirs, Volume II, page 443, uses the following language: "Griffin's Division, in backing to get out of the way of a severe cross-fire of the enemy, was found marching away from the fighting." He adds, however, that after awhile it was "brought back" and did excellent service. This is an extraordinary statement,—or at any rate it is to be hoped it is not an ordinary one in writing history,—to put down authoritatively as the record of our conduct and spirit that day.

"Backing to get out of the way of fire?" Griffin's Division? At what point in their history? "Backing from a cross-fire" here? The fire first followed was that of Munford's cavalry on their front and right while advancing according to orders; and "backing" from this would have thrown them directly on the celebrated "angle,"—where indeed they did arrive most timely, and on purpose to meet a "cross-fire," which they did not back out of. "Away from the fighting?" Let Ayres, and Ransom, and Wallace, and Wood, and Sheridan, answer. "Found." By whom? "Brought back." By what? They were found at the "angle," and brought themselves there ahead of the finders. Saul, the seeker of old, got more lost than the domestic wanderers he was after: they were in their place before he was; but the seeker found a kingdom, and doubtless forgave himself and the asses.

But this is a very serious charge against Griffin's Division, and in time of active service would warrant a court of inquiry. And even now the statement of one so revered cannot but be injurious to its reputation, and its honor.

To have stated this authoritatively as fact without being sure of it is so unlike the truthfulness and magnanimity of that great character, we are forced to believe he has here fallen before his only weakness,—that of trusting too implicitly to those whom he liked. If General Grant was to honor us by his notice at all, we should suppose he would acquaint himself with the facts. He seems, however, on so comparatively unimportant a topic, to have innocently absorbed the impression made upon him by parties interested in justifying an arbitrary act of authority. If General Grant could have looked into the case, he would have seen that this statement was not only unjust, but the very reverse of truth. The pressing sense of his approaching end compelled General Grant to finish his book in haste. However painful it be to review words written under circumstances so affecting, it is but just to inquire into the grounds of the accusation.

Griffin's orders were to follow Crawford; but the spirit of his position was that of a reserve; and this is held in hand ready to go in at a critical moment when and where most needed. All the facts necessary to adduce are that this division strictly, and with painstaking fidelity,—not in stupid quiescence,—followed its orders, until a moment came when it promptly acted in accordance with the spirit of its orders and of the whole plan of battle. It was "reserved" for that very kind of thing. And no one can say it fell short of its duty or the standard of its ancient honor.

The evidence is explicit and ample that the head of this division was at the angle of the works with Ayres and helped him to carry it. This is directly testified to by commanding officers of the "Maryland Brigade" on Ayres' right, and of the 4th Delaware on Gwyn's right, who say that Griffin's troops were on the flank and rear of the rebel line at the angle before they attacked it in front.[1] This is confirmed by officers of highest character in Ransom's Brigade on the left of the angle.[2] General Ayres says substantially the same in his testimony

[1] Colonel Stanton, who succeeded Bowerman in command of Ayres' Second Brigade, says the enemy were struck on their left and rear and forced in confusion on his front at the angle. Captain Buckingham, commanding 4th Delaware, the extreme right of Ayres' Division, says our troops had struck the enemy's works from the north at the time he reached them in front, facing west.

[2] Captain Faucette, 56th North Carolina, Ransom's Brigade, fully confirms this; and Honorable Thomas R. Roulac, 49th North Carolina, says that when the angle was carried, his troops had been attacked from the north and west, as well as on their proper front; and this by troops he saw moving down on them from the north, and that it was a "hand to hand" fight, "with clubbed muskets." See also North Carolina Regiments; 1861-65; Vol. III, p. 143.

before the Warren Court.[1] General Sheridan himself admits this.[2] It is evident, however, that in recounting his impression of the fight at the angle he failed to give prominence to the fact,—of no consequence to him, or to the general result, as to the particular troops engaged; and moreover, if acknowledged, making against his charge that Warren did not bring in his other divisions to support Ayres,—that Griffin's troops quite as much as Ayres' took part in carrying that angle. Indeed, he most probably regarded the troops of Griffin's whom he met here as part of Ayres' command. For this would explain most of the discrepancies in his statements compared with established and admitted facts.

But in truth the fight was by no means over when the angle was carried. Although tactically the result was a foregone conclusion when this was done, and although the fighting there was for a few minutes sharp, yet the hard fighting was in the whole field where the enemy made their successive stands with such courage and desperation. Griffin's part in this, and even Crawford's, cannot be ignored.

But it is insisted that Crawford's Division marched out of the fight. What is true is that it did not swing in promptly on Ayres' when he changed front to the left. That was an error, and an inexcusable departure from positive orders, not being warranted by the developments of the battle. But something is to be said about its cause, and its practical results. The diagram indicated to Crawford that his division would strike the enemy first at the "angle." Encountering serious resistance on crossing the White Oak Road, and naturally drawn towards it, he kept on, expecting perhaps that he was shortly to encounter the main force of the enemy in their works, and not observing the more severe attack which fell on Ayres' left,—where, indeed, the general orders for the battle should have prepared him to understand it, and take accordant action. In such case, Griffin would have taken in hand what was opposing Crawford. But the enemy before him led him to a wider sweep, in the course of which he confronted not only the two thousand dismounted cavalry, but at length large

---

[1]Ayres says Chamberlain's troops at the angle were somewhat in advance of his at the critical moment. Warren Court Records, p. 267 and p. 1080.

[2]Testimony, Warren Court Records, p. 123.

bodies of the infantry broken from their first hold and trying to make a stand on the Ford Road. He had fighting all the way around. Calling our fight at the angle, on our extreme left, "the front," and saying that General Warren was not "in the fight," while it might be pardoned as an excited ejaculation in the heat of battle, will not stand as sober truth, or as the premise for so violent a conclusion. And all those people who ring changes on the "obliquing off" of Crawford and Griffin from the center of action; "marching away from the fighting," or "drifting out of" what they call (by a familiar figure of speech) "the fight," do not tell us that this appearance was because Ayres was suddenly compelled to make a square change of front, and those who did not instantly conform and follow might seem to be obliquing to the right, when in fact they were "swinging to the left" according to orders,—unfortunately by too wide a sweep, having a very active enemy in their front. In this concern, some minds were unduly affected by that very natural notion that *the* fight is where they are; although in the case of General Sheridan it must be admitted that "the point was well taken." Crawford's wide movement was undoubtedly an error, and a costly one for Warren; but the simple fact that Crawford lost more men in the battle than both the other divisions together,—more indeed than all the rest, cavalry and infantry together,—goes to show that some of the fight was where he was.

These accusations against the conduct of each of Warren's Divisions, while susceptible of being magnified and manipulated so as to produce a certain forensic effect, are of no substantial weight. Even if true in the sharpest sense, they would be over-strained and uncalled for considering how the battle ended, and by whom it was mainly fought.

The broad ground of reason,—and a valid one if substantiated by fact,—for dissatisfaction with General Warren's conduct in the battle, and for his removal from command in consequence, would be that he was not in proper position during the battle to command his whole corps, and did not effectually command it. That at a sharp and critical point he was not present where General Sheridan wanted him is another matter, which does not in itself support the former conclusion.

In a military and highly proper sense, General Warren was responsible for the conduct of his corps, and ultimately for that of each of his divisions. There are two ways in which such control might be exercised: by prevention, or by correction. It was Crawford's duty to keep his vital connection with Ayres, and, if in any way it should be broken, to be on the alert to see and to act. Warren should hold him responsible for that. And if he could not at the start rouse Crawford, whose peculiarities he knew, to a vivid conception of the anatomy and physiology of the case, he should have had a staff officer charged with the duty of keeping Crawford closed on Ayres, while he himself at the point where he could keep in touch with his whole corps should hold Griffin under his hand as the ready and trusted reserve prepared for the unexpected.

It may be questioned, perhaps, whether it was wise to give Crawford that front line and wheeling flank in a movement of such importance, and make him a guide for Griffin. It would have been better, (as Griffin and Ayres said later in the day), to put Griffin on Ayres' right, in the order in which, curiously enough, Griffin's Brigades put themselves as if by some spiritual attraction, or possibly only common sense.

But it may be justly said that, whatever errors the development of the battle disclosed, Warren should have made his troops conform to the state of facts. He did. We can well understand how exasperating it must have been to General Sheridan when Ayres was so suddenly, and it seems unexpectedly, struck on the left flank, to find the largest division of the corps not turning with him, but drawing away from the tactical focus and the close envelopment of it intended, and getting into the place on wheeling flank which was assigned to Mackenzie's cavalry, and crowding Mackenzie "out of the fight." Griffin, when the exigencies on the left disclosed this error, hastened to put in his rear brigade,—the nearest—now become the leading one. Warren with the same intent, passing him, pushed on for Crawford with feverish effort not short of agony. Indeed he did more than could be legally required. He performed acts of "supererogation,"—voluntary works and above the commandments,—which certainly should have saved him from perdition. He undertook the duties of staff-officer for Crawford. He got hold of Kellogg's Brigade and posted it as a "marker" in the midst of the Sydnor woods, while he went off to find the rest of Crawford, and make him execute the grand left wheel; when one of Sheridan's staff coming along, astonished at this dumb-show, a brigade stationary, "marking time" at such a crisis, orders the marker into the "fight;" which the gallant commander begins right there, but ends soon after with a more exacting antagonist and with equal glory.

Meantime finding Crawford disporting himself on the tangent of a two-mile curve, Warren stuck to him like a tutor, leading him in on a quick radius to the supposed center,—which, be it borne in mind, we were all the time shifting off to the westward, making his route exhibit all the marvels of the hyperbola. His guide had gone into the vortex, and all he could do, in coming back with Crawford's recovered men, was to follow the fire, which we were battering off to the Forks. The cyclone had become a cycloid. So that Crawford was constantly obstructed by fugitives from the fight crowding him worse and worse all the way around; and when at last he struck the enemy's works, it was by no fault of Warren's that he struck them at their western end, near the Gilliam field, instead of at the left and center through the Sydnor fields. Things being as they were, Warren got his corps into the "fight" as quickly and effectively as he or anybody else possibly could.

But it is charged that the failure to close quickly on Ayres imperiled the result of the whole battle.[1] Recalling the fact that Griffin did not fail to close very promptly on Ayres, striking the "return" before Ayres struck the "angle," and the fact that the battle went on in the general way intended, only by a wider sweep and more complete envelopment, we should give attention to this remark, made in a manner so forcible. General Sheridan's judgment as a tactician can hardly be questioned; nor can his deliberate statement of it. But as we are now on the line of hypothesis, we may be entitled to consider what would have been the result in case Ayres had been withstood, or even repulsed, in his first attack. In the assertion before us, no account is made of Griffin's troops. Is it assumed that they were a flock of stray sheep, engaged in backing out of fire? What they would do may be judged from what they did. And can any one suppose the enemy would consider themselves in a very triumphant position between three bodies of our troops:—Ayres in front; the cavalry in rear; and two divisions of the Fifth Corps on their left flank as they would

---

[1]General Sheridan says: "If Ayres had been defeated, Crawford would have been captured: the battle would have been lost." Testimony, Warren Court Records, p. 125.

then front? How long does any one believe it would be, at such a signal, before the whole Fifth Corps and our cavalry also would whirl in, and catch the enemy in a maelstrom of destruction? What did happen, as it was, would have happened quicker had Ayres fared harder.

Or suppose Ayres was not so fortunately struck from the extended out-work, and had marched past the left of the enemy's entrenched line two hundred and fifty yards away, as he says he was doing.[1] Being on Griffin's left, he must have struck the left flank of the "return," and soon the rear of the enemy's main line on the White Oak Road. Griffin would then have been in immediate connection and would have swung with him. It would have taken a little longer; but the enemy would have been enveloped all the same. Sheridan's brilliant tactics would have been triumphant. Only Warren would have shared the glory.

Another consideration. Take things exactly as they were said to be,—Ayres at the "angle;" Griffin and Crawford out. What if those three Confederate brigades, ordered out of the Claiborne entrenchments that afternoon to fall on the flank of the Fifth Corps attacking at Five Forks, had come straight down, and not gone a long roundabout way as they did, striking too late and too far away for any good or harm,—what would have been the effect in such case had not these two divisions of the Fifth Corps been out there to stop them?

But suppose, again, all had gone as ordered and intended, and Crawford and Griffin had swung in on the rear of White Oak Road. Would it not have been awkward to have these five thousand fresh men[2] come down on the backs of our infantry, while having its hands full in front? What could Mackenzie have done with these men and Fitzhugh Lee's cavalry together? Lucky was it for us, in either case, that these five thousand infantrymen did not get down there. Lucky would it have been in such case, that Crawford and Griffin

---

[1]Testimony, Warren Court Records, p. 255. Major Benyaurd, Corps of Engineers, says Ayres' left passed the "Bass" house to our right of it. Warren Court Records, p. 160.

[2]General Hunton, before the Warren Court, placed the numbers of these three brigades, when they attacked us the day before, first at seven thousand five hundred, but was induced by the effect of cross examination afterwards to reduce this to five thousand. Records, pp. 629 and 630.

should happen to be out as flankers.

So much for the tactics of that battle. In spite of errors it was a great victory. It was Sheridan's battle. The glory of it is his. With his cavalry there was no error nor failure. Their action was not less than magnificent; the central thought carried into every brilliant act;—a picture to satisfy any point of view, idealist or impressionist.

As to the strategic merits of the battle, a few reflections may be permitted. Undoubtedly, as things were, it was an important battle. But our isolated position there invited fresh attack; and we only escaped it by the blundering or overcautious course of the forces sent out by Lee from the Claiborne front that afternoon, and which in Sheridan's solicitude we were pushed out to meet that night.[1] Then, too, we were much further off from the Petersburg front, and the opportunity for concerted action with the other corps in the line for general assault. And finally, we were in no more advantageous position now than we should be if we had turned the Claiborne flank of the enemy's entrenchments, and cut the Southside Road at Sutherland's the day before. Indeed, the very first thing we did the next morning after Five Forks was to move back to turn this same flank on the Claiborne Road and gain possession of Sutherland's. But Miles had taken care of this, as we might have done before him. Only Lee had now got a day's start of us; the head of his column well out on its retreat, necessitated not by Five Forks alone but by gallant work along our whole confronting line,—which might have been done the day before, and saved the long task of racing day and night, of toils and tribulations and losses recorded and unrecorded, which brought fame to Appomattox, and the end of deeds rewarded and unrewarded.

A study of this battle shows vexing provocations, but does not show satisfactory reasons for the removal of General Warren from command of the Fifth Corps. The fact is that much of the dissatisfaction with him was of longer standing. We recall the incident that General Sheridan did not wish to have the Fifth Corps with him at the start; also the suggestion by General Grant that Sheridan might have occasion to

[1]The right of the enemy's entrenchments on the Claiborne Road after they were driven in on the afternoon of March 31, was by no means strongly held. Testimony of General Hunton, Warren Court Records, p. 629.

remove him, and the authority to do so; then the keen disappointments of the Dinwiddie overture the day before, and the exasperation at Warren's not reporting to Sheridan that night. We recall General Griffin's remark in the morning that something like this would happen before the day was through. We recur also to the complaints earlier noticed. There was an unfavorable judgment of Warren's manner of handling a corps; an uncomfortable sense of certain intellectual peculiarities of his; a dislike of his self-centered manner and temperament and habit generally, and his rather injudicious way of expressing his opinion on tender topics. There was a variety of antagonism towards General Warren stored up and accumulating in General Sheridan's mind, and the tension of a heated moment brought the catastrophe.

No one can doubt General Sheridan's "right" to remove Warren; but whether he was right in doing so is another question, and one involving many elements. It is necessary that a chief commander, who is under grave responsibilities, should have the power to control and even displace the subordinates on whom he depends for the execution of his plans. Nor is it to be expected that he can properly be held to give strict account of action so taken, or be called upon to analyze his motives and justify himself by reasons to be passed upon by others. In this case, there are many subjective reasons, —influences acting on the mind of General Sheridan himself and not easily made known to others,—impressions from accounts of previous action, the appearance of things at the moment, and his state of mind in consequence,—which go to strengthen the favorable presumption accorded to his act. But as to the essential equity of it, the moral justification of it, opinions will be governed by knowledge of facts, and these extending beyond the incidents or accidents of this field.

The simple transfer of a corps commander is not a disgrace, nor necessarily an injury. General Warren had no vested right to the command of the Fifth Corps. And if Sheridan expected to have this corps with him in this campaign, in which he held assurances of a conspicuous and perhaps preeminent part, and General Warren was to him a *persona non grata*, we cannot wonder that he should wish to remove him. He had already objected to having this corps with him; but after trial he did not send back the corps, but its commander. It was the time, place and manner of this removal, the implications involved in it, and the vague reasons given for it, which made the grievance for General Warren. He was immediately assigned to another command; but even if Grant had restored him to the Fifth Corps, this would not wipe out that record, which stood against his honor. It is highly probable that a court martial would not have found him guilty of misconduct warranting such a punishment as dismissal from his command. There was not then, as there is not now, any tribunal with power to change the conclusion so summarily given by Sheridan, or to annul or mitigate the material effects of it. But such reasons as were given for this affected Warren's honor, and hence he persistently invoked a court of inquiry. All that he could hope for from such a court was the opportunity thus given for the facts and measurably the motives and feelings affecting the case to be brought out and placed upon the public records.

The posture of the parties before that court was peculiar. The members of the court were general officers of the active army. The applicant was then a lieutenant-colonel of engineers. The respondent—virtually the defendant—was lieutenant-general of the armies of the United States,—the superior of course, and the commander, of every member of the court, as also of most of the witnesses before it, then in the military service. The "next friend" and chief witness,—called by the applicant, but necessarily for the respondent,—was General Grant, ex-president of the United States, who still carried an immense prestige and influence. The traditions of the whole War Department were for sustaining military authority. We could not expect this court to bring in a verdict of censure on General Sheridan, or anything that would amount to that. We can only wonder at the courage of all who gave Warren any favorable endorsement or explanation, and especially of the court which found so little to censure in the conduct of General Warren as commander of the Fifth Corps in those last three days. The court sustained General Sheridan in his right, but General Warren felt that the revelation of the facts was of the nature of vindication. It came too late to save much of his life; it may have saved what was dearer.

I am by no means sure but that injustice must be taken by a military officer as a necessary part of his risks, of the conditions and chances of his service, to be suffered in the same way as wounds and sicknesses, in patience and humility.

But when one feels that his honor and the truth itself are impugned, then that larger personality is concerned wherein one belongs to others and his worth is somehow theirs. Then he does not satisfy himself with regret,—that strange complex feeling that something is right which is now impossible,—and even the truth made known becomes a consolation.

The Fifth Corps had an eventful history. Two passages of it made a remarkable coincidence. It was its fortune to lose two of its commanders,—the first and the last in the field of action,—by measures so questionable as to call for a court of review, by which, long after, both were substantially vindicated: Fitz John Porter, accounted the most accomplished corps commander on the Peninsula, and "heir apparent" to the command of the army, and Warren, whom Grant says he had looked upon for commander of the army in case anything should take from the field the sterling Meade. Who from such beginning could have foretold the end! And Meade,—he, too, went from the Fifth Corps to the command of the army, and found there a troubled eminence and an uncrowned end.

Shakespeare tells us, poetizing fate or faith:

"There's a Divinity that shapes our ends,
Rough-hew them how we will."

To our common eyes it often seems a dark divinity that rules; and the schoolmaster might interchange the verbs.

6

APPOMATTOX

I am to speak of what came under my observation in the action at Appomattox Courthouse and the circumstances attending the surrender of the Army of Northern Virginia, April 9, 1865.

You will understand that I am not attempting to present matters upon a uniform scale or to mark the relative merits of participants. This is only the story of what I saw and felt and thought,—in fact, my personal experience, including something of the emotions awakened and the reflections suggested by that momentous consummation.

In order that you may understand the pressure of conditions and the temper of our spirits in this last action, permit me to recur briefly to the situation of affairs. The great blow had been struck, the long hold loosened. Lee's communications had been cut; his intrenched lines broken and overrun; his right rolled up; Richmond and Petersburg evacuated by the Confederate forces and officials, and in our possession; his broken army in full retreat, or rather, desperately endeavoring to get off,—either to Danville, to effect a junction with Johnston in North Carolina, or to Lynchburg, where they might rally for one more forlorn but possibly long resistance. Meade with two corps of the Army of the Potomac—the Second and Sixth—was pressing Lee's rear; while Sheridan with his cavalry—three divisions—and our Fifth Corps of infantry under Griffin was making a flying march to circumvent Lee's path and plans; our combined forces all the while seeking to draw him to final battle, or compel him to surrender.

The 8th of April found the Fifth Corps at Prospect Station, on the South Side Railroad, nearly abreast of the head of Lee's retreating column, while Meade was with his two corps close upon Lee's rear at New Store, ten miles north of us, across the Appomattox. At noon of this day General Ord, of the Army of the James, joined us with two divisions of the Twenty-fourth Corps under General Gibbon, and Birney's Division of the Twenty-fifth Corps,—colored troops; Ord, by virtue of seniority, becoming commanding officer of the whole. He was a stranger to us all, but his simple and cordial manner towards Sheridan and Griffin, and even to us subordinates, made him welcome. We pushed on,—the cavalry ahead.

The Fifth Corps had a very hard march that day,—made more so in the afternoon and night by the lumbering obstructions of the rear of Ord's tired column, by courtesy given the road before us, the incessant check fretting our men almost to mutiny. We had been rushed all day to keep up with the cavalry, but this constant checking was worse. We did not know that Grant had sent orders for the Fifth Corps to march all night without halting; but it was not necessary for us to know it. After twenty-nine miles of this kind of marching, at the blackest hour of night, human nature called a halt. Dropping by the roadside, right and left, wet or dry, down went the men as in a swoon. Officers slid out of saddle, loosened the girth, slipped an arm through a loop of bridle-rein, and sunk to sleep. Horses stood with drooping heads just above their masters' faces. All dreaming,—one knows not what, of past or coming, possible or fated.

Scarcely is the first broken dream begun when a cavalry man comes splashing down the road, and vigorously dismounts, pulling from his jacket front a crumpled note. The sentinel standing watch by his commander, worn in body but alert in every sense, touches your shoulder. "Orders, sir, I think!" You rise on elbow, strike a match, and with smarting, streaming eyes read the brief, thrilling note, from Sheridan—like this, as I remember: "I have cut across the enemy at Appomattox Station, and captured three of his trains. If you can possibly push your infantry up here to-night, we will have great results in the morning." Ah, sleep no more! The startling bugle notes ring out "The General"—"To the march!" Word is sent for the men to take a bite of such as they had for food: the promised rations would not be up till noon, and by that time we should be—where? Few try to eat, no matter what. Meanwhile,

almost with one foot in the stirrup you take from the hands of
the black boy a tin plate of nondescript food and a dipper of
miscalled coffee,—all equally black, like the night around. You
eat and drink at a swallow; mount, and away to get to the
head of the column before you sound the "Forward." They are
there—the men: shivering to their senses as if risen out of the
earth, but something in them not of it! Now sounds the
"Forward," for the last time in our long-drawn strife; and they
move—these men—sleepless, supperless, breakfastless, sore-
footed, stiff-jointed, sense-benumbed, but with flushed faces
pressing for the front.

By sunrise we have reached Appomattox Station, where
Sheridan has left the captured trains. A staff-officer is here to
turn us square to the right,—to the Appomattox River, cutting
across Lee's retreat. Already we hear the sharp ring of the
horse-artillery, answered ever and anon by heavier field guns;
and drawing nearer, the crack of cavalry carbines; and unmistakably, too, the graver roll of musketry of infantry. There is
no mistake. Sheridan is square across the enemy's front, and
with that glorious cavalry alone is holding at bay all that is
left of the proudest army of the Confederacy. It has come at
last,—the supreme hour! No thought of human wants or weakness now: all for the front; all for the flag, for the final stroke
to make its meaning real. These men of the Potomac and the
James, side by side, at the double in time and column, now one
and now the other in the road or the fields beside. One
striking feature I can never forget,—Birney's black men abreast
with us, pressing forward to save the white man's country.

I had two brigades, my own and Gregory's, about midway of our hurrying column. Upon our intense procession
comes dashing out of a woods road on the right a cavalry staff-
officer. With sharp salutation he exclaims: "General Sheridan
wishes you to break off from this column and come to his
support. The rebel infantry is pressing him hard. Our men are
falling back. Don't wait for orders through the regular channels, but act on this at once!"

Sharp work now! Guided by the staff-officer, at cavalry
speed we break out from the column and push through the
woods, right upon Sheridan's battle-flag gleaming amidst the
smoke of his batteries in the edge of the open field. Weird-
looking flag it was: fork-tailed, red and white, the two bands
that composed it each charged with a star of the contrasting

color; two eyes sternly glaring through the cannon-cloud. Beneath it, that storm-centre spirit, that form of condensed energies, mounted on the grim charger, Rienzi, that turned the battle of the Shenandoah,—both, rider and steed, of an unearthly shade of darkness, terrible to look upon, as if masking some unknown powers.

Right before us, our cavalry, Devins' Division, gallantly stemming the surges of the old Stonewall Brigade, desperate to beat its way through. I ride straight to Sheridan. A dark smile and impetuous gesture are my only orders. Forward into double lines of battle, past Sheridan, his guns, his cavalry, and on for the quivering crest! For a moment it is a glorious sight: every arm of the service in full play,—cavalry, artillery, infantry; then a sudden shifting scene as the cavalry, disengaged by successive squadrons, rally under their bugle-calls with beautiful precision and promptitude, and sweep like a storm-cloud beyond our right to close in on the enemy's left and complete the fateful envelopment.

We take up the battle. Gregory follows in on my left. It is a formidable front we make. The scene darkens. In a few minutes the tide is turned; the incoming wave is at high flood; the barrier recedes. In truth, the Stonewall men hardly show their well-proved mettle. They seem astonished to see before them these familiar flags of their old antagonists, not having thought it possible that we could match our cavalry and march around and across their pressing columns.

Their last hope is gone,—to break through our cavalry before our infantry can get up. Neither to Danville nor to Lynchburg can they cut their way; and close upon their rear, five miles away, are pressing the Second and Sixth Corps of the Army of the Potomac. It is the end! They are now giving way, but keep good front, by force of old habit. Half way up the slope they make a stand, with what perhaps they think a good omen,—behind a stone wall. I try a little artillery on them, which directs their thoughts towards the crest behind them, and stiffen my lines for a rush, anxious for that crest myself. My intensity may have seemed like excitement. For Griffin comes up, quizzing me in his queer way of hitting off our weak points when we get a little too serious; accusing me of mistaking a blooming peach tree for a rebel flag, where I was dropping a few shells into a rallying crowd. I apologize—I was a little near-sighted, and hadn't been experienced in long-range fighting. But as for peaches, I was going to get some if the "pits didn't sit too hard on our stomachs."

But now comes up Ord with a positive order: "Don't expose your lines on that crest. The enemy have massed their guns to give it a raking fire the moment you set foot there." I thought I saw a qualifying look as he turned away. But left alone, youth struggled with prudence. My troops were in a bad position down here. I did not like to be "the under dog." It was much better to be on top and at least know what there was beyond. So I thought of Grant and his permission to "push things" when we got them going; and of Sheridan and his last words as he rode away with his cavalry, smiting his hands together—"Now smash 'em, I tell you; smash 'em!" So we took this for orders, and on the crest we stood. One booming cannon-shot passed close along our front, and in the next moment all was still.

We had done it,—had "exposed ourselves to the view of the enemy." But it was an exposure that worked two ways. For there burst upon our vision a mighty scene, fit cadence of the story of tumultuous years. Encompassed by the cordon of steel that crowned the heights about the courthouse, on the slopes of the valley formed by the sources of the Appomattox, lay the remnants of that far-famed army, counterpart and companion of our own in momentous history,—the Army of Northern Virginia—Lee's army!

It was hilly, broken ground, in effect a vast amphitheater, stretching a mile perhaps from crest to crest. On the several confronting slopes before us dusky masses of infantry suddenly resting in place; blocks of artillery, standing fast in column or mechanically swung into park; clouds of cavalry, small and great, slowly moving, in simple restlessness;—all without apparent attempt at offence or defence, or even military order.

In the hollow is the Appomattox,—which we had made the dead-line for our baffled foe, for its whole length, a hundred miles; here but a rivulet that might almost be stepped over dry-shod, and at the road crossing not thought worth while to bridge. Around its edges, now trodden to mire, swarms an indescribable crowd: worn-out soldier struggling to the front; demoralized citizen and denizen, white, black, and all shades between,—following Lee's army, or flying before these suddenly confronted, terrible Yankees pictured to them as demon-shaped and bent; animals too, of all forms and grades; vehicles of every description and non-description,—public and domestic, four-wheeled, or two, or one,—heading and moving in every direction, a swarming mass of chaotic confusion.

All this within sight of every eye on our bristling crest. Had one the heart to strike at beings so helpless, the Appomattox would quickly become a surpassing Red Sea horror. But the very spectacle brings every foot to an instinctive halt. We seem the possession of a dream. We are lost in a vision of human tragedy. But our light-twelve Napoleon guns come rattling up behind us to go into battery; we catch the glitter of the cavalry blades and brasses beneath the oak groves away to our right, and the ominous closing in on the fated foe.

So with a fervor of devout joy,—as when, perhaps, the old crusaders first caught sight of the holy city of their quest,—with an up-going of the heart that was half pæan, half prayer, we dash forward to the consummation. A solitary field-piece in the edge of the town gives an angry but expiring defiance. We press down a little slope, through a little swamp, over a bright swift stream. Our advance is already in the town,—only the narrow street between the opposing lines, and hardly that. There is wild work, that looks like fighting; but not much killing, nor even hurting. The disheartened enemy take it easy; our men take them easier. It is a wild, mild fusing,—earnest, but not deadly earnest.

A young orderly of mine, unable to contain himself, begs permission to go forward, and dashes in, sword-flourishing as if he were a terrible fellow,—his demonstrations seemingly more amusing than resisted; for he soon comes back, hugging four sabres to his breast, speechless at his achievement.

We were advancing,—tactically fighting,—and I was somewhat mazed as to how much more of the strenuous should be required or expected. But I could not give over to this weak mood.

My right was "in the air," advanced, unsupported, towards the enemy's general line, exposed to flank attack by troops I could see in the distance across the stream. I held myself on that extreme flank, where I could see the cavalry which we had relieved, now forming in column of squadrons ready for a dash to the front, and I was anxiously hoping it would save us from the flank attack. Watching intently, my eye was caught by the figure of a horseman riding out between those lines, soon joined by another, and taking a direction across the cavalry front towards our position. They were nearly a mile away, and I curiously watched them till lost from sight in the nearer broken ground and copses between.

Suddenly rose to sight another form, close in our own front,—a soldierly young figure, handsomely dressed and mounted,—a Confederate staff-officer undoubtedly, to whom some of my advanced line seemed to be pointing my position. Now I see the white flag earnestly borne, and its possible purport sweeps before my inner vision like a wraith of morning mist. He comes steadily on,—the mysterious form in gray, my mood so whimsically sensitive that I could even smile at the material of the flag,—wondering where in either army was found a towel, and one so white. But it bore a mighty message,—that simple emblem of homely service, wafted hitherward above the dark and crimsoned streams that never can wash themselves away.

The messenger draws near, dismounts; with graceful salutation and hardly suppressed emotion delivers his message: "Sir, I am from General Gordon. General Lee desires a cessation of hostilities until he can hear from General Grant as to the proposed surrender."

What word is this! so long so dearly fought for, so feverishly dreamed, but ever snatched away, held hidden and aloof; now smiting the senses with a dizzy flash! "Surrender"? We had no rumor of this from the messages that had been passing between Grant and Lee, for now these two days, behind us. "Surrender"? It takes a moment to gather one's speech. "Sir," I answer, "that matter exceeds my authority. I will send to my superior. General Lee is right. He can do no more." All this with a forced calmness, covering a tumult of heart and brain. I bid him wait a while, and the message goes up to my corps commander, General Griffin, leaving me mazed at the boding change.

Now from the right come foaming up in cavalry fashion the two forms I had watched from away beyond. A white flag again, held strong aloft, making straight for the little group beneath our battle-flag, high borne also,—the red Maltese cross on a field of white, that had thrilled hearts long ago. I see now that it is one of our cavalry staff in lead,—indeed I recognize him, Colonel Whitaker of Custer's staff; and, hardly keeping pace with him, a Confederate staff-officer. Without dismounting, without salutation, the cavalryman shouts: "This is unconditional surrender! This is the end!" Then he hastily introduces his companion, and adds: "I am just from Gordon and Longstreet. Gordon says 'For God's sake, stop this infantry, or hell will be to pay!' I'll go to Sheridan," he adds, and dashes away with the white flag, leaving Longstreet's aide with me.[1]

I was doubtful of my duty. The flag of truce was in, but I had no right to act upon it without orders. There was still some firing from various quarters, lulling a little where the white flag passed near. But I did not press things quite so hard. Just then a last cannon-shot from the edge of the town plunges through the breast of a gallant and dear young officer in my front line,—Lieutenant Clark, of the 185th New York,—the last man killed in the Army of the Potomac, if not the last in the Appomattox lines. Not a strange thing for war,—this swift stroke of the mortal; but coming after the truce was in, it seemed a cruel fate for one so deserving to share his country's joy, and a sad peace-offering for us all.

Shortly comes the order, in due form, to cease firing and to halt. There was not much firing to cease from; but "halt," then and there? It is beyond human power to stop the men, whose one word and thought and action through crimsoned years had been but forward. They had seen the flag of truce, and could divine its outcome. But the habit was too strong; they cared not for points of direction, but it was forward still,—forward to the end; forward to the new beginning; forward to the Nation's second birth!

But it struck them also in a quite human way. The more the captains cry "Halt! the rebels want to surrender," the more the men want to be there and see it. Still to the front, where the real fun is! And the forward takes an upward turn. For when we do succeed in stopping their advance, we cannot keep their arms and legs from flying.

To the top of fences, and haystacks, and chimneys they clamber, to toss their old caps higher in the air, and leave the earth as far below them as they can. Dear old General Gregory gallops up to inquire the meaning of this strange departure from accustomed discipline. "Only that Lee wants time to sur-

---

[1] I think the first Confederate officer who came was Captain P. M. Jones, now U. S. District Judge in Alabama; the other, Captain Brown of Georgia.

render," I answer with stage solemnity. "Glory to God!" roars
the grave and brave old General, dashing upon me with impetuosity that nearly unhorsed us both, to grasp and wring my
hand, which had not yet had time to lower the sword. "Yes,
and on earth peace; good will towards men," I answered, bringing
the thanksgiving from heavenward, manward.

"Your legs have done it, my men," shouts the gallant,
gray-haired Ord, galloping up cap in hand, generously forgiv-
ing our disobedience of orders, and rash "exposure" on the
dubious crest. True enough, their legs had done it,—had
"matched the cavalry" as Grant admitted, had cut around
Lee's best doings, and commanded the grand halt. But other
things too had "done it"; the blood was still fresh upon the
Quaker Road, the White Oak Ridge, Five Forks, Farmville,
High Bridge, and Sailor's Creek; and we take somewhat gravely
this compliment of our new commander, of the Army of the
James. At last, after "pardoning something to the spirit of
liberty," we get things "quiet along the lines."

A truce is agreed upon until one o'clock,—it is now ten.
A conference is to be held,—or rather colloquy, for no one here
is authorized to say anything about the terms of surrender.
Six or eight officers from each side meet between the lines,
near the courthouse, waiting Lee's answer to Grant's summons to surrender. There is lively chat here on this unaccustomed opportunity for exchange of notes and queries.

The first greetings are not all so dramatic as might be
thought, for so grave an occasion. "Well, Billy, old boy, how
goes it?" asks one loyal West Pointer of a classmate he had
been fighting for four years. "Bad, bad, Charlie, bad I tell you;
but have you got any whisky?" was the response,—not poetic,
not idealistic, but historic; founded on fact as to the strength of
the demand, but without evidence of the questionable maxim
that the demand creates the supply. More of the economic
truth was manifest that scarcity enhances value.

Everybody seems acquiescent, and for the moment
cheerful,—except Sheridan. He does not like the cessation of
hostilities, and does not conceal his opinion. His natural disposition was not sweetened by the circumstance that he was
fired on by some of the Confederates as he was coming up to
the meeting under the truce. He is for unconditional surrender, and thinks we should have banged right on and settled all
questions without asking them. He strongly intimates that

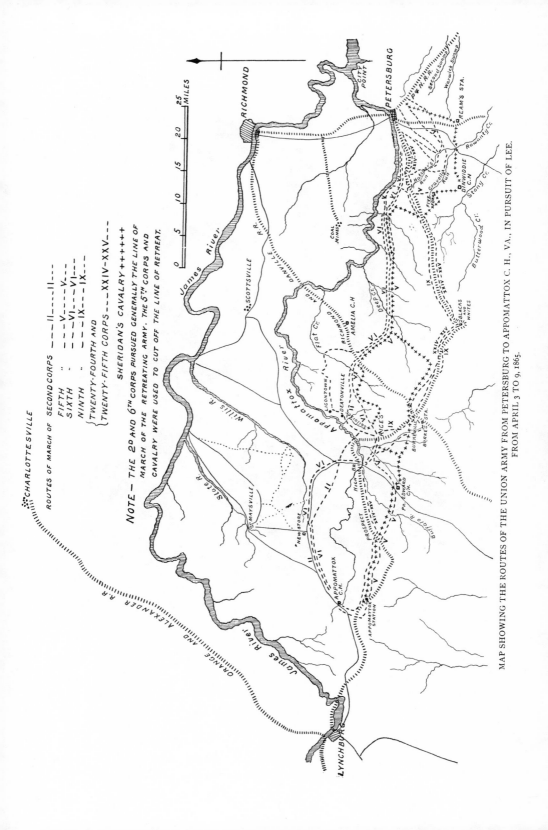

MAP SHOWING THE ROUTES OF THE UNION ARMY FROM PETERSBURG TO APPOMATTOX C. H., VA., IN PURSUIT OF LEE. FROM APRIL 3 TO 9, 1865.

ROUTES OF MARCH OF SECOND CORPS ——— II ———
FIFTH   "   — — V— — —
SIXTH   "   — VI — — VI — —
NINTH   "   — — IX — — IX — —

TWENTY-FOURTH AND
TWENTY-FIFTH CORPS — — XXIV-XXV — — —

SHERIDAN'S CAVALRY + + + + +

NOTE — THE 2D AND 6TH CORPS PURSUED GENERALLY THE LINE OF MARCH OF THE RETREATING ARMY. THE 5TH CORPS AND CAVALRY WERE USED TO CUT OFF THE LINE OF RETREAT.

Brevet Major General Joshua L. Chamberlain, 1865
(Courtesy Pejepscot Historical Society)

some of the free-thinking rebel cavalry might take advantage of the truce to get away from us. But the Confederate officers, one and all, Gordon, Wilcox, Heth, "Rooney" Lee, and all the rest assure him of their good faith, and that the game is up for them.

But suddenly a sharp firing cuts the air about our ears,—musketry and artillery,—out beyond us on the Lynchburg Pike, where it seems Sheridan had sent Gregg's command to stop any free-riding pranks that might be played. Gordon springs up from his pile of rails with an air of astonishment and vexation, declaring that for his part he had sent out in good faith orders to hold things as they are. And he glances more than inquiringly at Sheridan. "Oh, never mind," says Sheridan, "I know about it. Let 'em fight!" with two simple words added, which literally taken are supposed to express a condemnatory judgment, but in Sheridan's rhetoric convey his appreciation of highly satisfactory qualities of his men, —especially just now.

One o'clock comes; no answer from Lee. Nothing for us but to shake hands and take arms to resume hostilities. As I turned to go, General Griffin said to me in a low voice, "Prepare to make, or receive, an attack in ten minutes!" It was a sudden change of tone in our relations, and brought a queer sensation. Where my troops had halted, the opposing lines were in close proximity. The men had stacked arms and were resting in place. It did not seem like war we were to recommence, but wilful murder. But the order was only to "prepare," and that we did. Our troops were in good position,—my advanced line across the road; and we stood fast intensely waiting. I had mounted and sat looking at the scene before me, thinking of all that was impending and depending; when I felt coming in upon me a strange sense of some presence invisible but powerful—like those unearthly visitants told of in ancient story, charged with supernal message. Disquieted, I turned about; and there behind me, riding in between my two lines, appeared a commanding form, superbly mounted, richly accoutred; of imposing bearing, noble countenance, with expression of deep sadness overmastered by deeper strength. It is no other than Robert E. Lee! And seen by me for the first time within my own lines. I sat immovable, with a certain awe and admiration. He was coming, with a single staff officer[1] (Footnote appears on Page 152) for the great appointed meeting which was to determine momentous issues.

Not long after, by another inleading road, appeared another form—plain, unassuming, simple, and familiar to our eyes; but to the thought as much inspiring awe as Lee in his splendor and his sadness. It is Grant! He, too, comes with a single aide, a staff-officer of Sheridan's.[2]   Slouched hat without cord; common soldier's blouse, unbuttoned, on which, however, the four stars; high boots, mud-splashed to the top, trousers tucked inside; no sword, but the sword-hand deep in the pocket; sitting his saddle with the ease of a born master; taking no notice of anything, all his faculties gathered into intense thought and mighty calm. He seemed greater than I had ever seen him,—a look as of another world about him. No wonder I forgot altogether to salute him. Anything like that would have been too little.

He rode on to meet Lee at the courthouse. What momentous issues had these two souls to declare! Neither of them, in truth, free, nor held in individual bounds alone; no longer testing each other's powers and resources; no longer weighing the chances of daring or desperate conflict. Instruments of God's hands, they were now to record His decree!

But the final word is not long coming now. Staff officers are flying, crying "Lee surrenders!" Ah, there was some kind of strength left among those worn and famished men belting the hills around the springs of the Appomattox, who rent the air with shouting and uproar, as if earth and sea had joined the song. Our men did what they thought their share, and then went to sleep, as they had need to do; but in the opposite camp they acted as if they had got hold of something too good to keep, and gave it to the stars.

Besides, they had a supper that night,—which was something of a novelty. For we had divided rations with our old antagonists now that they were by our side as suffering brothers. In truth, Longstreet had come over to our camp that evening with an unwonted moisture on his martial cheek and compressed words on his lips: "Gentlemen, I must speak plainly; we are starving over there. For God's sake, can you send us something?" We were men; and we acted like men, knowing

---

[1]Colonel Marshall, chief of staff.

[2]Colonel Newhall.

we should suffer for it ourselves. We were too short-rationed also, and had been for days, and must be for days to come. But we forgot Andersonville and Belle Isle that night, and sent over to that starving camp share and share alike for all there with ourselves; nor thinking the merits of the case diminished by the circumstance that part of these provisions was what Sheridan had captured from their trains the night before.

At last we sleep—those who can. And so ended that 9th of April, 1865,—Palm Sunday—in that obscure little Virginia village now blazoned for immortal fame. Graver destinies were determined on that humble field than on many of classic and poetic fame. And though the issue brought bitterness to some, yet the heart of humanity the world over thrilled at the tidings. To us, I know, who there fell asleep that night, amidst memories of things that never can be told, it came like that Palm Sunday of old, when the rejoicing multitude met the meekly riding King, and cried "Peace in Heaven; glory in the highest!"

Late that night I was summoned to headquarters, where General Griffin informed me that I was to command the parade on the occasion of the formal surrender of the arms and colors of Lee's army. He said the Confederates had begged hard to be allowed to stack their arms on the ground where they were, and let us go and pick them up after they had gone; but that Grant did not think this quite respectful enough to anybody, including the United States of America; and while he would have all private property respected, and would permit officers to retain their side arms, he insisted that the surrendering army as such should march out in due order, and lay down all tokens of Confederate authority and organized hostility to the United States, in immediate presence of some representative portion of the Union army. Griffin added in a significant tone that Grant wished the ceremony to be as simple as possible, and that nothing should be done to humiliate the manhood of the Southern soldiers.

We felt this honor, but fain would share it. We missed our Second and Sixth Corps. They were only three miles away, and just moving back to Burkeville. We could not but feel something more than a wish that they should be brought up to be participants in a consummation to which they perhaps more than any had contributed. But whatever of honor or privilege came to us of the Fifth Corps was accepted not as

for any pre-eminent work or worth of ours, but in the name of
the whole noble Army of the Potomac; with loving remembrance of every man, whether on horse or foot or cannon-
caisson, whether with shoulder-strap of office or of knapsack,—of
every man, whether his heart beat high with the joy of this
hour, or was long since stilled in the shallow trenches that
furrow the red earth from the Antietam to the Appomattox!

On the morning of the 11th our division had been moved
over to relieve Turner's of the Twenty-Fourth Corps, Army of
the James, near the courthouse, where they had been receiving some of the surrendered arms, especially of the artillery on
their front, while Mackenzie's cavalry had received the surrendered sabres of W. H. F. Lee's command.

At noon of the 11th these troops of the Army of the
James took up the march to Lynchburg, to make sure of that
yet doubtful point of advantage.   Lee and Grant had both
gone,—Lee for Richmond to see his dying wife, Grant for Washington, only that once more to see again Lincoln living.   The
business transactions had been settled; the parole papers made
out; all was ready for the last turn,—the dissolving-view of the
Army of Northern Virginia.

It was now the morning of the 12th of April.   I had been
ordered to have my lines formed for the ceremony at sunrise.
It was a chill gray morning, depressing to the senses.   But our
hearts made warmth.   Great memories uprose; great thoughts
went forward.   We formed along the principal street, from the
bluff bank of the stream to near the courthouse on the left,—to
face the last line of battle, and receive the last remnant of the
arms and colors of that great army ours had been created to
confront for all that death can do for life.   We were remnants
also,—Massachusetts, Maine, Michigan, Maryland, Pennsylvania, New York,—veterans, and replaced veterans; cut to pieces,
cut down, consolidated, divisions into brigades, regiments into
one gathered by State origin, back to their birth place; this
little line—quintessence or metempsychosis of Porter's old corps
of Gaines' Mill and Malvern Hill; men of near blood born,
made nearer by blood shed.   Those facing us—now thank God,
the same.

Our earnest eyes scan the busy groups on the opposite
slopes, breaking camp for the last time,—taking down their
little shelter-tents and folding them carefully, as precious things,
then slowly forming ranks as for unwelcome duty.   And now

they move. The dusky swarms forge forward into gray columns of march. On they come, with the old swinging route step, and swaying battle-flags. In the van, the proud Confederate ensign,—the great field of white and for canton the star-strewn cross of blue on a field of red, this latter escutcheon also the regimental battle-flags—following on crowded so thick, by thinning out of men, that the whole column seemed crowned with red. At the right of our line our little group mounted beneath our flags, the red maltese cross on a field of white, erewhile so bravely borne through many a field more crimson than itself, its mystic meaning now ruling all.

This was the last scene of such momentous history that I was impelled to render some token of recognition; some honor also to manhood so high.

Instructions had been given; and when the head of each division column comes opposite our group, our bugle sounds the signal and instantly our whole line from right to left, regiment by regiment in succession, gives the soldier's salutation,—from the "order arms" to the old "carry"—the marching salute. Gordon at the head of the column, riding with heavy spirit and downcast face, catches the sound of shifting arms, looks up, and, taking the meaning, wheels superbly, making with himself and his horse one uplifted figure, with profound salutation as he drops the point of his sword to the boot toe; then facing to his own command, gives word for his successive brigades to pass us with the same position of the manual,—honor answering honor. On our part not a sound of trumpet more, nor roll of drum; not a cheer, nor word nor whisper of vain-glorying, nor motion of man standing again at the order; but an awed stillness rather and breath-holding, as if it were the passing of the dead!

As each successive division masks our own, it halts the men face inward towards us across the road, twelve feet away; then carefully "dress" their line, each captain taking pains for the good appearance of his company, worn and torn and half starved as they were. The field and staff take their positions in the intervals of regiments; generals in rear of their commands. They fix bayonets, stack arms; then, hesitatingly, remove cartridge-boxes and lay them down. Lastly,—reluctantly, with agony of expression,—they tenderly fold their flags, battle-worn and torn, blood-stained, heart-holding colors, and lay them down; some frenziedly rushing from the ranks, kneeling over them, clinging to them, pressing them to their lips with burning tears. And only the Flag of the Union greets the sky!

What visions thronged as we looked into each others' eyes! Here pass the men of Antietam, the Bloody Lane, the Sunken Road, the Cornfield, the Burnside Bridge; the men whom Stonewall Jackson on the second night at Fredericksburg begged Lee to let him take and crush the two corps of the Army of the Potomac huddled in the streets in darkness and confusion; the men who swept away the Eleventh Corps at Chancellorsville; who left six thousand of their companions around the bases of Culp's and Cemetery Hills at Gettysburg; these survivors of the terrible Wilderness, the Bloody Angle at Spotsylvania, the slaughter pen of Cold Harbor, the whirlpool of Bethesda Church!

Here comes Cobb's Georgia Legion, which held the stone-wall on Marye's Heights at Fredericksburg, close before which we piled our dead for breastworks so that the living might stay and live.

Here too come Gordon's Georgians and Hoke's North Carolinians, who stood before the terrific mine explosion at Petersburg, and advancing retook the smoking crater and the dismal heaps of dead—ours more than theirs—huddled in the ghastly chasm.

Here are the men of McGowan, Hunton, and Scales, who broke the Fifth Corps lines on the White Oak Road, and were so desperately driven back on that forlorn night of March 31st by my thrice-decimated brigade.

Now comes Anderson's Fourth Corps,—Only Bushrod Johnson's division left, and this the remnant of those we fought so fiercely on the Quaker Road, two weeks ago, with Wise's Legion, too fierce for its own good.

Here passes the proud remnant of Ransom's North Carolinians we swept through Five Forks ten days ago,—and all the little that was left of this division in the sharp passages at Sailor's Creek five days thereafter.

Now makes its last front A. P. Hill's old corps,—Heth now at the head, since Hill had gone too far forward ever to return: the men who poured destruction into our division at Shepardstown Ford, Antietam, in '62, when Hill reported the Potomac running blue with our bodies; the men who opened the desperate first day's fight at Gettysburg, where withstanding them so stubbornly our Robinson's Brigades lost 1185 men, and the Iron Brigade alone 1153,—these men of Heth's Division here too losing 2850 men, companions of these now looking into our faces so differently.

What is this but the remnant of Mahone's Division, last seen by us at the North Anna? Its thinned ranks of worn, bright-eyed men recalling scenes of costly valor and ever remembered history.

Now the sad great pageant,—Longstreet and his men! What shall we give them for greeting that has not already been spoken in volleys of thunder and written in lines of fire on all the river-banks of Virginia? Shall we go back to Gaines' Mill and Malvern Hill? Or to the Antietam of Maryland, or Gettysburg of Pennsylvania?—deepest graven of all. For here is what remains of Kershaw's Division, which left 40 percent of its men at Antietam, and at Gettysburg with Barksdale's and Semmes' Brigades tore through the Peach Orchard, rolling up the right of our gallant Third Corps, sweeping over the proud batteries of Massachusetts,—Bigelow and Philips,—where under the smoke we saw the earth brown and blue with prostrate bodies of horses and men, and the tongues of overturned cannon and caissons pointing grim and stark in the air.

Then in the Wilderness and at Spotsylvania, Kershaw again, in deeds of awful glory, and, thereafter, for all their losses, holding their name and fame, until fate met them at Sailor's Creek, where all but these, with Kershaw himself, and Ewell, and so many more, gave up their arms and hopes,—all, indeed, but manhood's honor.

With what strange emotion I looked into these faces before which in the mad assault on Rives' Salient, June 18, '64, I was left for dead under their eyes! It is by miracles we have lived to see this day,—any of us standing here.

Now comes the sinewy remnant of fierce Hood's Division, which at Gettysburg we saw pouring through the Devil's Den, and the Plum Run gorge; turning again by the left our stubborn Third Corps, then swarming up the rocky bastions of Round Top, to be met there by equal valor, which changed Lee's whole plan of battle, and perhaps the story of Gettysburg.

Ah, is this Pickett's Division?—this little group, left of those who on the lurid last day of Gettysburg breasted level cross-fire and thunderbolts of storm, to be strewn back drifting wrecks, where after that awful, futile, pitiful charge we buried them in graves a furlong wide, with names unknown!

Met again in the terrible cyclone-sweep over the breast-works at Five Forks; met now, so thin, so pale, purged of the mortal,—as if knowing pain or joy no more. How could we help falling on our knees,—all of us together,—and praying God to pity and forgive us all!

Thus, all day long, division after division comes and goes,—the surrendered arms being removed by our wagons in the intervals, the cartridge-boxes emptied in the street when the ammunition was found unserviceable, our men meanwhile resting in place.

When all is over, in the dusk of evening, the long lines of scattered cartridges are set on fire; and the lurid flames wreathing the blackness of earthly shadows give an unearthly border to our parting.

Then, stripped of every token of enmity or instrument of power to hurt, they march off to give their word of honor never to lift arms against the old flag again till its holders release them from their promise. Then, their ranks broken,—the bonds that bound them fused away by forces stronger than fire,—they are free at last to go where they will; to find their homes, now most likely stricken, despoiled by war.

Twenty-seven thousand men paroled; seventeen thousand stand of arms laid down or gathered up; a hundred battle-flags. But regiments and brigades—or what is left of them—have scarce a score of arms to surrender; having thrown them away by road and riverside in weariness of flight or hopelessness of heart, disdaining to carry them longer but to disaster. And many a bare staff was there laid down, from which the ensign had been torn in the passion and struggle of emotions, and divided piece by piece,—a blurred or shrunken star, a rag of smoke-stained blue from the war-worn cross, a shred of deep-ened dye from the rent field of red,—to be treasured for pre-cious keepsakes of manhood's test and heirlooms for their chil-dren.

Nor blame them too much for this; nor us for not blam-ing them more. Although, as we believed, fatally wrong in striking at the old flag, misreading its deeper meaning and the innermost law of the people's life, blind to the signs of the times in the march of man, they fought as they were taught, true to such ideals as they saw, and put into their cause their best. For us they were fellow-soldiers as well, suffering the fate of arms. We could not look into those brave, bronzed faces, and those battered flags we had met on so many fields where glorious manhood lent a glory to the earth that bore it, and think of personal hate and mean revenge. Whoever had misled these men, we had not. We had led them back, home. Whoever had made that quarrel, we had not. It was a remnant of the inherited curse for sin. We had purged it away, with blood-offerings. We were all of us together factors of that high will which, working often through illusions of the human, and following ideals that lead through storms, evolves the enfranchisement of man.

Forgive us, therefore, if from stern, steadfast faces eyes dimmed with tears gazed at each other across that pile of storied relics so dearly there laid down, and brothers' hands were fain to reach across that rushing tide of memories which divided us yet made us forever one.

It was our glory only that the victory we had won was for country; for the well-being of others, of these men before us as well as for ourselves and ours. Our joy was a deep, far, unspoken satisfaction,—the approval, as it were, of some voiceless and veiled divinity like the appointed "Angel of the Nation" of which the old scriptures tell—leading and looking far, yet mindful of sorrows; standing above all human strife and fierce passages of trial; not marking faults nor seeking blame; transmuting into factors of the final good corrected errors and forgiven sins; assuring of immortal inheritance all pure purpose and noble endeavor, humblest service and costliest sacrifice, unconscious and even mistaken martyrdoms offered and suffered for the sake of man.

7

THE GRAND REVIEW OF THE
ARMY OF THE POTOMAC
MAY 23, 1865

I read to you from manuscripts dimmed with long, lone companionship with me, the story of my last vision of the Army of the Potomac,—the vision of its march out of momentous action into glorious dream.

This is not an essay in composition,—military, historic or artistic. I had only sought to hold fast the image which passed before my eyes. But this will no less be truth,—one aspect of *the* truth, which in its manifold, magnificent wholeness it would take the notes and memories of thousands to portray. It will be manifest that I cannot undertake to reduce all the features of the picture to a common scale, nor to exhibit merit equitably. Some points, no doubt, are set in high light, under the emotion which atmospheres them; but it is not meant to throw others into shadow. If, in so rapid and condensed a passage, only familiar and prominent commanders can be named, it is not that I forget that in every grade and all through the ranks are men whose names deserve remembrance as immortal as their devotion was sublime. Neither can I forget, while yielding to none in my appreciation of the honor due to "the man behind the musket," that the military efficiency of such is largely affected by the instruction, discipline and influence of those in authority and responsibility over them; and their success and fame largely due to the manner in which they are "handled." A command is likely to be what its commander is. There are crises when confidence in his ability turns the scale of battle. There are supreme moments when the sudden sweep to the front by a commanding character strikes the heart and exalts the spirit of men so that they do superhuman things. Such are the men who are to pass before us.

It is the Army of the Potomac. After years of tragic history and dear-bought glories, gathering again on the banks of the river from which it took its departure and its name; an army yet the same in name, in form, in spirit, but the deep changes in its material elements telling its unspeakable vicissitudes; having kept the faith, having fought the good fight, now standing up to receive its benediction and dismissal, and bid farewell to comradeship so strangely dear.

We were encamped on Arlington Heights, opposite the Capital. As yet there are but two corps up,—the Second and the Fifth. The Sixth had been sent back from Appomattox to Danville, to secure the fruits of the surrender, and stand to the front before the falling curtain of the Confederacy. They had fulfilled that duty, and on this very day were setting forth for this final station. Of those that had come up, all the detachments had been called in. My division that left Appomattox five thousand strong now mustered twice that number. The ranks stood full,—what there were of the living,—for one more march together, one last look and long farewell.

Troops that had been with us and part of us in days of need and days of glory, were brought with us again: the Cavalry Corps, and the Ninth Corps, with a division of the Nineteenth. The Ninth, by the circumstance of its commander outranking all other generals except Grant, although of late often with us, was not incorporated with our army until the twenty-fourth of May, 1864, when Burnside magnanimously waived his rank and with his corps became part and parcel of our army through the terrible campaign of that dark year, and until relieved at Burkeville a few days after the surrender at Appomattox. To these old companions General Meade with generous courtesy gave the post of honor and precedence. Sherman's great army had lately come up, and was encamped on the river bank at no great distance below.

A mighty spectacle this: the men from far and wide, who with heroic constancy, through toils and sufferings and sacrifices that never can be told, had broken down the Rebellion, gathered to give their arms and colors and their history to the keeping of a delivered, regenerated nation.

For our review the order of march was to be the follow-ing: Headquarters of the Army of the Potomac; the cavalry corps; the provost marshal's brigade; the engineer brigade; the Ninth Corps with a division of the Nineteenth; then the Army of the Potomac, that stood here upon the earth,—the Fifth Corps and the Second; the infantry and artillery, and ambu-lances too—great sharers of eventful service.

The Ninth Corps crossed the Potomac on the afternoon of the twenty-second and went into bivouac east of the Capitol. The engineer brigade, the provost guard and the escort moved to bivouac near Long Bridge, to start at 3.30 in the morning for their rendezvous at the foot of the Capitol front, ready to follow the cavalry ordered to be there at 9 A.M. At 4 A.M., of the twenty-third, the Fifth Corps began its march over Long Bridge, Canal Bridge and Maryland Avenue to First Street, East, moving "left in front" in order to draw out easily, right in front, for the ceremonial column. The Second Corps, leaving camp at 7 A.M., followed the Fifth to the vicinity of the Capi-tol, ready to follow in review.

The movement was to be up Pennsylvania Avenue. The formation was in column by companies closed in mass, with shortened intervals between regiments, brigades and divisions; the company fronts equalized to twenty files each, so the num-ber of companies corresponded to the total numbers of the regiment,—some having twelve or fifteen companies, so many had gathered now for the grand muster-out.

Six ambulances were to follow each brigade, moving three abreast. The artillery brigades were to accompany their respective corps. The infantry were to take "route step" and right shoulder arms until reaching the State Department build-ing, where they take the cadenced step and the shoulder arms,—later known as the "carry." Here also the "guide left" was to be taken, as the reviewing stand was in front of the President's house. He was the proper reviewing officer; but arrangements were made for the accommodation also of the cabinet, the foreign diplomatic corps, the governors of states and other distinguished personages and high officials. In the salute, drums were to ruffle and colors dip, but only mounted officers were to salute. The bands were not to turn out in front of the reviewing officer, as is the custom in reviews. All precautions were taken to preserve relative distances, so as to avoid crowding, confusion and delay in the marching column.

In my command we were well aware of quite an anxiety among officers and men of the army generally to look their very best, and more, too, on this occasion; for new uniforms, sashes, epaulettes, saddle housings and other gay trappings almost disguised some of our hardiest veterans, who were not insensible to the new order of spectators before whom they were now to pass their ordeal. I hesitate to admit that in the revulsion from this on the part of the officers and men of my division, there might be a scornful pride more sinful than that of vanity. We knew many a dude in dress who expressed in this way a consciousness of personal worth which rang true in the tests of battle. We could not pretend to be better,—proud of our humility. Perhaps we thought we could not look equal to what we deemed our worth, and possibly our reputation; so we resolved to do nothing for show, but to look just what we were, and be judged by what we wore; letting our plainness tell its own story. The men brought themselves up to regulation field inspection; themselves, their dress and accouterments clean and bright; but all of every-day identity. And for officers no useless trappings, rider or horse; plain, open saddle, with folded gray army blanket underneath; light, open bridle with simple curb and snaffle-rein; service uniform,—shoulder-strap, belts, scabbards, boots and spurs of the plainest,—no sashes, no epaulettes;—light marching order, just as in the field, but clean and trim. No doubt this might make us somewhat conspicuous, as things were; but homeliness was a character we thought we could maintain, even "before company."

It was a clear, bright morning, such as had so often ushered in quite other scenes than this. At nine o'clock the head of column moved. First Meade,—commanding all—our old Fifth Corps commander, knightly in bearing as ever, grave of countenance now, thoughtful perhaps with foreshadowings; with him rode his principal staff, chivalrous "Andy Webb," in earlier days familiar friend, inspector of our corps,—since that, meeting with his superb brigade the death-defying valor of Pickett's charge,—now rightly chief-of-staff of the army; grim old Hunt, chief of artillery, whose words were like his shot, whose thunder-sweeps had shaken hearts and hills from Antietam to Appomattox; Seth Williams, adjutant-general, steadfast as the rocky crests of Maine from which he came, whose level head had balanced the disturbances and straightened the confusions of campaigns and changes of commanders through

our whole history. And following these heads of staff, all the
gallant retinue well-known to us all.

Now move the cavalry: survivors and full-blown flower
of the troopers, Joe Hooker, in the travailing winter of 1862
and 1863 had redeemed from servitude as scattered orderlies
and provost-guards at headquarters and loose-governed cities,
and transformed into a species of soldier not known since the
flood-times of Persia, the Huns of Attila or hordes of Tamerlane;
cavalry whose manœuvres have no place in the tactics of modern Europe; rough-riders, raiders, scouts-in-force, cutting communications, sweeping around armies and leagues of entrenched
lines in an enemy's country,—Stoneman and Pleasanton, and
Wilson, Kilpatrick, Custer, and alas, Dahlgren!

And when the solid front of pitched battle opposes, then
terrible in edge and onset,—as in the straight-drawn squadron
charges at Brandy Station,—the clattering sweep at Aldie,—the
heroic lone-hand in the lead at Gettysburg, holding back the
battle till our splendid First Corps could surge forward to meet
its crested wave, and John Buford and John Reynolds could
shake hands! Through the dark campaign of 1864, everywhere giving account of themselves as *there*. At last in 1865
sweeping over the breastworks at Five Forks down upon the
smoking cannon and serried bayonets; thence swirling around
Sailors' Creek and High Bridge, and finally at Appomattox by
incredible marches circumventing Lee's flying column, and
holding at bay Stonewall Jackson's old corps, with Hill's and
Anderson's, under Gordon;—alone, this cavalry, until our infantry overtaking the horses, force the flag of truce to the
front, and all is over! Fighters, firm, swift, superb,—
cavalry—chivalry!

Sheridan is not here. He is down on the Rio Grande,—a
surveyor, a draughtsman, getting ready to illustrate Seward's
diplomatic message to Napoleon that a French army cannot
force an Austrian emperor on the Mexican Republic. Crook, so
familiar to our army, is not here, preferring an "engagement"
elsewhere and otherwise; for love, too, bears honors, to-day.
Soldierly Merritt is at the head; well-deserving of his place.
Leading the divisions are Custer, Davies and Devin,—names
known before and since in the lists of heroes. Following also,
others whom we know,—Gibbs, Wells, Pennington, Stagg of
Michigan, Fitzhugh of New York, Brayton Ives of Connecticut.
Dashing Kilpatrick is far away. Grand Gregg we do not see;

nor level-headed Smith, nor indomitable "Prin." Cilley, with
his 1st Maine Cavalry; these now sent to complete the peace
around Petersburg.

Now rides the provost marshal general, gallant George
Macy of the 20th Massachusetts, his right arm symbolized by
an empty sleeve pinned across his breast.

Here the 2d Pennsylvania Cavalry, and stout remnants
of the 1st Massachusetts, reminding us of the days of Sargent
and "Sam" Chamberlain. Here, too, the 3d and 10th U. S.
Infantry, experienced in stern duties.

Now with heads erect and steady eyes, marches the
Signal Corps; of those that beckoned us to the salvation of
Round Top; and disclosed movements and preparations other-
wise concealed in the dense maze and whirl of battle from the
Wilderness to the Chickahominy; then from their lofty observa-
tories watching the long ferment on the Appomattox shores.
What message do your signals waft us now?

Here come the engineers with their great unwieldy pontoons grotesque to the eye,—grand to the thought! Had we not
smiled at them—the huge dromedary caravans, struggling along
the road, or sliding, leviathan-like down the slopes of half-
sheltered river-coves, launching out to their perilous, importu-
nate calling? Did not the waters of all Virginia's rivers know
of their bulk and burden? Had we not seen them,—*not
smiling,*—time and time again, spanning the dark
Rappahannock?—as in December, '62, Sumner and Howard
launched them from the exposed bank opposite Fredericksburg
into the face of Lee's army—vainly opposing,—bridging the
river of death, into the jaws of hell! Had we not a little later,
a mile below, crowded over the hurriedly laid, still swaying,
boat-bridge, raked and swept by the batteries on Marye's
Heights, and rushed up the bloody, slippery slopes to the dead-
line stone wall? And on the second midnight after, shall we
forget that forlorn recrossing, in murk and rain, on the last
pontoon bridge left, and this muffled with earth to dull our
stealthy, silent tread, and already half-loosened, and ready to
cut free and swing from the touch of that fateful shore? And
what of that rear-guard covering the retreat from Chancellorsville
in 1863, seeking the bridge-end and in utter blackness of darkness, and driving storm of rain and rushing river, *not finding it*
because the swelling torrent was roaring twenty feet between
it and the shore; and when gained by manly resolution or

demoniac instinct, already half a ruin, the lashings of chess
and rail loosened by rush and pressure of previous passers;
crowded plank in heaps and gaps yard wide, amid the yawn-
ing, dizzying surges in the pitchy blackness, where only the
sagacious horse could smell the distances, and leap the chasms,
followed by the trusting "brotherhood" of man. "Great arks"
indeed they were, these boats, borne above the waters of desolation, and bearing over manhood fit to replenish and re-people
the war-whelmed earth!

Last, looming above the broad waters of the James,
your thread-like bridge swaying beneath the mighty tread,—our
horses hardly able to keep their feet,—bearing us over to the
gloomy tests of Petersburg,—the long beginning of the end.

And where are the brave young feet that pressed your
well-laid plank at Germanna and Ely's Ford of the Rapidan on
that bright morning a summer ago? To what shores led that
bridge?

No, we do not smile to-day at the ungainly pontoons!
God rest their bodies now! if perchance they have no souls
except what have gone into the men who bore them, and
whom in turn they bore.

Now rises to its place the tried and tested old Ninth
Corps, once of Burnside and Reno; now led by Parke, peer of
the best; with Willcox and Griffin of New Hampshire and Curtin
leading its divisions,—Potter still absent with cruel wounds,
and Hartranft detached on high service elsewhere,—and its
brigade commanders General McLaughlen and Colonels
Harriman, Ely, Carruth, Titus, McCalmon and Matthews. These
are the men of the North Carolina expedition, of Roanoke and
New Berne, who came up in time of sore need to help our army
at Manassas and Chantilly; and again at South Mountain and
Antietam. After great service in the west, with us again in the
terrible campaign of '64; then in the restless, long-drawn, see-
saw action on the Petersburg lines; through the direful "crater;" at last in the gallant onset on the enemy's flank and the
pressing Southside pursuit,—part of us until all was over.

So they are ours,—these men of the Ninth Corps, and
our proud hearts yearn forward to them as they are whelmed
in tumultuous greeting along the thronging avenue. Noble
men! As they move out past the head of our waiting column,
I look at them with far-running thought. Earnestly remembered by the older regiments of my division; for sent to support

the Ninth Corps at the Burnside Bridge when it was so gallantly carried at the bayonet point by Potter's 51st New York
and Hartranft's 51st Pennsylvania, Burnside pushed across
the Antietam our single division to replace that whole corps on
those all-important heights where he was expecting a heavy
attack. How full the intervening years have been! How strained
and sifted the ranks! Of those two remembered regiments to-
day, there stand,—the 51st New York, one hundred and twenty
men; the 51st Pennsylvania, forty men!

Here too, a remnant, the 36th Massachusetts; long ago
shipmates with us of the 20th Maine on the transport that
bore us forth in '62 to fields and fortunes far apart,—now at
last united again. We remember how that splendor of equip-
ment and loftiness of bearing made us feel very green and
humble,—but we are somehow equalized now! Of them was
Major Henry Burrage, now proudly riding, acting assistant
adjutant-general of his brigade,—foretokening his place and
part in the Loyal Legion of Maine!

Here comes our 31st Maine, brave Daniel White's; consolidated with it now the 32d, those left from its short, sharp
experience with Wentworth and John Marshall Brown, at such
dear cost leading,—both Bowdoin boys, one the first adjutant
of the 20th. Here passes steadily to the front as of yore the
7th Maine Battery; Twitchell, my late college friend, at the
head;—splendid recessional,—for I saw it last in '64 grimly
bastioning the slopes above Rives' Salient, where darkness fell
upon my eyes, and I thought to see no more.

Following, in Dwight's Division of the Nineteenth Corps,
other brave men, known and dear: a battalion of the 1st Maine
Veterans, under Captain George Brown; the brigades of stalwart George Beal and clear-eyed "Jim" Fessenden, my college
classmate; the sturdy 15th Maine from its eventful experiences
of the Gulf under steadfast-hearted Isaac Dyer, Murray and
Frank Drew; soldierly Nye with the 29th, made veterans on
the Red River and Shenandoah; royal Tom Hubbard, with his
30th, once Frank Fessenden's, whom Surgeon Seth Gordon
saved; a third of them now of the old 13th,—these too, of the
Red River, Sabine Cross Roads and Grand Ecore, and thence
to the Virginia valleys; rich in experiences, romantic and Roman!

And now it is the Fifth Corps. The signal sounds. Who
is that mounting there? Do you see him? It is Charles Griffin.

How lightly he springs to the saddle. How easy he sits,—straight and slender, chin advanced, eyes to the front,—pictured against the sky. Well we know him. Clear of vision, sharp of speech, true of heart, clean to the center. Around him groups the staff, pure-souled Fred Locke at their head.

My bugle calls. Our horses know it. The staff gather,—Colonel Spear, Major Fowler, Tom Chamberlain my brave young brother, of the First. The flag of the First Division, the red cross on its battle-stained white, sways aloft; the hand of its young bearer trembling with his trust, more than on storm-swept fields. Now they move,—all,—ten thousand hearts knitted together. Up the avenue, into that vast arena, bright with color,—flowers, garlands, ribbons, flags; and flecked with deeper tones. Windows, balconies, house-tops, high and far, thronged with rich-robed forms, flushed faces, earnest eyes. Now it seems a tumult of waters; we pass like the children of Israel walled by the friendly Red Sea. Around us and above, murmurs, lightnings and thunders of greeting. The roar of welcome moves forward with our column. Those in the street-ways press upon us; it almost needs the provost-guard to clear our way.

Now a girlish form, robed white as her spirit, presses close; modest, yet resolute, eyes fixed on her purpose. She reaches up towards me a wreath of rare flowers, close-braided, fit for viking's arm-ring, or victor's crown. How could I take it? Sword at the "carry" and left hand tasked, trying to curb my excited horse, stirred by the vastness, the tumult, the splendor of the scene. He had been thrice shot down under me; he had seen the great surrender. But this unaccustomed vision,—he had never seen a woman coming so near before,—moved him strangely. Was this the soft death-angel—did he think?—calling us again, as in other days? For as often as she lifted the garland to the level of my hand, he sprang clear from earth: heavenwards, doubtless,—but was not heaven nearer just then? I managed to bring down his fore-feet close beside her, and dropped my sword-point almost to her feet, with a bow so low I could have touched her cheek. Was it the garland's breath or hers that floated to my lips? My horse trembled. I might have solved the mystery, could I have trusted him. But he would not trust me. All that was granted me was the Christian virtue of preferring another's good and passing the dangerous office of receiving this mishap

Brevet Major General Joshua L. Chamberlain, 1865
(Courtesy Pejepscot Historical Society)

Brevet Major General Joshua L. Chamberlain, 1866
(Courtesy Pejepscot Historical Society)

token to the gallant young aide behind me. And I must add I did not see him again for some time! All this passed like a flash in act; but it was not quite so brief in effect. From that time my horse was shy of girls,—sharp eyes out for soft eyes,—I dare say, for his master's peace and safety!

All the way up the avenue a tumult of sound and motion. Around Griffin was a whirlpool; and far behind swelled and rolled the generous acclaim. At the rise of ground near the Treasury a backward glance takes in the mighty spectacle; the broad avenue for more than a mile solid full, and more,—from wall to wall, from door to roof, with straining forms and out-welling hearts. In the midst on-pressing that darker stream, with arms and colors resplendent in the noonday sun; an army of tested manhood, clothed with power, crowned with glory,—marching to its dissolution!

At this turn of the avenue, our bugle rings out the signal: "Prepare for Review!" The bands strike the cadenced march; the troops take up the step; the lines straighten; the column rectifies distances; the company fronts take perfect "dress," guide left, towards the side of the reviewing stand ahead, arms at the ceremonial "carry."

All is steadiness, dignity, order now. We are to pass in final review. The culminating point is near; the end for us nearing; a far-borne vision broods upon our eyes; world-wide and years-long thought,—deep, silent, higher than joy!

Still there is some marching more, in this restrained, cadenced order. We approach the region of the public offices and higher residential quarter, welcomed by yet fairer forms and more finely balanced salutations. Ah! women sitting at the balconied windows, with straining eyes and handkerchiefs now waving, then suddenly, at some face seen,—or not seen where once belonging,—pressed to faces bowed and trembling. Some of you I have seen where the earth itself was trembling, beneath the greetings wherewith man meets man with wrath and wreck,—you and those like you,—for heaven, too, is wide,—searching under the battle smoke to find a lost face left to be unknown; bending to bind up a broken frame made in God's image; or skillfully as divinely taught, fashioning the knot to check an artery's out-rushing life,—nay, even pressing tender fingers over it till what you deemed better help could come; to catch a dying message, or breathe a passing prayer; or perchance no more than give a cup of water to men now of

God's "little ones,"—so done unto his Christ!

You in my soul I see, faithful watcher by my cot-side long days and nights together through the delirium of mortal anguish,—steadfast, calm and sweet as eternal love. We pass now quickly from each other's sight; but I know full well that where beyond these passing scenes you shall be, there will be heaven!

But now we come opposite the reviewing stand. Here are the President, his cabinet, ambassadors and ministers of foreign lands, generals, governors, judges, high officers of the nation and the states. But we miss the deep, sad eyes of Lincoln coming to review us after each sore trial. Something is lacking to our hearts now,—even in this supreme hour. Already the simple, plain, almost threadbare forms of the men of my division have come into view, and the President and his whole great company on the stand have risen and passed to the very front edge with gracious and generous recognition. I wheel my horse, lightly touching rein and spur to bring his proud head and battle-scarred neck to share the deep salutation of the sword. Then riding past, I dismount at the President's invitation, and ascend the stand. Exchanging quick greetings, I join them at the front. All around I hear the murmured exclamations: "This is Porter's old division!" "This is the Fifth Corps!" "These are straight from Five Forks and Appomattox!" It seemed as if all remained standing while the whole corps passed. Surely all of them arose as each brigade commander passed, and as some deep-dyed, riven color drooped in salutation; and the throng on the stand did not diminish, although for more than three hours the steady march had held them before ours came to view.

For me, while this division was passing, no other thing could lure my eyes away, whether looking on, or through. These were my men; and those who followed were familiar and dear. They belonged to me, and I to them by bonds birth cannot create nor death sever. More were passing here than the personages on the stand could see. But to me so seeing, what a review,—how great, how far; how near! It was as the morning of the resurrection.

The brigades to-day are commanded by General Pearson, General Gregory and Colonel Edmunds, veterans of the corps. First is the Third Brigade, bearing the spirit and transformed substance of Porter's old division of Yorktown, and Morell's at

Gaines' Mill and Malvern Hill. These are of the men I stood with at Antietam and Fredericksburg, and Chancellorsville and Gettysburg. Of that regiment—the 20th Maine—a third were left on the slopes of Round Top, and a third again in the Wilderness, at Spotsylvania, the North Anna, Cold Harbor and the Chickahominy; to-day mingling in its ranks the remnants of the noble 2d, and 1st Sharpshooters. Beside it still, the 118th Pennsylvania, sharing all its experiences from the day when these two young regiments took ordeal together in the floods of waters beneath and of fiery death above in the testing passage of Shepardstown Ford in 1862. More Pennsylvania veterans yet; the storied 83d and 91st, and brilliant 155th Zouave, and the shadow of the stalwart 62d, gone, and 21st Cavalry passed on. With these the 1st and 16th Michigan, ever at the front, the keen-eyed 1st and 2d Sharpshooters and proud relics of the 4th, left from the Wheat-field of Gettysburg. Here is the trusted, sorely-tried 32d Massachusetts, with unfaltering spirit and ranks made good from the best substance of the 18th, wakening heart-held visions. These names and numbers tell of the men who had opened all the fiery gateways of Virginia from the York River to the Chickahominy, and from the Rapidan to the Appomattox.

Now Gregory's New York Brigade,—the 187th, 188th, and 189th, young in order of number, but veteran in experience and honor; worthy of the list held yet in living memory, the 12th, 13th, 14th, 17th, 25th, and 44th, one by one gone before.

One more brigade yet, of this division; of the tested last that shall be first; the splendid 185th New York, and fearless, clear brained Sniper still at their head; the stalwart fourteen company regiment, the 198th Pennsylvania, its gallant field officers gone,—brave veteran Sickel falling with shattered arm, and brilliant young Adjutant McEwen, shot dead,—both within touch of my hand in the sharp rally on the Quaker Road; and Major Glen since commanding, cut down on the height of valor, colors in hand, leading a charge I ordered in a moment of supreme need. Captain John Stanton, lately made major, leads to-day. These also coming into the bloody field of the dark year 1864; but soon ranked with veterans and wreathed with honor. In the last campaign opening with the brilliant victory on the enemy's right flank; of the foremost in the cyclone sweep at Five Forks, and at Appomattox first of the

infantry to receive the flag of truce which bespoke the end.
Each of these brigades had been severally in my command;
and now they were mine all together, as I was theirs. So has
passed this First Division,—and with it, part of my soul.

But now comes in sight a form before which the tumult
of applause swells in mightier volume. It is Ayres, born soldier, self-commanding, nerve of iron, heart of gold,—a man to
build on. What vicissitudes had he not seen since Gettysburg!
Of those three splendid brigades which followed the white
maltese cross to the heights of Round Top, compact in spirit,
and discipline and power, only *two regiments* now hold their
place; the 140th and 146th New York,—and of these both
colonels killed, at the head of their heroes,—O'Rorke at
Gettysburg and Jenkins in the Wilderness. Where are the
regulars, who since 1862 had been ever at our side?—the ten
iron-hearted regiments that made that terrible charge down
the north spur of Little Round Top into the seething furies at
its base, and brought back not one-half of its deathless offering. Like Ayres it was,—in spirit and in truth,—when asked
at the Warren Court,—years after, then reviewing the Five
Forks battle, "Where were your regulars then?" to answer with
bold lip quivering, "Buried, sir, at Gettysburg!" Whereat there
was silence,—and something more. And of what were not then
buried, fifteen hundred more were laid low beneath the flaming scythes of the Wilderness, Spotsylvania and the other bloody-
fields of that campaign. And the government, out of pride and
pity, sent the shredded fragments of them to the peaceful forts
in the islands of New York harbor,—left there to their thoughts
of glory.[1]

Their places had been taken by two brigades from the
old First Corps,—dearly experienced there; the thrice-honored
Maryland Brigade, 1st, 4th, 7th and 8th; in whose latest action
I saw two of its brigade commanders shot down in quick succession; and the gallant little Delaware Brigade, with its proud
record of loyalty and fidelity, part of the country's best history.
Brave Dennison and Gwyn, generals leading these two brigades today; both bearing their honors modestly, as their hardly
healed wounds manfully.

[1]The losses of the regulars must in honor be here recalled.
At Gettysburg, 829; The Wilderness, 295; Spotsylvania, 420; North Anna, 44;
Bethesda Church, 165; The Weldon Road, 480; Peebles' Farm, 76; a total of 2,309.

Now the First Brigade; this of New York,—the superb
5th, 140th and 146th and the 15th Artillery, their equal in
honor. At the head of this, on the fire-swept angle at Five
Forks the high-hearted Fred Winthrop fell; then Grimshaw
and Ayres himself led on to the first honors of that great day.
At its head on this great day rides the accomplished General
Joe Hayes, scarcely recovered from dangerous wounds. It was
a hard place for brigade commanders,—the Fifth Corps,—in
those "all summer" battles,—and for colonels, too.

So they pass, those that had come to take the place of
the regulars; they pass into immortal history. Oh, good people
smiling, applauding, tossing flowers,waving handkerchiefs from
your lips with vicarious suggestion,—what forms do you see
under that white cross, now also going its long way?

But here comes the Third Division, with Crawford, of
Fort Sumter fame; high gentleman, punctilious soldier, familiar to us all. Leading his brigades are the fine commanders,
dauntless Morrow, of the "Iron Brigade," erect above the scars
of Gettysburg, the Wilderness and Petersburg; resolute Baxter,
and bold Dick Coulter,—veterans, marked, too, with wounds.
Theirs is the blue cross,—speaking not of the azure heaven,
but of the down-pressing battle smoke. And the men who in
former days gave fame to that division,—the Pennsylvania
Reserves of the Peninsula, Antietam and Gettysburg, with
their strong *"esprit de corps"* and splendor of service,—only the
shadow of them now. But it is of sunset gold.

Here draws near a moving spectacle indeed, the last of
the dear old First Corps; thrice decimated at Gettysburg in
action and passion heroic, martyr-like, sublime: then merged
into the Fifth, proudly permitted to bear its old colors, and in
the crimson campaign of 1864 fought down to a division; in the
last days the ancient spirit shining in the ranks where its
scattered regiments are absorbed in other brigades,—shining
still to-day! But where are my splendid six regiments of them
which made that resolute, forlorn-hope charge from the crest
they had carried fitly named "Fort Hell," down past the spew-
ing dragons of "Fort Damnation" into the miry, fiery pit before
Rives' Salient of the dark June 18. Two regiments of them,
the 121st Pennsylvania, Colonel Warner, and 142d Pennsylvania, Colonel Warren, alone I see in this passing pageant,—worn,
thin hostages of the mortal. I violate the courtesies of the
august occasion. I give them salutation before the face of the

reviewing officer,—the President himself,—asking no permission—no forgiveness.

Here, led by valiant Small, that 16th Maine, which under heroic Tilden held its appointed station on the fierce first day of Gettysburg, obedient to the laws, like Spartans, for their loyalty and honor's sake; cut through, cut down, swept over, scattered, captured; so that at dreary night-fall the hushed voices of only four officers and thirty-eight men answered the roll-call. With them the 94th New York, which under Colonel Adrian Root shared its fate and glory.

And here are passing now those yet spared from earth and heaven of that "Iron Brigade," of Meredith's, on whose list appear such names as Lucius Fairchild, Henry Morrow, Rufus Dawes and Samuel Williams, and such regiments as the 19th Indiana, 24th Michigan, and 2d, 6th and 7th Wisconsin, which on the first day's front line with Buford and Reynolds, in that one fierce onset at Willoughby's Run, withstood overwhelming odds, at the cost of highest manliness and the loss of a thousand, a hundred and fifty-three manly men;—that of the 24th Michigan largest of all,—three hundred and sixty-five,—eighty-one out of every hundred of that morning roll-call answering at evening, otherwhere. One passing form to-day holds every eye. Riding calmly at the head of the 7th Wisconsin is Hollon Richardson, who at Five Forks sprang to take on himself the death-blow struck at Warren as he leaped the flaming breast-works in the lurid sunset of his high career.

Pass on, men, in garb and movement to some monotonous: pass on, men, modest and satisfied; as if those looking on knew what you are!

And now, Wainwright, with the artillery of the corps; guns whose voices I should know among a hundred;—"D" of the Fifth Regular, ten-pounder guns, which Hazlett lifted to the craggy crest of Little Round Top; its old commander, Weed, supporting; whence having thundered again his law to a delivered people, God called them both to their reward. "L" of the 1st Ohio, perched on the western slope, hurling defiance at deniers. I see not Martin of the 3d Massachusetts, whose iron ploughed the gorge between Round Top and the Devil's Den. But "B" of the 4th Regular is here, which stood by me on the heart-bastioned hillock in the whirlwind of the Quaker Road. And here the 5th Massachusetts which wrought miracles of valor all the way from the Fifth Corps right, across the valley of death at Gettysburg, to the North Anna; where, planted in my very skirmish line, Phillips, erect on the gun-carriage, launched percussion into buildings full of sharpshooters picking off my best men. And where is Bigelow of the 9th Massachusetts, who on the exposed front fell back only with the recoil of his guns before the hordes swarming through the Peach Orchard, giving back shot, shrapnel, canister, rammer, pistol and saber, until his battery,—guns, limbers, horses, men,—and he himself, were a heap of mingled ruin? Which, also, a year after, with Mink's 1st New York and Hart's 15th, came to support the charge at the ominous Fort Hell; whence Bigelow, with watchful eyes, sent his brave men down through hissing canister, and enfilading shell, and blinding turf and pebbles flying from the up-torn earth, to bring back my useless body from what else were its final front.

Roar on, ye throngs around and far away; there are voices in my ear out-thundering yours!

All along in the passing column I have exchanged glances with earnest, true-hearted surgeons, remembered too well, but never too much loved and honored; with faithful chaplains, hospital attendants and ambulance men, never to be forgotten,—of the few who know something of the unrecorded scenes in the rear of a great battle. I have caught glances also from bright-eyed young staff officers who in the kaleidoscope changes of eventful years had been of my field family. Their look was sometimes confidential, as if slyly reminding me of the salutary discipline of camp, when they were turned out at reveille roll-call to "get acquainted with the men;" and after guard-mounting the college men of them called up to demonstrate Euclid's *"pons asinorum"* with their scabbards in the sand; and for those who were not men of Bowdoin or Amherst or Yale or Columbia, the test commuted to shivering with pistol shot the musty hard-tack tossed in air, or at race-course gallop, spitting with saber-point the "Turk's head" of a junk of "condemned" pork on the commissary's hitching-post, or picking up a handkerchief from the ground, riding headlong, at Tartar speed. Other pranks, of spontaneous and surreptitious discipline, when they thought it necessary to teach a green quarter-master how to ride, by deftly tucking dry pine cones under his saddle-cloth. You are ready to do it again, I see,—you demure pretenders;—or something the sequence of this skill, more useful to your fellow-man!

Have they all passed,—the Fifth Corps? Or will it ever pass? Am I left alone, or still with you all? You, of the thirteen young colonels, colleagues with me in the courts-martial and army schools of the winter camps of 1862: Vincent, of the 83d Pennsylvania, caught up in the fiery chariot from the heights of Round Top; O'Rorke, of the 140th New York, pressing to that glorious defense, swiftly called from the head of his regiment to serener heights; Jeffords, of the 4th Michigan, thrust through by bayonets as he snatched back his lost colors from the deadly reapers of the Wheat-field; Rice, of the 44th New York, crimsoning the harrowed crests at Spotsylvania with his life-blood,—his intense soul snatched far otherwhere than his last earthly thought,—"Turn my face towards the enemy!" Welch, of the 16th Michigan, first on the ramparts at Peebles' Farm, shouting "On, boys, and over!" and receiving from on high the same order for his own daring spirit; Prescott, of the 32d Massachusetts, who lay touching feet with me after mortal Petersburg of June 18, under the midnight requiem of the somber pines,—I doomed of all to go, and bidding him stay,—but the weird winds were calling otherwise; Winthrop, of the 12th Regulars, before Five Forks just risen from a guest-seat at my homely luncheon on a log, within a half hour shot dead in the fore-front of the whirling charge. These gone;—and of the rest, Varney, of the 2d Maine, worn down by prison cruelties, and returning, severely wounded in the head on the storm-swept slopes of Fredericksburg, and forced to resign the service; Hayes, of the 18th Massachusetts, cut down in the tangles of the Wilderness; Gwyn, of the 118th Pennsylvania, also sorely wounded there; Herring, of the same regiment, with a leg off at Dabney's Mill; Webb, then of the corps staff, since, highly promoted, shot in his uplifted head, fronting his brigade to the leaden storm of Spotsylvania; Locke, adjutant-general of the corps,—a bullet cutting from his very mouth the order he was giving on the flaming crests of Laurel Hill!

You thirteen: seven, before the year was out, shot dead at the head of your commands; of the rest, every one desperately wounded in the thick of battle; I last of all, but here today,—with you, earthly or ethereal forms.

"*Waes Hael!*"—across the rifts of vision—"Be Whole again, My Thirteen!"

Pardon me, gentlemen on the platform! Pardon me, ministers of the old world, and masters of the new. I had lost myself for a little, and dreamed it was my review!

But what draws near heralded by tumult of applause, but when well-recognized greeted with mingled murmurs of reverence? It is the old Second Corps,—of Sumner and of Hancock,—led now by one no less honored and admired,—Humphreys, the accomplished, heroic soldier; the noble and modest man. He rides a snow-white horse, followed by his well-proved staff, like-mounted, chief of them the brilliant Frank Walker, capable of higher things,—and "Joe Smith," chief commissary, with a Medal of Honor for gallant service beyond duty,—a striking group, not less to the eye in color and composition, than to the mind in character. Above them is borne the corps badge, the cloverleaf,—peaceful token, but a triple mace to foes,—dear to thousands among the insignia of our army, as the shamrock to Ireland or rose and thistle of the British empire.

Here comes the First Division,—that of Richardson, and Caldwell, and Barlow and Miles; but at its head to-day we see not Miles, for he is just before ordered to Fortress Monroe to guard "Jeff Davis" and his friends,—President "Andy Johnson" declaring he "wanted there a man who would not let his prisoners escape." So Ramsay of New Jersey is in command on this proud day. Its brigades are led by McDougal, Fraser, Nugent and Mulholland;—whereby you see the shamrock and thistle are not wanting even in our field. These are the men we saw at the sunken road at Antietam, the stone wall at Fredericksburg, the Wheat-field at Gettysburg, the Bloody Angle at Spotsylvania, the swirling fight at Farmville, and in the pressing pursuit along the Appomattox before which Lee was forced to face to the rear, and answer Grant's first summons to surrender. We know them well. So it seems do these thousands around.

These pass; or rather, do not pass, but abide with us; while crowd upon our full hearts the stalwart columns of the Second Division,—the division of the incisive Barlow,—once of Sedgwick and Howard and Gibbon. These men bring thoughts of the terrible charge at the Dunker church at Antietam, and that still more terrible up Marye's Heights at Fredericksburg, and the check given to the desperate onset of Pickett and Pettigrew in the consummate hour of Gettysburg. We think, too, of the fiery mazes of the Wilderness, the death-blasts of Spotsylvania, and murderous Cold Harbor; but also of the brilliant fights at Sailor's Creek and Farmville, and all the splendid action to the victorious end. Here is the seasoned remnant of the "Corcoran Legion," the new brigade, which rushing into the terrors of Spotsylvania, halted a moment while its priest stood before the brave, bent heads and called down benediction.

Webb's Brigade of the Wilderness is commanded to-day by Olmstead; the second, by McIvor; veteran colonels from New York; the third by Colonel Woodall of Delaware. This brigade knows the meaning of that colorless phrase, "the casualties of the service," showing the ever shifting elements which enter into what we call identity. Here are all that is left of French's old division at Antietam, and Hays' at Gettysburg, who was killed in the Wilderness, Carroll's Brigade at Spotsylvania, where he was severely wounded; Smyth's at Cold Harbor, killed at Farmville. Into this brigade Owen's, too, is now merged. They are a museum of history.

Here passes led by staunch Spaulding the sterling 19th Maine,—once gallant Heath's,—conspicuous everywhere, from the death-strewn flank of Pickett's charge, through all the terrible scenes of "Grant's campaign," to its consummation at Appomattox. In its ranks now are the survivors of the old Spartan 4th, out of the "Devil's Den," where Longstreet knew them.

Heads uncover while passes what answers the earthly roll-call of the immortal 5th New Hampshire, famed on the stubborn Third Corps front at Gettysburg, where its high-hearted Colonel Cross fell leading the brigade; among the foremost in the sad glory of its losses,—two hundred and ninety-five men having been killed in its ranks.

What is that passing now, the center of all eyes,—that little band so firmly poised and featured they seem to belong elsewhere? This is what was the 1st Minnesota,—sometimes spoken of, for valid reasons, as the 1st Maine,—more deeply known as of Gettysburg, where in the desperate counter-charge to stay an overwhelming onset, they left eighty-three men out of every hundred! With ever lessening ranks but place unchanged at the head of its brigade from Bull Run to Appomattox, to-day a modest remnant, Colonel Hausdorf proudly leads on its last march, the 1st Minnesota.

What wonder that as such men pass, the out-poured greetings take on a strangely mingled tone. You could not say from what world they come, or to what world they go. Not without deep throbbings under our breath,—ours who in heart belong to them,—as if answering some far-off drum-beat "assembly" summons.

But now comes on with veteran pride and far-preceding heralding of acclaim, the division which knows something of the transmigration of souls; having lived and moved in different bodies, and under different names, knowing, too, the tests of manhood, and the fate of suffering and sacrifice; but knowing most of all the undying spirit which holds fast its loyalty and faces ever forward. This is the division of Mott,—himself commanding to-day, although severely wounded at Hatcher's Run on the sixth of April last. These are all that is left of the old commands of Hooker and Kearney, and later, of our noble Berry, of Sickles' Third Corps. They still wear the proud "Kearney patch,"—the red diamond. Birney's Division, too, has been consolidated with Mott's; and the brigades are now commanded by the chivalrous De Trobriand, and the sterling soldiers, Pierce of Michigan and McAllister of New Jersey. Their division flag now bears the mingled symbols of the two corps, the Second and Third,—the diamond and the trefoil.

Over them far floats the mirage-like vision of them on the Peninsula, and then at Bristow, Manassas and Chantilly; and again the solid substance of them at Chancellorsville, and on the stormy front from the Plum Run gorge to the ghastly Peach Orchard where the earth shone red with the bright facings of their brave Zouaves thick-strewn amidst the blue, as we looked down from smoking Round Top. Then in the consolidation for the final trial, bringing the prestige, and spirit, and loyalty of their old corps into the Second,—making this the strongest corps in the army,—adding their splendid valor to the fame of this in which they merged their name.

Now come those heavy artillery regiments which the exigencies of the service drew suddenly to unexpected and unfamiliar duty, striking the fight at its hottest in the cauldron of Spotsylvania, and obeying orders literally, suffered loss beyond all others there; the 1st Massachusetts losing three hundred, and the 1st Maine four hundred and eighty-one officers and men in that single action. This same 1st Maine, afterwards in the rashly-bidden, futile charge at Petersburg, June 18, 1864, added to its immortal roll six hundred and thirty-two lost in that lost assault. Proudly rides Russell Shepherd at their head,—leaving the command of a brigade to lead these men to-day. Deep emotions stir at the presence of such survivors,—cherishing the same devotion and deserving the same honor as those who fell.

Here passes the high-borne steadfast-hearted 17th Maine from the seething whirlpool of the Wheat-field of Gettysburg to the truce-compelling flags of Appomattox. To-day its ranks are honored and spirit strengthened by the accession of the famous old 3d Regiment,—that was Howard's. Some impress remains of firm-hearted Roberts, brave Charley Merrill, keen-edged West, and sturdy William Hobson; but Charley Mattocks is in command in these days,—a man and a soldier, with the unspoiled heart of a boy. Three of these college mates of mine. What far dreams drift over the spirit, of the days when we questioned what life should be, and answered for ourselves what we would be!

But now passes the artillery,—guns all dear to us; but we have seen no more of some, familiar and more dear: Hall's 2d Maine, that was on the cavalry front on the first day of Gettysburg, grand in retreat as in action, afterwards knowing retreat only in sunset bugle-call; Stevens' 5th Maine, that tore through the turmoil of that tragic day, and gave the Louisiana "Tigers" another cemetery than that they sought on the storied hill; roaring its way through the darkness of 1864, holding all its ancient glory. Most of the rest we knew had gone to the "reserve."

The pageant has passed. The day is over. But we linger, loath to think we shall see them no more together,—these men, these horses, these colors afield. Hastily they have swept to the front as of yore; crossing again once more the long bridge and swaying pontoons, they are on the Virginia shore, waiting as they before had sought, the day of the great return.

———————

But we were to have one great day more. The Sixth Corps had come up from its final service of perfecting the surrender, and on this bright morning of June 8 was to be held in review by honoring thoughts and admiring eyes. We who had passed our review were now invited spectators of this. But there was something more. Something the best in us would be passed in review to-day.

The military prestige of this corps was great, and its reputation was enhanced by Sheridan's late preference, well-known. The city, too, had its special reasons for regard. The Sixth Corps had come up from its proud place in the battle lines in days of fear and peril, to save Washington. Besides, this corps was part of the great Army of the Potomac.

The President and all the dignitaries were on the reviewing stand as before. Multitudes were filling the streets, and the houses bloomed their welcome from basement to summit. The ordering was much as before. Column of companies; files equalized. Space now permits some features of a regular review. Instead of close order, the column moves at wheeling distance of its subdivisions; all commissioned officers salute; division and brigade commanders after passing the reviewing stand, turn out and join the reviewing officer; the bands also at this point wheel out and continue playing while their brigade is passing. The ambulances, engineers and artillery follow as before.

The symbol of the flag of this corps is the Greek cross,—the "square" cross, of equal arms. Symbol of terrible history in old world conflicts,—Russian and Cossack and Pole; token now of square fighting, square dealing, and loyalty to the flag of the union of freedom and law.

These are survivors of the men in early days with Franklin and Smith and Slocum and Newton. Later, and as we know them best, the men of Sedgwick; but alas, Sedgwick leads no more, except in spirit. Unheeding self he fell smitten by a sharpshooter's bullet, in the midst of his corps. Wright is commanding since, and to-day, his chief-of-staff, judicial Martin McMahon. These are the men of Antietam and the twice wrought marvels of courage at Fredericksburg, and the long tragedy of Grant's campaign of '64; then in the valley of the Shenandoah with Sheridan in his rallying ride, and in the last campaign storming the works of Petersburg—losing eleven hundred men in fifteen minutes; masters at Sailor's Creek, four days after, taking six thousand prisoners, with Ewell and five of his best generals,—of them the redoubtable Kershaw; in the van in the pursuit of Lee, and with the Second Corps pressing him to a last stand, out of which came the first message of surrender.

First comes the division of Wheaton; at its head, under

Penrose, the heroic New Jersey Brigade which at the Wilderness and Spotsylvania lost a thousand, one hundred and forty-three officers and men. Next, and out of like experiences, the brigades of Edwards and Hamblen,—representing the valor of Massachusetts, Rhode Island, Connecticut, Pennsylvania and Wisconsin.

Now passes Getty's Division. Leading is Warner's Brigade, from its great record of the Wilderness, Spotsylvania and Cold Harbor; then the magnificent First Vermont Brigade, under that sterling soldier, General Lewis Grant; as their proud heads pass, we think of the thousand six hundred and forty-five laid low at the Salient of Spotsylvania. Now we think we see the shadow of that "Light Division" with Burnham storming Marye's Heights in the Chancellorsville campaign of '63. For here, last, is the Third Brigade,—once of Neill and Bidwell,—with the fame of its brave work all through Grant's campaign, led now by Sumner's 1st Maine Veterans, of which it is enough to say it is made up of the old 5th, and 6th, and 7th Maine,—the hearts of Edwards and Harris and Connor still beating in them. Can history connote or denote anything nobler in manliness and soldiership, than has been made good by these? Commanding is the young general, Tom Hyde, favorite in all the army; prince of staff-officers, gallant commander, alert of sense, level of head, sweet of soul.

The infantry column is closed by Ricketts' Division: its brigades commanded by Truman Seymour and Warren Keifer,—names known before and since. These men too, knowing what was done and suffered,—shall we say in vain?—in that month under fire from the Wilderness to Cold Harbor; in these two battles losing out of their firm-held ranks a thousand, eight hundred and twenty-five men; knowing also of the valley of the Shenandoah and the weary windings of the Appomattox. Of the heart of the country,—these men; Vermont, New York, New Jersey, Ohio, Pennsylvania, Maryland. These twelve regiments were to close that grand procession of muskets, tokens of a nation's mighty deliverance, now to be laid down; tokens also of consummate loyalty and the high manhood that seeks not self but the larger, deeper well-being which explains and justifies personal experience.

Now follows the artillery brigade, under Major Cowan; eight batteries representing all the varieties of that field service, and the contributions of Rhode Island, Vermont, New

York and New Jersey, and the regulars. What story of splendors and of terrors do these grim guns enshrine!

Now, last of all, led by Major Van Brocklin, the little phalanx of the 50th New York Engineers, which had been left to help the Sixth Corps pass once more the turbid rivers of Virginia. Here again, the train of uncouth pontoons; telling of the mastery over the waters as of the land. This last solemn passage now, waking memories of dark going and dark returning, deep slumbering in our souls. Thanks and blessing, homely pontoons! Would to God we had a bridge so sure, to bear us over other dark waters,—out of the pain,—into the Peace!

Home again, Sixth Corps! Home to your place in our hearts! Encamp beside us once more; as for so long we have made sunshine for each others' eyes, and watched with hushed voices guarding their rest; and wakened to the same thrilling call, guided on each other through maze of darkness to fronts of storm and over walls of flame!

Sit down again, Sixth Corps! with the Fifth and Second, holding dear to thought the soul and symbol of the vanished First and Third. Sit down again together, Army of the Potomac! all that are left of us,—on the banks of the river whose name we bore, into which we have put new meaning of our own. Take strength from one more touch, ere we pass afar from the closeness of old. The old is young to-day; and the young is passed. Survivors of the fittest; for the fittest, it seems to us, abide in the glory where we saw them last,—take the grasp of hands, and look into the eyes,—without words! Who shall tell what is past and what survives? For there are things born but lately in the years, which belong to the eternities.

A

DEDICATION OF THE TWENTIETH MAINE MONUMENTS AT GETTYSBURG
October 3, 1889

General Chamberlain's Address:

A quarter of a century ago on this rugged crest you were doing what you deemed your duty. To-day you come with modest main, with care more for truth than for praise, to retrace and record the simple facts—the outward form—of your movements and action. But far more than this entered into your thought and motive, and far greater was the result of the action taken than any statistical description of it could import.

You were making history. The world has recorded for you more than you have written. The centuries to come will share and recognize the victory won here, with growing gratitude. The country has acknowledged your service. Your State is proud of it. This well-earned and unsought fame has moved you already to acknowledge your deserts. Your own loyal and loving zeal for justice has indeed anticipated the State's recognition. At your own cost you set your monument here to mark the ground where faithful service and devotion wrought a result so momentous.

To-day your historians have recalled the facts. On that line which has been so patiently and candidly investigated and as far as possible freed from doubt and unclearness, your admirable record leaves little to be desired. But as this is suitable, if not final, opportunity for accurate and complete statement of these facts, I may be indulged in a remark or two germane to this matter, which recent visits and this occasion itself suggests.

I am certain that the position of this monument is quite

to the left of the centre of our regimental line when the final charge was ordered. Our original left did not extend quite to the great rock which now supports this memorial of honor. When we changed front with our left wing and extended it by the flank and rear, the color was brought to mark the new centre, which was to become the salient of our formation; and it was placed, I was sorry to do it, on the smooth and open slope, and in a position completely exposed. Beyond this the left was refused and extended in single rank. When the charge was made I was beside the color-bearer, and I know well that we struck the enemy where their line was open to view, and the ground comparatively unobstructed. The color advanced in the direction of the proper front of the right wing, and passed the rock altogether to our left. I am not at all criticizing the judgment of our comrades who selected the great boulder for the base of the monument. It was entirely fitting to mark it with that honor, as it became so conspicuous an object during the terrible struggle—the centre and pivot of the whirlpool that raged around.

I take note also of the surprise of several officers to hear that it was some other than a single one of them who came to me in the course of the fight with information of the enemy's extended movements to envelop our left. Now, as might well be believed of such gentlemen and soldiers, they are all right; no one of them is wrong.

It was quite early in the action, and while as yet only our right wing was hotly engaged, that an officer from that centre reported to me that a large body of the enemy could be seen in his front, moving along the bottom of the valley below us, deliberately towards our extreme left and rear. I sprang upon a rock in our line, which allowed me to see over the heads of those with whom we were then engaged, and the movement and intent of the enemy was plain to be seen. It was this timely knowledge that enabled me to plan the prompt movement which you so admirably executed—that rapid change of front, doubling back upon ourselves, and the single rank formation, which proved so effectual for our stubborn resistance.

Sometime after this, and while we were hard pressed upon all sides, an officer from the extreme left reported to me, with great anxiety, that the enemy were outflanking our left, thrown back as it was. I found the situation critical, and

immediately ordered the right company to repair to the extreme left in support, and sent to the commanding officer of
the 83d Pennsylvania Regiment, asking him to extend his left
to cover the ground vacated on our right. But as I found this
movement produced much confusion, and this withdrawal was
likely to be misconstrued into a retreat, I was obliged to coun-
termand the order, and let the left wing hold on as best it
could, and as best it did.

One more matter. In the third fierce onset of the enemy, through a rift in the rolling smoke I saw with consterna-
tion that our centre was nearly shot away, and the color guarded
only by a little group, who seemed to be checking the enemy
by their heroic bearing and not by numbers, and I sent the
adjutant to the commanding officer of the color company, to
ask him to hold on if he possibly could, till I could reinforce
him from some other regiment. So little expectation had I that
the adjutant could live to reach the spot, I pressed into my
service a trusted sergeant and despatched him with the same
message. Meantime the crash had come, and out of the flame
and smoke emerged that centre, bearing the color still aloft,
forced back, pressed in upon itself, but solid and firm, an
impregnable front, face to the foe. The enemy on their part
had also recoiled, and were gathering in the low shrubbery for
a new assault. Our ammunition was gone. It was manifest
that we could not stand before the wave that was ready to roll
upon us. Knowing all this I resolved upon the desperate chances
of a counter-charge with the bayonet. I at once sent to the left
wing to give them notice and time for the required change of
front. Just then the brave and thoughtful young Lieutenant,
commanding the color company, came up to me and said, "I
think I could press forward with my company, if you will
permit me, and cover the ground where our dead and wounded
are." "You shall have the chance," was my answer, "I am
about to order a charge. We are to make a great right wheel."
What he did, you who know him know. What you did, the
world knows.

I am sorry to have heard it intimated that any hesitated when that order was given. That was not so. No man
hesitated. There might be an appearance of it to those who
did not understand the whole situation. The left wing bent
back like an ox-bow, or sharp lunette, had to take some little
time to come up into the line of our general front, so as to form

the close, continuous edge which was to strike like a sword-cut upon the enemy's ranks. By the time they had got up and straightened the line, the centre and salient, you may be sure, was already in motion. Nobody hesitated to obey the order. In fact, to tell the truth, the order was never given, or but imperfectly. The enemy were already pressing up the slope. There was only time or need for the words, "Bayonet! Forward to the right!" The quick witted and tense-nerved men caught the words out of my lips, and almost the action out of my hands.

So much in elucidation of facts. You see there may be stories apparently not consistent with each other, yet all of them true in their time and place, and so far as each actor is concerned.

And while every one here, officer and soldier, did more than his duty, and acted with utmost intelligence and spirit, you must permit me to add the remark that I commanded my regiment that day.

Words elsewhere spoken by me to-day in our State's behalf strive to express the motive and purpose of this great struggle, and the character and consequence of the victory vouchsafed us. It is there I speak of country; here it needs only that I speak of you, and of ground made glorious by you and yours.

The lesson impressed on me as I stand here and my heart and mind traverse your faces, and the years that are gone, is that in a great, momentous struggle like this commemorated here, it is character that tells. I do not mean simply nor chiefly bravery. Many a man has that, who may become surprised or disconcerted at a sudden change in the posture of affairs. What I mean by character is a firm seasoned substance of soul. I mean such qualities or acquirements as intelligence, thoughtfulness, conscientiousness, right-mindedness, patience, fortitude, long-suffering and unconquerable resolve.

I could see all this on your faces when you were coming into position here for the desperate encounter; man by man, file by file, on the right into line. I knew that you all knew that was staked on your endurance and heroism. Some of you heard Vincent say to me, with such earnest and prophetic eyes, pointing to the right of our position and the front of the oncoming attack, "You understand, Colonel, this ground must be held at all costs!" I did understand; with a heavy weight on my mind and spirit. You understood; and it was done. Held, and at what cost! Held, and for what effect!

There is no need that I should recount to the friends who stand around us here, what would have happened had this little line—this thin, keen edge of Damascus steel—been broken down from its guard. All can see what would have come of our Brigade swallowed up; of Weed's, struck in the rear; of Hazlitt's guns, taken in the flank and turned to launch their thunder-bolts upon our troops, already sore pressed in the gorge at our feet, and the fields upon the great front and right. Round Top lost—the day lost—Gettysburg lost—who can tell or dream what for loss thence would follow!

I do not know whether any friends who now stand here on this calm and sunny day, comprehend how the weight of such a responsibility presses upon the spirit. We were young then. We do not count ourselves old yet; and these things were done more than twenty-six years ago. We believe we could do them now; but we wonder how we could have done them then. Doubtless the spring and elasticity of youth helped us bear the burden and recover from the shock. But something more than youthful ardor and dash was demanded for such a test. And that was yours. In thought, in habit, in experience, in discipline, you were veterans. It was a matter, as I have said, of character. It was the soul of youth suddenly springing into the flush and flower of manhood. It was the force of the characters you had formed in the silent and peaceful years by the mother's knee and by the father's side, which stood you in such stead in the day of trial. And so it is. We know not of the future, and cannot plan for it much. But we can hold our spirits and our bodies so pure and high, we may cherish such thoughts and such ideals, and dream such dreams of lofty purpose, that we can determine and know what manner of men we will be whenever and wherever the hour strikes, that calls to noble action. This predestination God has given us in charge. No man becomes suddenly different from his habit and cherished thought. We carry our accustomed manners with us. And it was the boyhood you brought from your homes which made you men; which braced your hearts, which shone upon your foreheads, which held you steadfast in mind and body and lifted these heights of Gettysburg to immortal glory.

This Round Top spur, as it is easy to see to-day, was a commanding position in that battle, and confessedly the key of the field for that day's fight. It is deliberately so pronounced in official papers by the leaders on both sides. I stood on that summit not long ago with Longstreet and officers of our own army, not so much disposed as he by the events of that day's fighting, to praise the Fifth Corps, and they one and all acknowledged that this was by nature and in fact the supreme position. One of the ablest of the southern historians, describing in his impassioned style the fight which circled and flamed around this crest, says, "That was the glittering coronet we longed to clutch." The glittering coronet was won, but not by them. All honor to those who seeing it, seized it in thought; who gained it, who held it, who glorified it. All honor to Warren, first and last, and now forever, of the Fifth Corps; to Vincent, to Rice, to Hazlitt, to Weed, to Ayres,—chief commanders here. Peace be to their spirits where they have gone. Honor and sacred remembrance to those who fell here, and buried part of our hearts with them. Honor to the memory of those who fought here with us and for us, and who fell elsewhere, or have died since, heart-broken at the harshness or injustice of a political government. Honor to you, who have wrought and endured so much and so well. After life's fitful fever, may you, also, sleep well. And so, farewell.

B

DEDICATION OF THE MAINE MONUMENTS AT GETTYSBURG
Evening of October 3, 1889

The day, one of the most beautiful of October, was used for the regimental reunions and for visiting places of interest upon the field. It was the rare pleasure of the company to hear the stories of many exciting scenes of the battle from the lips of narrators, who had also been actors in those scenes.

In the evening the general dedicatory exercises occurred in the Gettysburg Courthouse before a large audience. The programme was carried out as arranged. Major Greenlief T. Stevens, secretary of the executive committee, called the assembly to order and in a brief and fitting manner introduced General Joshua L. Chamberlain as president of the day who, on taking the chair, made the following address—

General Chamberlain's Address:

The State of Maine stands here to-day for the first time in her own name. In other days she was here indeed—here in power—here in majesty—here in glory; but as elsewhere and often in the centuries before, with that humility which is perhaps the necessary law of human exaltation, her worth merged in a name mightier than her own, so here, content to be part of that greater being that she held dearer than self, but which was made more worthy of honor by her belonging to it—the United States of America. For which great end, in every heroic struggle from the beginning of our history until now,—a space of more than 200 years,—she has given her best of heart and brain and poured out her most precious blood.

190

To-day she stands here, in a service of mingled recognitions; humbly submitting to that mysterious law of sacrifice and suffering for the deliverance from evil; bending sorrowfully above the dust to which have returned again the priceless jewels offered from her bosom; proud that it was her part and lot that what was best in her giving and what was immortal in her loss should be builded into the nation's weal; and stretching out her hand, of justice and of grace, to raise along these silent lines of battle monuments eloquent of her costly devotion and of the great reward. She stands here—not ashamed when the roll of honor is called, to speak her own name, and answer, Here!

The organization of the army of the Union was a counterpart of that of the Union itself. In its ultimate elements and separate units of organization, the personal force and political authority of each State were present; but they were merged and mingled in another order, which took another and higher name when exercised jointly,—in a single aim, for the common weal. For reasons various but valid, the regiments and batteries of the several States were, for the most part, separated in assignment, distributed to different brigades, divisions, corps, armies. Some sad suggestions there were among these reasons; for one, the care that in some great disaster the loss might not fall too heavily on the families of one neighborhood. But there was a greater reason. Our thoughts were not then of States as States, but of the States united,—of that union and oneness in which the People of the United States lived and moved and had their being. Our hearts beat to that one high thought; our eyes saw but the old flag; and our souls saw it, glorious with the symbols of power and peace and blessing in the forward march of man.

But now that this victory is won, this cause vindicated, and the great fact of the being and authority of the People of the United States has been thus solemnly attested,—the moral forces summoning, and as it were consecrating the physical as token and instrument of their convictions,—now, the several States that stood as one in that high cause come here in their own name,—in the noblest sphere of their State rights,—to ratify and confirm this action of their delegates; to set these monuments as seals to their own great deeds, and new testament of life.

To-day we stand on an awful arena, where character

which was the growth of centuries was tested and determined by the issues of a single day. We are compassed about by a cloud of witnesses; not alone the shadowy ranks of those who wrestled here, but the greater parties of the action—they for whom these things were done. Forms of thought rise before us, as in an amphitheatre, circle beyond circle, rank above rank; The State, The Union, The People. And these are One. Let us—from the arena,—contemplate them, the spiritual spectators.

There is an aspect in which the question at issue might seem to be of forms, and not of substance. It was, on its face, a question of government. There was a boastful pretense that each State held in its hands the death-warrant of the Nation; that any State had a right, without show of justification outside of its own caprice, to violate the covenants of the constitution, to break away from the Union, and set up its own little sovereignty as sufficient for all human purposes and ends; thus leaving it to the mere will or whim of any member of our political system to destroy the body and dissolve the soul of the Great People. This was the political question submitted to the arbitrament arms. But the victory was of great politics over small. It was the right reason, the moral consciousness and solemn resolve of the people rectifying its wavering exterior lines according to the life-lines of its organic being.

There is a phrase abroad which obscures the legal and the moral questions involved in the issue,—indeed, which distorts and falsifies history: "The War between the States." There are here no States outside of the Union. Resolving themselves out of it does not release them. Even were they successful in intrenching themselves in this attitude, they would only relapse into territories of the United States. Indeed, several of the States so resolving were never in their own right either States or Colonies; but their territories were purchased by the common treasury of the Union, and were admitted as States out of its grace and generosity. Underneath this phrase and title,—"The War between the States,"—lies the false assumption that our Union is but a compact of States. Were it so, neither party to it could renounce it at his own mere will or caprice. Even on this theory the States remaining true to the terms of their treaty, and loyal to its intent, would have the right to resist force by force, to take up the gage of battle thrown down by the rebellious States, and compel them to return to their duty and their allegiance. The Law of Nations would have accorded the loyal States this right and remedy.

But this was not our theory, nor our justification. The flag we bore into the field was not that of particular States, no matter how many nor how loyal, arrayed against other States. It was the flag of the Union, the flag of the people, vindicating the right and charged with the duty of preventing any factions, no matter how many nor under what pretense, from breaking up this common Country.

It was the country of the South as well as of the North. The men who sought to dismember it, belonged to it. Its life was a larger life, aloof from the dominance of self-surroundings; but in it their truest interests were interwoven. They suffered themselves to be drawn down from the spiritual ideal by influences of the physical world. There is in man that peril of the double nature. "But I see another law," says St. Paul, "I see another law in my members, warring against the law of my mind."

There is here, I admit, an intrinsic confusion, one arising out of the very nature of the case; for both sides claimed to be fighting for the same things: "self-government," "freedom,"— if that means liberty to act one's own will,—and even "constitutional rights." But the simple fact is,—and a most momentous one,—that the same human life runs in many spheres; and here people were feeling and thinking and seeing and acting in one sphere and capacity on one side, and in another on the other side. Temperament, education, habit, have place sometimes in mighty consequences. Here, one party limited their interests by the bounds of States, the other by the bounds of Country comprehending the rights of Man. The truth is, our political life and being are in two capacities,—people of the States, and people of the United States. Every man and woman of us lives in both at once. In the ruling sentiments of a complex people the likenesses may be very great, yet some small differences become the starting-points for great issues of right and wrong,—pivots on which mighty movements swung.

No, not a war between the States; but a war between the Spheres!

No one of us would disregard the manly qualities and earnest motives among those who permitted themselves to strike at the life of the Union we held so vital and so dear, and thus made themselves our foes. Truly has it been said that the best of virtues may be enlisted in the worst of causes.

Had the question of breaking up this Union been submitted to the people of the South as American citizens, I do not believe it possible that such a resolution could have been taken. But the leaders in that false step knew how to take advantage of instincts deeply planted in every American heart; and by perverting their State Governments, and making their conspiracy seem to be the act and intent of the States, sprung an appeal to the sentiment of loyalty to the principle of local self-government; and the thrilling reveille of cannon swept the heart strings of a chivalrous and impressionable people. There are times when it is more natural to act than to reason, and easier to fight than to be right. But the men that followed that signal made a terrible mistake. Misled by fictions; mistaught as to fact and doctrine by their masters of political history and public law; falsely fired by misdirected sentiment; mazed in the strange contradiction that they were at once the champions of democracy and the exponents of aristocratic superiority, they heeded not the calm, true life rolling on deep within,—the mightier solution of differences,—the great coherence of affinity, stronger by counterpoise of attractions and interfusion of unlikenesses, than any mere aggregation of sameness of elements. They did not recognize the providential facts of history, beyond the wilfulness of man,—that interior constitution, formative and directive of all others,—that deeper organic law,—that divinely pressing ideal, by which a Nation grows.

There was no war between the States. It was a war in the name of certain States to destroy the political existence of the United States, in membership of which alone, on any just theory of the government, their own sovereignty as States inhered, and could make itself effectual. To this absurd pass did that false theory come,—a war of States against the people; and if successful, the suicide of States.

Our enemies, it is true, by their choice of field, secured the opportunity to say they were resisting an invader; that they were fighting for their native soil and birthright; for their homes and all that men hold dear in them. We understand the power of sentiments like these, even when abused and played upon by indirection.

The State is dear to all of us. It is the guardian of what we may call home rights; the almoner of home-born charities; the circle within which likeness of material, identity of interests and sympathy of sentiment make a crystal unity. Were our own State attacked in its high place and rightful function, we should defend it as valiantly as our brethren of the South were made to think they were defending theirs. But no such assault was made. We fought against no State; but for its deliverance. We fought the enemies of our common Country, to overthrow the engines and symbols of its destruction wherever found upon its soil. We fought no better, perhaps, than they. We exhibited, perhaps, no higher individual qualities. But the cause for which we fought was higher; our thought was wider. We too were fighting for birthright and native soil; for home and all the sanctities of life, wide over the land, and far forward through the years to come. For all this belongs to us, and we to it. That thought was our power. We took rank by its height, and not of our individual selves.

It is something great and greatening to cherish an ideal; to act in the light of the truth that is far-away and far above; to set aside the near advantage, the momentary pleasure; the snatching of seeming good to self, and to act for remoter ends, for higher good, and for interests other than our own.

To us this people in its life on earth was a moral personality, having a character and a commission; hence responsibility; hence duty; hence right, and its authority. The Union was the body of a spiritual Unity. Of this we were part, —responsible to it and for it,—and our sacrifice was its service.

Our personality exists in two identities,—the sphere of self, and the sphere of soul. One is circumscribed; the other moving out on boundless trajectories; one is near, and therefore dear; the other far and high, and therefore great. We live in both, but most in the greatest. Men reach their completest development, not in isolation nor working within narrow bounds, but through membership and participation in life of largest scope and fullness. To work out all the worth of manhood; to gain free range and play for all specific differences, to find a theatre and occasion for exercise of the highest virtues, we need the widest organization of the human forces consistent with the laws of cohesion and self-direction. It is only by these radiating and reflected influences that the perfection of the individual and of the race can be achieved.

A great and free country is not merely defense and protection. For every earnest spirit, it is opportunity and inspiration. In its rich content and manifold resources, its bracing atmosphere of broad fellowship and friendly rivalry, impulse is given to every latent aptitude and special faculty. Meantime enlarged humanity reflects itself in every participant. The best of each being given to all, the best of all returns to each. So the greatness as well as the power of a country broadens every life and blesses every home. Hence it is that in questions of rank, of rights, and duties, Country must stand supreme.

The thought goes deeper. There is a mysterious law of our nature that, in this sense of membership and participation, the spirit rises to a magnitude commensurate with that of which it is part. The greatness of the whole passes into the consciousness of each; the power of the whole seems to become the power of each, and the character of the whole is impressed upon each. The inspiration of a noble cause involving human interests wide and far, enables men to do things they did not dream themselves capable of before, and which they were not capable of alone. The consciousness of belonging, vitally, to something beyond individuality; of being part of a personality that reaches we know not where, in space and in time, greatens the heart to the limits of the soul's ideal, and builds out the supreme of character.

It was something like this, I think, which marked our motive; which made us strong to fight the bitter fight to the victorious end, and made us unrevengeful and magnanimous in that victory.

We rose in soul above the things which even the Declaration of Independence pronounces the inalienable rights of human nature, for the securing of which governments are instituted among men. Happiness, liberty, life, we laid on the altar of offering, or committed to the furies of destruction, while our minds were lifted up to a great thought and our hearts swelled to its measure. We were beckoned on by the vision of destiny; we saw our Country moving forward, charged with the sacred trusts of man. We believed in its glorious career; the power of high aims and of strong purpose; the continuity of great endeavor; the onward, upward path of history, to God. Every man felt that he gave himself to, and belonged to, something beyond time and above place,—something which could not die.

These are the reasons, not fixed in the form of things, but formative of things, reasons of the soul, why we fought for

the Union. And this is the spirit in which having overcome the
dark powers of denial and disintegration, having restored the
people of the South to their place and privilege in the Union,
and set on high the old flag telling of one life and one body,
one freedom and one law, over all the people and all the land
between the four great waters, we now come, as it were, home;
we look into each other's eyes; we speak in softer tones; we
gather under the atmosphere of these sacred thoughts and
memories,—like the high, pure air that shines down upon us
to-day, flooding these fields where cloud and flash and thun-
der-roll of battle enshrouded us and them in that great three
days' burial,—to celebrate this resurrection; to rear on these
far-away fields memorials of familiar names, and to honor the
State whose honor it was to rear such manhood, and keep such
faith, that she might have part in far-away things.

But there are other reasons, more determinate and tan-
gible, reasons embodied in positive forms, which are matters of
knowledge and understanding.   I have said that the issue
brought upon us was a question of politics. Every one knows
that I do not mean that this was a party question, as to what
particular set of persons or policies should have control of the
Government. And when I say that it was a political question,
this is not saying that it was not also a moral question. For I
do not think that politics and morals are so utterly alien and
exclusive, one from the other, as some find it necessary to
maintain. It is true that on one side politics is concerned with
forms, methods, measures; and herein acts chiefly upon economic and tactical considerations. Still, all these must be con-
formable, or at least not alien, to the great constructive principle which holds to the motive and to the final cause of action.

Politics, I believe, is the organization of the human
elements and powers for the promotion of right living, and to
secure the noblest ends of living attainable in human character.   It is, then, a domain which on its higher side takes
cognizance not alone of rights, but of rightness, and of human
worth, and of a nobleness which has a moral and divine ideal.
The sphere of politics, therefore, is the highest range of thought
and action, and the widest field of practical ethics set before
the mind of man for its earthly career.

The issue before us, while having its ultimate ground in
reason and great ethics, and the perfectibility of man, was
practically one of positive, public law. It was an issue, as we

believed, to enforce the performance of constitutional obligations undertaken deliberately and freely and under solemn pledges, as the expression of the deepest convictions of the mind and conscience of the people. If we were right, then there was such a being and power on this earth as the People of the United States of America. If we were wrong, then there was no such People, but a chaos of jarring elements and antagonizing interests. The forces ranged themselves across this line. It became the test of what we call Loyalty. This was a positive, practical question. The test was sharp. The answer must be final.

That question has been answered; at the cost of toil and treasure, of blood and tears. The people have made themselves the expounders of their Constitution. The decision has been accepted by clear, constitutional and legal enactment; confirmed by the supreme judicial tribunals of the land; and, we fervently trust, sealed by the benediction of the Most High. We are one People; and the law of its spirit is supreme over the law of its members.

But grave responsibilities come with great victory. The danger is not so much, I think, from renewed attacks of those who lost, as from the tendencies of power on the part of those who won. It should be distinctly borne in mind that we were not antagonizing the principle of local self-government. Our triumph was for all the people, and in full recognition of the value in our political system of recognizing local centres of influence and of government. The "lost cause" is not lost liberty and right of self-government. What is lost is slavery of men and supremacy of States.

It was necessary for us to save the Union. In the stress and sharpness of the conflict we were forced to strain to the utmost all the central powers of the Government, and leave it to the after-wisdom of the People to restore the equilibrium of powers, to see to it that the abnormal necessities of war should not be made precedents for the law of life and growth. Necessity is a dangerous plea for the privilege of power; especially when the sole judge of it is the power pretending it. In times of peace, when the free faculties of the people are proceeding by natural and spiritual laws of growth, the powers of government should be jealously guarded, and its agents held close to the thought and purpose of the people. The national authority we have vindicated by the war, means in the last analysis that

Congress is the sole judge of its own powers, and sole educator of its own will. This is a tremendous trust. God grant that it be ever exercised, not in willfulness of power nor by force of chance majorities, nor to favor particular or partisan interests, but with the large and long look, and with the deep sense of constitutional obligation and of supreme trusts, for the common well-being.

To this end the place of the State in our political system is one of vital importance. The inter-action of local and national capacities is a peculiarity in our system, without parallel and but little understood in other lands, and liable to be too little regarded in our own. We make much account of checks and balances in the separation of the three Departments of the Government—Legislative, Executive and Judicial. A similar theory does not hold England from pressing steadily towards a concentration of power in the hands of her House of Commons, now practically absolute. We rely justly on the lines of division between State and National powers, a wisdom to which England has not yet attained, but of which the skillful recognition makes the strength of the German Empire of to-day, while the lack of it has held back the French Republic for a hundred years.

Local self-government alone could not have constructed this People; but without local self-government as an instrumentality in our representative system, neither Government nor people could hold together. The generative and formative forces are in the local centres. These vortexes of living energy, touching and interfusing, are rounded into oneness and bound together by the deep, central consciousness of mutual service and a common destiny. In the course of history, which we call the orderings of Providence, local traditions, sentiments, needs and aspirations have made up the strong composite character of this country. So long as the people of each decided local type and centre feel that in the institutions, laws and policies of the great People shaping the larger life, their own freedom is secured, their own thoughts and interests are represented, they will feel bound together by the central attraction of a vital force, and no lesser influence nor lower impulse can tempt away their loyalty, patriotism and pride of partnership.

But it is not enough that the State is supreme in its sphere, and that departments of government shall not encroach upon each other. Our strongest safeguard is in per-

sonal participation in the direction and destiny of the Nation.
It is not the separation of spheres and offices in the administrative order, but the interpenetration of State and National
capacities in the organic order. The political unit of organization is neither the individual nor the State; but the people of
each State,—each man acting, not in his personal capacity, but
in his political capacity; exercising not his isolated, "natural
rights" in the commonly conceived, fictitious, impossible sense,
but the powers and franchises recognized in him or conferred
upon him in the Constitution of his State, which is the appointed order of the common life. Our "self-government" is not
the aggregate will of so many Ishmaelites, but the political
people of the several States in their responsible character and
mature convictions, regulating the civil order in their own
State, and reaching out to their larger interests, administering
the great trusts of the Nation.   Just as in the sphere and
function of the States is the surest safeguard of liberty,—as
those who are to make and execute the laws which affect the
daily life and dearest interests are chosen from among citizens
whom the people know, and can trust and can vouch for,—so it
is within the power of the same people, acting yet through
their State organizations, to see to it that in the election of
Representatives, Senators and Presidents only such men are
chosen as well understand the delicate articulations by which
liberty is kept alive, who are brave to reverse the false maxim
that the law cares not for the least but only for the great, and
who represent not the mere will of a momentary majority, but
the heart and conscience of the manifold people which make
their vote the voice of God.

When the martyr President, standing on this hallowed
ground at the consecration of this cemetery, uttered that noble
climax of his immortal speech, "We here highly resolve that
the government of the people, by the people, and for the people,
shall not perish from the earth," he meant such a people as I
have described. Surely he did not mean in this sublime utterance to justify the rule of mob majority, nor to furnish a
watchword for revolutionists like those who a century ago in
France knew not how to overthrow tyranny without overturn-
ing also the foundations of society human and divine, nor a
pretext for the anarchist and dynamiters of to-day who in the
name of the people would let loose a riot of discordant and
irresponsible individualism—a carnival of savage greed and

frenzied passion.

He meant government; he meant a people holding its liberty under law; exercising its sovereignty by deliberation and delegation; respecting its minorities; checking its own caprice and facility of change; relegating great questions to its sober second thought; its consciousness alive in every part, but guided ever by great commanding convictions, and pressing forward as one for the goal of a common good.

Part and parcel of this political being of the people is this State of ours. As such she stood on these hills and slopes a generation ago, of the foremost of the people's defenders. Whether on the first, the second, or the third day's battle; whether on the right, caught and cut to pieces by the great shears-blades of two suddenly enclosing hostile columns; on the left, rolled back by a cyclone of unappeasable assault; or on the centre, dashed upon in an agony of desperation, terrible, sublime; wherever there was a front, the guns of Maine thundered and her colors stood. And when the long, dense, surging fight was over, and the men who made and marked the line of honor were buried where they fell, the name of Maine ran along these crests and banks, from the Cavalry Fields, Wolf's Hill, Culp's Hill, and the Seminary Ridge, down through the Cemetery, the Peach Orchard, the Wheat-field to the Devil's Den and the Round Top Crags—a blazonry of ennobled blood!

Now you have gathered these bodies here. You mark their names with head-stones, and compass them about with the cordon of the State's proud sorrow. You station them here, on the ground they held. Here they will remain, not buried but transfigured forms,—part of the earth they glorified,—part also of the glory that is to be.

No chemistry of frost or rain, no overlaying mould of the season's recurrent life and death, can ever separate from the soil of these consecrated fields the life-blood so deeply commingled and incorporate here. Ever henceforth under the rolling suns, when these hills are touched to splendor with the morning light, or smile a farewell to the lingering day, the flush that broods upon them shall be rich with a strange and crimson tone,—not of the earth, nor yet of the sky, but mediator and hostage between the two.

But these monuments are not to commemorate the dead alone. Death was but the divine acceptance of life freely offered by every one. Service was the central fact. That fact, and that truth, these monuments commemorate. They mark the centres around which stood the manhood of Maine, steadfast in noble service,—to the uttermost, to the uppermost! Those who fell here—those who have fallen before or since—those who linger, yet a little longer, soon to follow; all are mustered in one great company on the shining heights of life, with that star of Maine's armorial ensign upon their foreheads forever—like the ranks of the galaxy.

In great deeds something abides. On great fields something stays. Forms change and pass; bodies disappear; but spirits linger, to consecrate ground for the vision-place of souls. And reverent men and women from afar, and generations that know us not and that we know not of, heart-drawn to see where and by whom great things were suffered and done for them, shall come to this deathless field, to ponder and dream; and lo! the shadow of a mighty presence shall wrap them in its bosom, and the power of the vision pass into their souls.

This is the great reward of service. To live, far out and on, in the life of others; this is the mystery of the Christ,—to give life's best for such high sake that it shall be found again unto life eternal.

20th Maine Monument on Little Round Top, Gettysburg, PA.

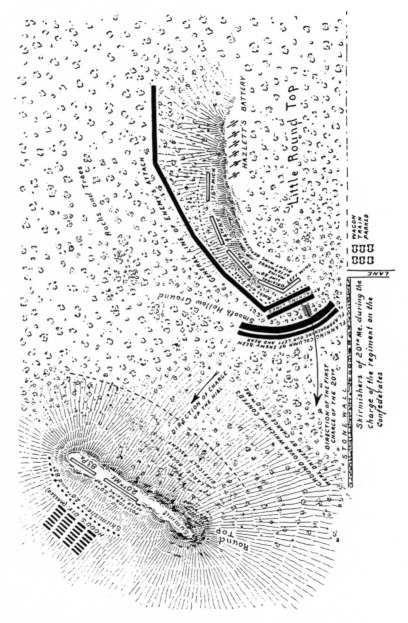

3D BRIGADE, 1ST DIVISION, 5TH CORPS IN ACTION, JULY 2, AND 3, 1863, AT GETTYSBURG, PA.

C

COLONEL CHAMBERLAIN'S REPORT ON THE BATTLE OF GETTYSBURG

Report of Colonel Joshua L. Chamberlain,
Twentieth Maine Infantry, on the Battle of Gettysburg
Field Near Emmitsburg, July 6, 1863

In compliance with the request of the colonel commanding the brigade, I have the honor to submit a somewhat detailed report of the operations of the Twentieth Regiment Maine Volunteers in the battle of Gettysburg on the 2d and 3d instant.

Having acted as the advance guard, made necessary by the proximity of the enemy's cavalry, on the march of the day before, my command on reaching Hanover, Pennsylvania just before sunset on that day, were much worn, and lost no time in getting ready for an expected bivouac. Rations were scarcely issued, and the men about preparing supper, when rumors that the enemy had been encountered that day near Gettysburg absorbed every other interest, and very soon orders came to march forthwith to Gettysburg.

My men moved out with a promptitude and spirit extraordinary, the cheers and welcome they received on the road adding to their enthusiasm. After an hour or two of sleep by the roadside just before daybreak we reached the heights southeasterly of Gettysburg at about 7 A.M., July 2.

Massed at first with the rest of the division on the right of the road, we were moved several times farther toward the left. Although expecting every moment to be put into action, and held strictly in line of battle, yet the men were able to take some rest and make the most of their rations.

Somewhere near 4 P.M. a sharp cannonade, at some distance to our left and front, was the signal for a sudden and rapid movement of our whole division in the direction of this firing, which grew warmer as we approached. Passing an open field in the hollow ground in which some of our batteries were going into position, our brigade reached the skirt of a piece of woods, in the farther edge of which there was a heavy musketry fire, and when about to go forward into line we received from Colonel Vincent, commanding the brigade, orders to move to the left at the double-quick, when we took a farm road crossing Plum Run in order to gain a rugged mountain spur called Granite Spur, or Little Round Top.

The enemy's artillery got range of our column as we were climbing the spur, and the crashing of the shells among the rocks and the tree tops made us move lively along the crest. One or two shells burst in our ranks. Passing to the southern slope of Little Round Top, Colonel Vincent indicated to me the ground my regiment was to occupy, informing me that this was the extreme left of our general line, and that a desperate attack was expected in order to turn that position, concluding by telling me I was to "hold that ground at all hazards." This was the last word I heard from him.

In order to commence by making my right firm, I formed my regiment on the right into line, giving such direction to the line as should best secure the advantage of the rough, rocky, and stragglingly wooded ground.

The line faced generally toward a more conspicuous eminence southwest of ours, which is known as Sugar Loaf, or Round Top. Between this and my position intervened a smooth and thinly wooded hollow. My line formed, I immediately detached Company B, Captain Morrill commanding, to extend from my left flank across this hollow as a line of skirmishers, with directions to act as occasion might dictate, to prevent a surprise on my exposed flank and rear.

The artillery fire on our position had meanwhile been constant and heavy, but my formation was scarcely complete when the artillery was replaced by a vigorous infantry assault upon the center of our brigade to my right, but it very soon involved the right of my regiment and gradually extended along my entire front. The action was quite sharp and at close quarters.

In the midst of this an officer from my center informed

me that some important movement of the enemy was going on in his front beyond that of the line with which we were engaged. Mounting a large rock, I was able to see a considerable body of the enemy moving by the flank in rear of their line engaged, and passing from the direction of the foot of Great Round Top through the valley toward the front of my left. The close engagement not allowing any change of front, I immediately stretched my regiment to the left, by taking intervals by the left flank, and at the same time "refusing" my left wing, so that it was nearly at right angles with my right, thus occupying about twice the extent of our ordinary front, some of the companies being brought into single rank when the nature of the ground gave sufficient strength or shelter. My officers and men understood my wishes so well that this movement was executed under fire, the right wing keeping up fire, without giving the enemy any occasion to seize or even to suspect their advantage. But we were not a moment too soon; the enemy's flanking column having gained their desired direction, burst upon my left, where they evidently had expected an unguarded flank, with great demonstration.

We opened a brisk fire at close range, which was so sudden and effective that they soon fell back among the rocks and low trees in the valley, only to burst forth again with a shout, and rapidly advanced, firing as they came. They pushed up to within a dozen yards of us before the terrible effectiveness of our fire compelled them to break and take shelter.

They renewed the assault on our whole front, and for an hour the fighting was severe. Squads of the enemy broke through our line in several places, and the fight was literally hand-to-hand. The edge of the fight rolled backward and forward like a wave. The dead and wounded were now in front and then in our rear. Forced from our position, we desperately recovered it, and pushed the enemy down to the foot of the slope. The intervals of the struggle were seized to remove our wounded (and those of the enemy also), to gather ammunition from the cartridge-boxes of disabled friend or foe on the field, and even to secure better muskets than the Enfields, which we found did not stand service well. Rude shelters were thrown up of the loose rocks that covered the ground.

Captain Woodward, commanding the Eighty-third Pennsylvania Volunteers, on my right, gallantly maintaining his fight, judiciously and with hearty co-operation made his movements conform to my necessities, so that my right was at no time exposed to a flank attack.

The enemy seemed to have gathered all their energies for their final assault. We had gotten our thin line into as good a shape as possible, when a strong force emerged from the scrub wood in the valley, as well as I could judge, in two lines in echelon by the right, and, opening a heavy fire, the first line came on as if they meant to sweep everything before them. We opened on them as well as we could with our scanty ammunition snatched from the field.

It did not seem possible to withstand another shock like this now coming on. Our loss had been severe. One-half of my left wing had fallen and a third of my regiment lay just behind us dead or badly wounded. At this moment my anxiety was increased by a great roar of musketry in my rear, on the farther or northerly slope of Little Round Top, apparently on the flank of the regular brigade, which was in support of Hazlett's battery on the crest behind us. The bullets from this attack struck into my left rear, and I feared that the enemy might have nearly surrounded the Little Round Top, and only a desperate chance was left for us. My ammunition was soon exhausted. My men were firing their last shot and getting ready to "club" their muskets.

It was imperative to strike before we were struck by this overwhelming force in a hand-to-hand fight, which we could not probably have withstood or survived. At that crisis I ordered the bayonet. The word was enough. It ran like fire along the line from man to man, and rose into a shout, with which they sprang forward upon the enemy, now not thirty yards away. The effect was surprising; many of the enemy's first line threw down their arms and surrendered. An officer fired his pistol at my head with one hand while he handed me his sword with the other. Holding fast by our right, and swinging forward our left, we made an extended "right wheel," before the enemy's second line broke, and fell back, fighting from tree to tree, many being captured, until we had swept the valley and cleared the front of nearly our entire brigade.

Meantime, Captain Morrill with his skirmishers (sent out from my left flank), with some dozen or fifteen of the U. S. Sharpshooters who had put themselves under his direction, fell upon the enemy as they were breaking, and by his demonstrations, as well as his well-directed fire, added much to the effect of the charge.

Having thus cleared the valley and driven the enemy up the western slope of the Great Round Top, not wishing to press so far out as to hazard the ground I was to hold by leaving it exposed to a sudden rush of the enemy, I succeeded (although with some effort to stop my men, who declared they were "on the road to Richmond") in getting the regiment into good order and resuming our original position.

Four hundred prisoners, including two field and several line officers, were sent to the rear. These were mainly from the Fifteenth and Forty-seventh Alabama regiments, with some of the Fourth and Fifth Texas. One hundred and fifty of the enemy were found killed and wounded in our front.

At dusk Colonel Rice informed me of the fall of Colonel Vincent, which had devolved the command of the brigade on him, and that Colonel Fisher had come up with a brigade to our support. These troops were massed in our rear. It was the understanding, as Colonel Rice informed me, that Colonel Fisher's brigade was to advance and seize the western slope of Great Round Top, where the enemy had shortly before been driven. But after considerable delay this intention for some reason was not carried into execution.

We were apprehensive that if the enemy were allowed to strengthen himself in that position he would have a great advantage in renewing the attack on us at daylight or before. Colonel Rice then directed me to make the movement to seize that crest.

It was now 9 P.M. Without waiting to get ammunition, but trusting in part to the very circumstance of not exposing our movement or our small front by firing, and with bayonets fixed, the little handful of 200 men pressed up the mountain side in every extended order, as the steep and jagged surface of the ground compelled. We heard squads of the enemy falling back before us, and, when near the crest, we met a scattering and uncertain fire, which caused us the great loss of the gallant Lieutenant Linscott, who fell, mortally wounded. In the silent advance in the darkness we laid hold of 25 prisoners, among them a staff officer of General (E. M.) Law, commanding the brigade immediately opposed to us during the fight. Reaching the crest, and reconnoitering the ground, I placed the men in a strong position among the rocks, and informed Colonel Rice, requesting also ammunition and some support to our right, which was very near the enemy, their movements and words even being now distinctly heard by us.

Some confusion soon after resulted from the attempt of some regiment of Colonel Fisher's brigade to come to our support. They had found a wood road up the mountain, which brought them on my right flank, and also in proximity to the enemy, massed a little before. Hearing their approach, and thinking a movement from that quarter could only be from the enemy, I made disposition to receive them as such. In the confusion which attended the attempt to form them in support of my right, the enemy opened a brisk fire, which disconcerted my efforts to form them and disheartened the supports themselves, so that I saw no more of them that night.

Feeling somewhat insecure in this isolated position, I sent in for the Eighty-third Pennsylvania, which came speedily, followed by the Forty-fourth New York, and, having seen these well posted, I sent a strong picket to the front, with instructions to report to me every half hour during the night and allowed the rest of my men to sleep on their arms.

At some time about midnight two regiments of Colonel Fisher's brigade came up the mountain beyond my left, and took position near the summit; but as the enemy did not threaten from that direction I made no effort to connect with them.

We went into the fight with 386, all told—358 guns. Every pioneer and musician who could carry a musket went into the ranks. Even the sick and footsore, who could not keep up in the march, came up as soon as they could find their regiments and took their places in line of battle, while it was battle, indeed. Some prisoners I had under guard under sentence of court-martial, I was obliged to put into the fight, and they bore their part well, for which I shall recommend a commutation of their sentence.

The loss, so far as I can ascertain it, is 136—30 of whom were killed, and among the wounded are many mortally.

Captain Billings, Lieutenant Kendall, and Lieutenant Linscott are officers whose loss we deeply mourn—efficient soldiers and pure and high-minded men.

In such an engagement there were many incidents of heroism and noble character which should have place even in an official report; but, under present circumstances, I am unable to do justice to them. I will say of that regiment that the resolution, courage, and heroic fortitude which enabled us to withstand so formidable an attack have happily led to so conspicuous a result, that they may safely trust to history to record their merits.

About noon on the 3d of July we were withdrawn, and formed on the right of the brigade, in the front edge of a piece of woods near the left center of our main line of battle, where we were held in readiness to support our troops, then receiving the severe attack of the afternoon of that day.

On the 4th we made 'a reconnaissance to the front, to ascertain the movements of the enemy, but finding that they had retired, at least beyond Willoughby's Run, we returned to Little Round Top, where we buried our dead in the place where we had laid them during the fight, marking each grave by a head-board made of ammunition boxes, with each soldier's name cut upon it. We also buried 50 of the enemy's dead in front of our position of July 2. We then looked after our wounded, whom I had taken the responsibility of putting into the houses of citizens in the vicinity of Little Round Top, and on the morning of the 5th took up our march on the Emmitsburg Road.

I have the honor to be
your obedient servant,
JOSHUA L. CHAMBERLAIN, Colonel,
Commanding Twentieth Maine Volunteers

D

LETTER FROM
COLONEL JOSHUA CHAMBERLAIN
TO GOVERNOR COBURN

Headquarters, 20th Maine Volunteers
In the field, July 21st 1863

To His Excellency Abner Coburn
Governor of Maine

Dear Governor,

I embrace a rare opportunity—namely a days halt within a few miles of our baggage—to write you in reference to the affairs of our Regiment in which, I am well aware, you feel the deepest interest.

In the first place, allow me to thank you for the honor you have done me in entrusting to my care this noble Regiment. I trust I shall be always worthy of the confidence you have thus placed in me. I consider it an officer's first duty to look after the welfare of his men. To this he is bound no less by the responsibility which the arbitrary nature of his power imposes, than by the regard he should have to the interests of the service in which he is engaged. My experience in several trying campaigns has taught me that the way to insure the efficiency of the army is to keep the <u>men</u> in the best possible condition, physically and mentally.

Within a month this Regiment has been engaged in the most active and honorable service—taking a conspicuous part in three fights in as many different states, within that time, and in all of them doing as well as the best. At the great battle of Gettysburg, however, the Regiment won distinguished honor. We were assigned to the extreme left of our line of battle, where the fiercest assault was made. A whole rebel brigade was opposed to this Regiment, charging on us with desperate fury, in column of Regiments, so that we had to contend with a <u>front</u> of <u>fresh</u> <u>troops</u> after each struggle. After two hours fighting on the defensive, our loss had been so great, and the remaining men were so much exhausted, having fired all our "sixty rounds" and all the cartridges we could gather from the scattered boxes of the fallen around us, friend and foe, I saw no way left but to take the <u>offensive</u> and accordingly, we charged on the enemy—trying "cold steel" on them. The result was we drove them entirely out of the field, killing and wounding one hundred and fifty of them and taking <u>three hundred</u> and <u>eight</u> prisoners and two hundred and seventy-five stand of arms. The prisoners taken were from five different Regiments from Alabama and Texas—twelve of the number were officers—some of the staff of the General commanding their Brigade. They admitted that they had charged on us with a Brigade, and said that they had fought a dozen battles, and never had been stopped before.

We were afterward ordered, or <u>asked</u>, to carry a height which afforded the Rebels a very advantageous position, and was considered by our Generals a strong point to carry; and exhausted as we were, the <u>one hundred and ninety-eight</u> bayonets I had left after that day's fighting, charged up that hill and carried every thing before them—taking many more prisoners and arms, but what is better taking the <u>heights</u> and holding them—the darkness which had now come on deceiving the enemy as to our numbers.

Our services have been officially acknowledged, though no partial friend has published our praises in the state whose name we are proud to bear, and which, we believe, we have not dishonored. I protected my men in every possible way but I grieve over the loss of thirty-two gallant fellows who fell on that field which their courage helped to make a "field of Honor," and I regret to lose the services of 102 who were wounded there. Besides this, in our other fights we had a loss of three killed and sixteen wounded and missing. I fear I have written too freely but this is not an "official" letter, and I know you desire to be informed reliably of the service rendered by your Regiments.

I am sorry to say that Lieutenant Colonel Gilmore was

obliged to leave us on our march through Maryland, and is now in Baltimore not yet fit for duty. We all suffered for want of <u>medical attendance</u>. Our toilsome and hurried marches broke down a great many, and I had to be Surgeon and father as well as colonel, to such an extent that I fell sick myself and came near dying, but was providentially able to lead my gallant fellows in to the fight. The surgeons recently appointed have reported, and we are highly gratified with their appearance.

I should be glad to have Reverend Mr. Brown whom you recommended with Hon. J. J. Perry and others, appointed Hospital Steward and ordered to report at once. I very much need a <u>field officer</u>. I had to go through the fights alone. Is there any objection to following the suggestion of Colonel Ames in the appointment of Major? I should heartily endorse that.

Very Respectfully,
Your Obedient Servant and friend
J. L. CHAMBERLAIN, Colonel,
20th Maine Volunteers

E

REPORT ON THE WHITE OAK ROAD AND FIVE FORKS CAMPAIGN

Camp of First Division, Fifth Corps
April 24, 1865

CAPTAIN: In compliance with orders just received, I have the honor to submit the following report of the operations of the First Brigade of this division from the 29th of March to the 9th of April, 1865:

The brigade broke camp on the morning of the 29th ultimo and marched at 6 A.M., by way of Arthur's Swamp and the old stage road and Vaughan Road, toward Dinwiddie Courthouse; turning to our right, we went into position near the Chappell house. Soon after this we returned to the Vaughan Road and moved up the Quaker Road in a northerly direction. On reaching Gravelly Run Major-General Griffin directed me to form my brigade in order of battle and advance against some works which were in sight on the opposite bank. Crossing the run, I sent Major E. A. Glenn, commanding the second battalion of the One Hundred and Ninety-eighth Pennsylvania Volunteers, forward with his command as skirmishers, and formed my lines, with Brevet Brigadier General H. G. Sickel, One Hundred and Ninety-eighth Pennsylvania, on the right, and Colonel G. Sniper, One Hundred and Eighty-fifth New York, on the left of the road. Major Glenn pushed forward vigorously and drove the enemy's skirmishers out of their works without any difficulty, and succeeded in pressing them through the woods and as far as the Lewis house. The enemy making considerable show of force in the edge of woods beyond, I halted Major Glenn and brought my line of battle up to supporting distance. Here I was directed to halt. In a short time I was ordered by General Griffin to resume the advance. There being at that time no firing of any consequence on the skirmish line I brought my line of battle up to that point, reformed it on the buildings, re-enforced the skirmishers by a company from the One Hundred and Eighty-fifth New York, and commenced a rapid advance with my whole command. The skirmishers reached the edge of woods before the firing became at all severe. I was exceedingly anxious that the troops should gain the cover of the woods before receiving the shock of the fire, but the obstacles to be overcome were so great that this could not be fully accomplished, and my men were obliged to gain the woods against a heavy fire. They advanced, however, with great steadiness and drove the enemy from their position and far into the woods. It was not long, however, before another attack was made upon us, evidently by a greatly superior force, and we became completely enveloped in a withering fire. We replied with spirit and persistency, holding our ground, taking rather the defensive at this stage of the action. In the course of half an hour my left became so heavily pressed that it gradually gave way, and at last was fairly turned, and driven entirely out of the woods to a direction parallel the road by which we advanced. This position could not be held ten minutes, and nothing but the most active exertions of field and staff officers kept the men where they were, the fire all the time being very severe. At this moment I sent a request for General Gregory, commanding Second Brigade, on my left, to attack the enemy in flank in their newly gained position. I was assured by Major-General Griffin, who was on the line, that if we would hold on five minutes be could bring up the artillery. Upon this I succeeded in rallying the men, and they once more gained the woods. Battery B of the Fourth U. S. Artillery now came into position and opened a most effective fire. By this assistance we held our line until the enemy fell heavily upon our right and center, and my men being by this time out of ammunition, many of them absolutely with out a cartridge, began to yield ground. Seeing that this was inevitable I dispatched an aide to General Gregory asking him for a regiment, and at the same time Major-General Griffin ordered up three regiments of the Third Brigade. These regiments came promptly to our assistance. I was at that moment endeavoring to reform my broken line, so as, at all events, to cover the artillery. The line was falling back in front of the Lewis house when Lieutenant-Colonel Doolittle of the One Hundred and Eighty-eighth New York, came up, gallantly leading his regiment, as also Colonel Partridge, Sixteenth Michigan; the One-Hundred and Fifty-fifth Pennsylvania and First Michigan came on in the most handsome manner, passing to my front, Brevet Brigadier-General Pearson, of the One Hundred and Fifty-fifth, grasping his color and dashing straight against the enemy's line. This assistance and the admirable service of the artillery compelled the enemy to abandon their position; otherwise I must have been driven entirely from the field.

This action lasted nearly two hours before any support reached us. I need not speak of the severity of the engagement, nor of the conduct of my officers and men, inasmuch as it was all under the eye and direction of the major-general commanding, who shared the dangers, as well as the responsibilities, of that field; but I may be permitted to mention the fact that more than 400 of my men and 18 officers killed and wounded marked our line with too painful destructiveness. Nor can I fail to speak of the steadfast coolness and courage of Brevet Brigadier-General Sickel, whose example and conduct made my efforts needless in that part of the line, until he was borne from the field severely wounded; the unflinching tenacity of Colonel Sniper at his perilous post, and the desperate bravery with which he rallied his men, seizing his color after it had fallen from the hands of three color-bearers and a captain, and bearing it into the very ranks of the enemy; the fiery courage of Major Glenn, which could scarcely be restrained; and of the heroic spirit of Major Maceuen, who fell dead foremost in the ranks of honor; nor shall I forget to name the young gentlemen of my staff—Lieutenants Walters and Vogel, my personal aides, both painfully wounded, but keeping the field to the last; Lieutenant Mitchell, my adjutant-general, and Lieutenant Fisher, pioneer officer—who rendered me essential aid in the hottest of the fire. Private Kelsey, my orderly, rode upon the enemy's line and captured, under my own eyes, an officer and five men, and brought them in.

Remaining on the ground that night and the next day, we buried our dead and 130 of the enemy's, and brought in the wounded of both parties.

On the morning of the 31st we moved up the Boydton Plank Road, and upon this nearly to Gravelly Run crossing, taking position on the left of the division and the corps. A sharp engagement commenced to our right, which resulted in the troops falling back through our lines in great confusion. I was desired by General Griffin to regain the field which these troops had yielded. My men forded a stream nearly waist deep, formed in two lines, Major Glenn having the advance, and pushed the enemy steadily before them. Major-General Ayres' Division supported me on the left in echelon by brigade, the skirmishers of the First Division, in charge of General Pearson, in their front. We advanced in this way a mile or more into the edge of the field it was desired to retake. Up to this time we had been opposed by only a skirmish line, but quite a heavy fire now met us, and a line of battle could be plainly seen in the opposite edge of woods and in a line of breast-works in the open field, in force at least equal to our own. I was now ordered by Major-General Warren to halt and take the defensive. My first line had now gained a slight crest in the open field, where they were subjected to a severe fire from the works in front and from the woods on each flank. As it appeared that the enemy's position might be carried with no greater loss than it would cost us merely to hold our ground, and the men were eager to charge over the field, I reported this to General Griffin, and received permission to renew the attack. My command was brought into one line and put in motion. A severe oblique fire on my right, together with the artillery which now opened from the enemy's works, caused the One Hundred and Ninety-eighth to waver for a moment. I then requested General Gregory, who reported to me with his brigade, to move rapidly into the woods on our right by battalion in echelon by the left, so as to break this flank attack, and possibly to turn the enemy's left at the same moment that I should charge the works directly in front at a run. This plan was so handsomely executed by all that the result was completely successful. The woods and the works were carried, with several prisoners and one battle-flag, and the line advanced some 300 yards across the White Oak Road.

My loss in this action was not more than seventy-five, but it included some of my best officers and men.

It would be unjust not to mention the services of Major Glenn and Colonel Sniper in this affair, whose bravery and energy I relied upon for the successful execution of my plans. I would also express my obligations to General Gregory for his quick comprehension of my wishes and for his efficient aid. I may be permitted also to mention the gallantry of Captain Fowler, assistant adjutant-general of division, who rode into the hottest fire to bring my orders, having his horse killed under him in doing so, and who by his conduct and bearing showed an example worthy of all praise.

During the night we buried our dead and cared for our wounded, and bivouacked on the line.

The brigade left bivouac on the White Oak Road early on the morning of the 1st and moved, with the rest of the division, toward Dinwiddie Courthouse, until we met General Sheridan with his cavalry. We then moved in connection toward Five Forks. Arriving at a point near Gravelly Run Church we were formed on the right of the Third Brigade of this division in three lines. Brevet Brigadier-General Gregory, commanding Second Brigade of this division, reported to me with his brigade, by order of General Griffin, and was placed upon the right flank of our lines, one regiment being deployed as skirmishers in our front, one on the flank faced outward, and one held in reserve. Mackenzie's cavalry was on our right. In this formation we advanced in the order designated. Our instructions were to keep closed to the left on the Third Brigade, and also to wheel to the left in moving, the design being to strike the enemy in flank. We advanced through an open wood with nothing but light skirmishes in our front for some time. The constant change of direction to the left made the march on the right flank exceedingly rapid. On coming out at a large opening it was discovered that the Third Division of the corps was no longer on the left of the First Division, as had been the order of movement, and the heavy firing was all concentrated at a point to our left and front, where the Second Division had struck the enemy's works. Seeing the division flag moving in that direction I immediately drew my brigade into the field by the left flank and formed them facing this fire, and General Griffin ordered me to move against the point. Brevet Major-General Bartlett advanced at the same time with three regiments of the Third Brigade immediately on my right. We moved up rapidly under the crest of a hill and charged the works, striking them obliquely in flank and reverse, the right of my line—the One Hundred and Eighty-

fifth New York (Colonel Sniper) and the first battalion of the
One Hundred and Ninety-eighth Pennsylvania (Major Glenn)
—passing down to the rear of the works, and the left—second
battalion of the One Hundred and Ninety-eighth (Captain
Stanton)—passing in front of them. The regiments of the Third
Brigade, striking farther up, met a very heavy flank fire on the
right, which broke us up somewhat, the extreme right falling
back and the remainder of the line showing strong disposition
to swing to the left into the works from which we had driven
the enemy, a position which would render them powerless
against the flank attack which was then commencing. It required the utmost personal efforts of every general and staff
officer present to bring our line to face perpendicularly to the
line of works, and to repulse the attack. General Bartlett
informing me of the imminent peril on his right, I directed my
two right regiments to sweep down the rear of the Twentieth
Maine and First Michigan and break the attack, General Gregory also pressing forward with his brigade in the same direction. In the attempt to do this the regiments of the several
brigades became somewhat mixed, but a new direction was
given to our line, and the enemy completely put to rout. In the
meantime, with one staff officer and Captain Brinton, of the
division staff, I assisted General Bartlett in collecting the stragglers from all commands who were seeking shelter in the edge
of the woods; these men, to the number of 150 or 200, were
formed and pushed in. While engaged in this I saw in the
open field in our rear the flag of General Gwyn, of the Second
Division, and dispatched Lieutenant Fisher, of my staff, to
request him to throw his brigade in as rapidly as possible in
the same direction as had been given to the troops already in.
This assistance was most cheerfully and promptly rendered,
and contributed in a good degree to our success. The confusion
of the battle at this moment was great; different commands
were completely mingled, but our line was still good. The men
of my own brigade were, for the most part, nearest to the line
of works though many of them were mixed with those of the
Twentieth Maine and of the Second Brigade. As the line all
merged into one the right of our line, consisting chiefly of the
Second and Third Brigade troops, struck a battery and wagons
on a road running perpendicular to the works, while Colonel
Sniper and Major Glenn, with their colors close together, came
upon the flank of other guns in position in the works. Two

battle-flags were taken here by the One Hundred and Eighty-fifth New York Volunteers, and a large number of prisoners. The whole line then pressed on, three brigades of the division as one, and driving the enemy far up the road to the distance, I should judge, of a mile or more. At dark I received an order from General Griffin to collect the troops of the division, and afterward from General Sheridan, to gather all the infantry that could be found and reform them in an open field to the left of the road, which was done; and we then encamped for the night along the works.

The prisoners captured by my brigade who cannot be claimed by other commands were nearly 900. Four battle-flags were taken; all these were turned over and receipted for except one battle-flag, which was torn up and distributed among the men before it could be properly taken charge of. My loss was not heavy in comparison with that of previous days, but cannot be considered otherwise than severe, inasmuch as it includes the name of so excellent a gentleman, and so thorough a soldier, as Major Edwin A. Glenn, commanding One Hundred and Ninety-eighth Pennsylvania Volunteers, who fell mortally wounded in the extreme advance. I have already recommended his promotion by brevet for distinguished gallantry at the battle of Lewis' farm and White Oak Road.

On the afternoon of the 2d we moved from the battle-field by the Church Road, my brigade leading the advance. Colonel Sniper deployed six companies as skirmishers, holding four as support. Flankers were thrown out on the right and left. We advanced but a short distance before we came upon a strong skirmish line of the enemy, who endeavored to oppose our crossing a small creek. Colonel Sniper, however, attacked them with a vigor which soon dislodged them, and drove them before him. At Church Road crossing on the South Side Railroad we captured a train of cars, which happened to be passing, in which were some Confederate officers and men. Crossing the railroad, I was then directed by Major-General Bartlett, commanding the division, to push out, if possible, to the Cox Road, crossing our direction at nearly right angle. The enemy here showed a disposition to make a stand, deploying a line in single rank, composed, as I judged, of about 1,500 dismounted cavalry. I immediately formed the two battalions of the One Hundred and Ninety-eighth Pennsylvania in line of battle, threw forward Lieutenant-Colonel Townsend's Regiment of General

Gregory's Brigade, which had reported to me, into a piece of woods to protect my right, and in this order pushed rapidly forward. The enemy fell back on Colonel Sniper's brisk fire, and, with a loss of only three men wounded, the road was secured. I was then ordered to make disposition to hold the road, which was done; the skirmish line being formed along a creek half a mile or more in advance. We remained in this position until General Sheridan came up, when we moved again down the Cox Road, with skirmishers and flankers as before, marching until night, and encamping on what is called the Namozine Road. On the morning of the 3d we moved out the Namozine Road toward Amelia Courthouse; bivouacked that night on the same road. Marched at 6 A.M. on the morning of the 4th, and after dark came upon the Danville Railroad at Jetersville, and made preparations to attack the enemy's trains in that vicinity. As the enemy appeared to be in force we threw up works, and remained on the alert during the night. The next day, the 5th, we were under arms nearly all day prepared to receive or make an attack. At about 1 o'clock I moved out the Amelia Courthouse Road to support a portion of our cavalry who were bringing in a large number of prisoners, and were severely attacked on the road. Returned to camp and remained during the night. The next day, the 6th, we marched in pursuit of the enemy in a westerly direction, passing through Paineville, my brigade in advance; firing was heard on our left. The skirmishers captured about 150 prisoners and several teams and our pioneers destroyed, by order of the corps commander, a large number of army wagons, gun carriages, and caissons which had been captured by our cavalry or abandoned by the enemy. Our march this day was very rapid and tiresome. After dark we encamped near Sailor's Creek. On the morning of the 7th we moved up the road by Sailor's Creek, and crossing the Lynchburg Railroad near Rice's Station, brisk firing was heard on our right. Marched to Prince Edward Courthouse and encamped for the night. On the 8th we moved by way of Prospect Station up the Lynchburg Pike, the Twenty-fourth Corps preceding. Our march was frequently obstructed and tedious. Bivouacked at midnight on the road. Information was here received that General Sheridan had met the enemy and captured several trains. Marched at 4 A.M. on the 9th to the vicinity of Appomattox Courthouse, being but a short distance, and found the cavalry warmly engaged. My

Head Quarters 1st Div. 5th A. C.
May 30 1865

Colonel,

As you are about to leave the military service of the United States with your Regt. I desire to tender to you the expression of my high appreciation of your character and services while you have been under my Command.

In every engagement with the enemy since your Regiment has been in the service, you have acquitted yourself with distinguished honor: at Watkin's Farm March 25th, at the Quaker road March 29th, at White Oak road March 31st, at Five Forks April 1st, and at Church road crossing on the Southside April 2, your conduct and that of your command was in the highest degree commendable. At Appomattox Court House April 9th your regt was in the advance line when the flag of truce came in, & you lost the last man killed in this war, before the surrender of Lee's army.

You may have the proud satisfaction of knowing that you have done your duty to your Regiment, to the army, + to the whole country.

I part with you with regret, and shall ever take pleasure in the recollection of the noble record of the 185 New York + its commander in this closing campaign.

I am, Colonel,
your friend + servt,
J. L. Chamberlain
Brig. Genl
Cmdg. 1st Div.
5th A.C.

Colonel Gustavus Sniper
Cmdg. 185 N.Y.V.

Letter from General Joshua Chamberlain to Colonel Gustavus Sniper, expressing appreciation for the Colonel's service to his regiment, the service and the country. General Chamberlain mentions the last man killed in the war before the surrender of Lee's Army.

brigade having the advance was filed to the right, moved to the rear of the cavalry, and formed on the right of the division and corps, in two lines. A heavy skirmish line was thrown forward, connecting with the Third Brigade skirmishers on the left, and our lines advanced against the enemy, relieving the cavalry, who reformed on my right. The skirmishers drove the enemy rapidly before them, while our line of battle was opened on by a battery in the town, my right being exactly in the line of fire. My skirmish line had reached the town, its right being at the house of Mrs. Wright, and my line of battle was rapidly closing on them, when a flag of truce came in with an aide of the commanding officer of the opposing forces, who was referred to the major-general commanding. I soon after received the order to halt my lines and to cease the skirmishing. During the conference which ensued we remained as we had halted, and afterward went into camp near the same ground. My loss this day was, 1 killed and 1 wounded, Lieutenant Hiram Clark, of the One Hundred and Eighty-fifth New York being instantly killed by a cannon-shot, just as the flag of truce came in.

> Respectfully submitted,
> J. L. CHAMBERLAIN
> Brigadier-General,
> Late Commanding First Brigade.

F

THE THIRD BRIGADE AT APPOMATTOX

At two o'clock on the morning of April 9, 1865, the Third Brigade, after a feverish march of twenty-nine miles, came to a halt, the rear brigade of the division column, which on such occasions has the hardest place of all. Worn out, body and spirit, by the vexations of a forced march over a course blocked every half hour by the nondescript and unaccountable obstacles of a lagging column in the road ahead, men made few preliminaries about "going into camp." That peculiar ingredient of humanity called the nervous system held an imperious precedence, not only over mind and matter, but over army regulations and discipline. There was no voice and ear for roll-calls, and even the command of empty stomachs did not avail with habit or instinct to grope among the jumbled remnants of the too familiar haversacks. Officers and men alike flung themselves right and left along the roadside, whether it were bank or ditch, in whatever order or disorder the column had halted. Horses and riders exchanged positions, the patient animals, with slackened girths, dozing with drooping head just over the faces of their masters. In an instant, as it were, the struggling, straggling hosts were wrapped in misty darkness and silence.

But suddenly and soon the bugles rang out "The General!" Orders came to march within an hour's time. Word had come from Sheridan that he was at Appomattox Station, and that if we could hurry up he could cut the head of Lee's column, then near Appomattox Courthouse. Such a summons itself gave something of the strength it demanded. Spirit triumphed over body, and seemed to be on the alert before the

222

latter could fully recover its senses. The time given was intended to provide for a meal, but that required also material, which indeed was now so simple as to quality and quantity as to make choice no task. Some of the younger regiments of the division were seen lighting dismal little fires to fry salt pork or steep some musty, sodden coffee. The Third Brigade, made up of veterans, spared their strength until the last for severer exercises. But this time patience did not attain to its perfect work. While sitting on their heels munching crumbs of hard tack and watching the coffee gradually "taking water," so as to produce a black liquid which could be sipped from the black tin dipper, word suddenly came that the Third Brigade was to take the head of the column, and must pull out at once. The glimmering daybreak made still more weird the scenes and sounds which betokened that untimely departure, and the glimmering breakfasts must have evoked similar wild sensations for the benighted stomachs of the Third Brigade. But a brisk march with a fight at the end was the best medicine for such a mood.

In three hours we were at Appomattox Station, and then learned that Sheridan, with the cavalry, had pushed on to Appomattox Courthouse, leaving word for us to follow with all possible dispatch. Indeed, there was no need of orders to this effect, for we now began to hear the boom of cannon ahead, and we knew that Sheridan and our glorious cavalry had cut across Lee's last line of retreat. Every heart beat high. No "obstacles" hindered that march. The head of the Fifth Corps ran past the rear of the Twenty-fourth, which had had the advance in the order of march. It was a triple column. The roads were taken mostly by whatever was to go on wheels, the men of both corps pressing along the fields on each side. We were evidently so near the "front" that General Bartlett thought it time to throw forward a "division" skirmish line, which he and General Griffin followed with characteristic eagerness. I was following with my own brigade and the Second (Gregory's), when there dashed out of a farm road on our right an officer of General Sheridan's staff, who gave me a hurried order to break off from the column at once, without waiting for communication with any immediate superiors, and hasten to the support of Sheridan, who was that moment forced to fall back somewhat before the desperate onset of Gordon's old "Stonewall Corps."

Now it was the "double-quick," indeed. This movement, of course, brought me on the ground our cavalry occupied, and on the enemy's left flank, at nearly the same time at which our skirmish line had struck them in their proper front, the direction of the Lynchburg Pike. Reaching the ground, I wheeled into double line of battle and gradually replaced our cavalry, which galloped off to our right, while the Third Brigade still poured in upon my left. In this way we pressed the enemy steadily back upon Appomattox Courthouse. There was gallant and wild work done there by the Third Brigade, as well as by the rest of the division.

Gordon had hoped to force his way through our cavalry before our infantry could get up, and reach Lynchburg with the resolute remnant of his famous old corps. But when there burst upon his front and flank these lines of ours they knew so well, that had so unexpectedly kept pace with the cavalry and marched around his retreating front, desperately as he had pressed his march, the veterans of Lee's army took in the situation as by instinct. Their resistance was mechanical and by force of habit or discipline. Their old dash and daring were gone. When our advance struck them at close quarters, they fell back in disorder or rendered themselves up as prisoners. As an example of this feeling, all that was left of an entire brigade surrendered to a single staff officer of the Third Brigade, who dashed up to them with the demand. It may well be believed that our men also were responsive to the logic of the situation. The end was now so near they could see through to it, and they were bound to "be there" themselves. Action there was of the most stirring kind, but of passion nothing. No man wantonly or in excitement struck at the life of his antagonist. It was an example of what is so strangely, and for want of an adequate word, called a "moral" effect.

When in the heat of the onset the flag of truce was seen coming in on our right, some deeper, inner sense seemed to stifle all the others. All was moving with such momentum, that when the order came at length to cease firing and to halt, it was next to impossible to stop the men. They saw well that we held the rebel army at bay, and what the consequence must soon be they did not need to be told; only whatever was to be done, they wanted to be there and have a hand in it. If there was anything to be seen, they had earned the right to front seats at the spectacle. But when at about four o'clock in the afternoon the brief, thrilling message was passed along the lines, "Lee surrenders!" there was a tumult as of an ocean let loose. Men went wild with the sweeping energies of that assurance, which answered so much of long-cherished hope and of long-endured suffering that had marked their loyal and brave career.

Now that they were no longer allowed to go forward and did not know how to go backward, there was no direction left but to go upward, and that way they took—to the top of fences, haystacks, roofs; and chimneys, that they might send their hallelujahs and toss their old caps higher toward heaven. The rebels over across the slender rivulets of the Appomattox were shouting their side of the jubilation, from whatever cause, whether cheering Lee as he rode over to speak a last word to them, or whether in deep truth they were heartily sick of the war and felt that their loyal spirit and manly energies were wasted in hopeless and perhaps mistaken cause. There is reason to believe the latter feeling was the motive of their exuberant demonstration, whose echoes rolled along the hillsides long after all was silent in our bivouac. For toward evening some of the rations that had been promised us for distribution at nine o'clock that morning, and from which we had double-quicked away, had now got up, and we could finish our breakfasts before lying down in peace at the close of that eventful day; and a certain deeper peace was ours, in that learning now of the starving condition of our surrendering foes, twenty thousand rations were sent over just as the day was done, into that camp of fellow-countrymen we had restored to brotherhood. Fitting token and emblem of the spirit in which that victory was won and that day ended! Here too was possibly one reason for the cheering that echoed in our ears as we fell asleep on that Palm Sunday evening.

All the next day, and the day after, measures were being determined as to the actual breaking up of Lee's army, and the return of ours. Grant and Lee had not lingered, after the main points were settled, nor indeed was Sheridan seen again on the field. Generals Griffin, Gibbon, and Merritt were appointed commissioners to arrange the final details.

All this while the visiting fever and the exchanging of tokens and souvenirs ran wild through both armies. Stringent measures had to be taken to prevent utter confusion in both camps, especially in ours, as it seemed to be understood that we were the hosts, and it was our "at home" reception. This spirit of exchange shortly passed into the spirit of trade; for our rations, after the best was done, were very short, and for three days afterwards it became necessary to forage the country far and wide to get even raw corn enough for man and beast. So the market "went up" decidedly on all sorts of farm produce. Hard tack was a luxury, and coffee and sugar at a high premium.

How or why it came about, I do not know, but on the evening of the 10th of April I was summoned to headquarters, and informed that I was to command the parade which was to receive the formal surrender of the arms and colors of the rebel army the next morning. This was an order, and to be received and obeyed without question. One request only I ventured to make of my corps commander. It was that, considering this occasion, I might resume command of my old brigade, the Third, from which I had been transferred in June, 1864, with which I had served up to that time since my entrance into the service. My request was granted, and on that evening I yielded the command of my gallant First Brigade, and went back to my veterans.

General Grant was a magnanimous man, great-minded and large-minded. He would have nothing done for show and no vain ceremony. He granted to officers the high privilege of retaining their swords, and all men who owned their horses were made welcome to keep them, as they would need them to plow their land. The rebels had begged to be spared the pain of actually laying down their arms and colors in the presence of our troops, and to be permitted to stack them in front of their own camps and march off, and let us go and pick them up after they had gone. But this would be to err too far on the side of mildness. So it was insisted that, while the surrendering army should be spared all that could humiliate their manhood, yet the insignia of the rebellion and the tokens of the power and will to hurt, lifted against the country's honor and life, must be laid down in due military form in presence of a designated portion of our army.

This latter office fell to our lot. It gave us, no doubt, a grateful satisfaction and permitted a modest pride, but it was not accepted as a token that we surpassed our comrades in merit of any kind.

We formed our line of battle on the southern margin of

the principal street in Appomattox Courthouse. Massachusetts on the right—her Thirty-second Regiment, with all that was left to us of her Ninth, Eighteenth, and Twenty-second; then Maine—her Twentieth Regiment, with the delivered remnant of her Second and her First Sharpshooters; Michigan next—her Sixteenth, with interminglings of her First and Fourth. On the left Pennsylvania—her One Hundred and Fifty-fifth holding also filaments which bound us with the Sixty-second, Eighty-third, Ninety-first, and One Hundred and Eighteenth, an immortal band, which held in it the soul of the famous "Light Brigade," and of the stern old First Division, Porter's, which was nucleus of the Fifth Corps, men among them who had fired the first shot at Yorktown, and others that had fired the last at Appomattox, and who thus bore upon their banners all the battles of that army.

By the courtesy of General Bartlett the First Brigade, which I had so long commanded, and the Second, which had been with me in this last campaign, were sent to me and held part in the parade, being formed on another line across the street and facing us. These were, with the exception of the One Hundred and Ninety-eighth Pennsylvania, composed of New York regiments,—the One Hundred and Eighty-fifth, One Hundred and Eighty-seventh, One Hundred and Eighty-eighth, and One Hundred and Eighty-ninth,—which in severe service had made themselves veterans worthy the fellowship of those sterling old New York regiments that had fulfilled their time and fame. Names and figures, all of these, dear to every heart that had shared their eventful and glorious history.

As we stood there in the morning mist, straining our eyes toward that camp about to break up for the last march, a feeling came over our hearts which led us to make some appropriate recognition of this great, last meeting.

We could not content ourselves with simply standing in line and witnessing this crowning scene. So instructions were sent to the several commanders that at the given signals, as the head of each division of the surrendering column approached their right, they should in succession bring their men to "attention" and arms to the "carry," then resuming the "ordered arms" and the "parade rest." And now we see the little shelter tents on the opposite slope melting away and carefully folded, being things which were needed by men as men and not as tokens of rebellion. Soon the gray masses are in motion—once more toward us—as in the days that were gone. A thrilling sight. First, Gordon, with the "Stonewall Corps"; then their First Corps,—Longstreet's,—no less familiar to us and to fame; then Anderson, with his new Fourth Corps; and lastly, A. P. Hill's Corps, commanded now by Heth, since Hill had fallen at one of the river fights a few days before. On they come with careless, swinging route step, the column thick with battle flags, disproportionate to their depleted numbers. As they come opposite our right our bugle sounds the signal, repeated along our line. Each organization comes to "attention," and thereupon takes up successively the "carry." The gallant General Gordon, at the head of the marching column, outdoes us in courtesy. He was riding with downcast eyes and more than pensive look; but at this clatter of arms he raises his eyes and, instantly catching the significance, wheels his horse with that superb grace of which he is master, drops the point of his sword to his stirrup, gives a command, at which the great Confederate ensign following him is dipped, and his decimated brigades, as they reach our right, respond to the "carry." All the while on our part not a sound of trumpet or drum, not a cheer, nor word nor motion of man, but awful stillness, as if it were the passing of the dead. Now and then a gust of wind would spring up from the south with strange greeting; our starry ensigns stiffen and fly out as if to welcome back the returning brothers. The ensigns of rebellion seem to shrink back and strain away from the fated farewell.

So a division at a time covers our front. They halt, face inward, some ten paces from us; carefully "dress" their lines, each captain as careful of his alignment as if at a dress parade. Then they fix bayonets, stack arms, then wearily remove their cartridge-boxes and hang them on the pile; lastly, reluctantly, painfully, they furl their battle-stained flags and lay them down; some, unable to restrain themselves, rushing from the ranks, clinging to them, kneeling over them and kissing them with burning tears. And then the Flag of the Union floats alone upon the field.

Then, stripped of every sign of the rebellion and token of its hate and will to hurt, they march off to give their word of honor never to lift arms against the old flag again, and are free to go where they will in the broad Republic.

Thus division after division passes, and it takes the whole day long to complete this deliverance. Twenty-seven thousand men paroled, one hundred and forty cannon and near that number of battle flags surrendered, but only about seventeen thousand stand of small arms. For sometimes a whole brigade, or what was left of it, had scarcely a score of arms to surrender, having thrown them away by roadside and riverside in weariness of flight or hopelessness of heart, or disdaining to carry them longer, only to be taken from them in token of a lost cause. After this it remained only to gather up what was serviceable of this material of war and to destroy the rest. Nothing was left which could be turned to use against the Union armies. The cartridge-boxes were emptied on the ground for the most part, burned, and after the troops had withdrawn at the first dusk of evening, it was a weird and almost sad sight to see the running flame with frequent bursts of lurid explosion along the lines where the surrendering army had stood; then only bits of leather writhing in the gray ashes.

All was over. With the dawn of morning the hillsides were alive with men, in groups or singly, on foot or horse making their way as by the instinct of an ant, each with his own little burden, each for his own little harbor or home.

And we were left alone and lonesome! The familiar forms that had long so firmly held our eyes, until they almost demanded the sight of them for their daily satisfaction, had vanished like a dream. The very reason of our existence seemed to have been taken away. And when on the morrow we took up our march again, though homeward, something was lacking in the spring and spice which had enlivened us through even the dreariest times. To be sure, the war was not over yet, but we felt that the distinctive work of the old Third Brigade was over. We were soon to be mustered out; but never to be again as if the Third Brigade had not become a part of our lives; a part of our souls. There were "thoughts that ran before and after," memories of things that cannot be told, and new purposes of manly living and hopes of useful service yet, in visions of a broader citizenship and the career of an enfranchised country.

G

THE LAST SALUTE OF THE ARMY OF NORTHERN VIRGINIA

Details of the Surrender of General Lee at Appomattox Courthouse April 9, 1865

The Battle of Five Forks, which occurred on the 1st of April, 1865, served to prove to General Grant the fact which General "Phil" Sheridan had advanced that the cutting of railroad lines between Petersburg and the South had made exceedingly difficult, if not practically impossible, the provisioning of the Confederate army, and that the departure of that command and its march toward Lynchburg might soon be expected.

The victory of Five Forks was so complete in every way as to wholly paralyze General Lee's plan for further delay, and it is not too much to say that the decision was at once made for the western movement of the Army of Northern Virginia toward a new supply base.

The battle of Sailor's Creek, with Ewell's surrender, and that of Farmville, followed quickly after, the Confederates being hard pressed on their left flank, and for them there was little rest owing to the continual hounding by Sherman's forces which seemed quite eager for constant combat.

The Fifth Army Corps had been detailed to work with Sheridan's Cavalry Division. The subsequent relief of General Warren is a matter of history, which there is no need of repeating.

General Griffin succeeded to command, and aided by the 6th, the 2d, and portions of the Army of the James, with other corps as fast as they could get to the scene, the military movements of that time form some of the most absorbing chapters of the Civil War which history has placed on record. Since the approach to Appomattox—for a hundred miles or more along this stream there had been terrible fighting—brought the head of each army very frequently in view, the strange spectacle of one army pressing with all energy in pursuit, while its antagonist was using its best efforts to get away and reach its delayed base of supplies, was presented to both sides.

On the terrible march to Appomattox Courthouse the Federal troops were ever shrouded in smoke and dust, and the rattle of firearms and the heavy roar of artillery told plainly of the intense scene which threatened to bring on yet one more general engagement.

Then came a moment which to me, at least, was more thrilling than any that had gone before. As we were hurrying on in response to Sheridan's hastily scribbled note for aid, an orderly with still another command from "Little Phil" came upon our bedraggled column, that of the 1st Division of the Fifth Army Corps, just as we were passing a road leading into the woods. In the name of Sheridan I was ordered to turn aside from the column of march, without waiting for orders through the regular channels, and to get to his relief.

The orderly said in a voice of greatest excitement that the Confederate infantry was pressing upon Sheridan with a weight so terrible that his cavalry alone could not long oppose it.

I turned instantly into the side road by which the messenger had come, and took up the "double-quick," having spared just time enough to send to General Gregory an order to follow me with his brigade.

In good season we reached the field where the fight was going on. Our cavalry had even then been driven to the very verge of the field by the old "Stonewall" Corps. Swinging rapidly into action the first line was sent forward in partial skirmish order, followed by the main lines, the 1st and 2d Brigades. Once, for some unknown reason, I was ordered back, but in the impetuosity of youth and the heat of conflict, I pushed on, for it seemed to me to be a momentous hour. We fought like demons across that field and up that bristling hill. They told us we would expose ourselves to the full fire of the Confederate artillery once we gained the crest, but push on we did, past the stone wall behind which the "Stonewall Corps" had hidden, driving them back to the crest of the ridge, down over it, and away.

We were gathering our forces for a last final dash upon the enemy. From the summit of the hill we could see on the opposite ridge a full mile across the valley the dark blotches of the Confederate infantry drawn up in line of battle; the blocks of cavalry further to our right, and lower down more cavalry, detached, running hither and thither as if uncertain just what to do.

In the valley, where flowed the now narrow Appomattox, along whose banks we had fought for weary miles, was a perfect swarm of moving men animals, and wagons, wandering apparently aimlessly about, without definite precision. The river sides were trodden to a muck by the nervous mass. It was a picture which words can scarce describe.

As we looked from our position we suddenly saw a couple of men ride out from the extreme left of the Confederate line, and even as we looked the glorious white of a flag of truce met our vision. At that time, having routed the Confederate forces on the hill, my brigade was left alone by Sheridan's cavalry, which had gone to the right to take the enemy in the flank.

I was on the right of the line as we stood at the crest of the hill. Near by us was the red Maltese cross of the Hospital Corps and straight toward this the two riders, one with the white flag, came.

When the men arrived, the one who carried the flag drew up before me, and, saluting with a rather stiff air—it was a strained occasion—informed me that he had been sent to beg a cessation of hostilities until General Lee could be heard from. Lee was even then said to be making a wide detour in the hope of attacking our forces from the rear. The officer who bore the flag was a member of the Confederate General Gordon's staff, but the message came to me in the name of General Longstreet.

At that time the command had devolved upon General Ord, and I informed the officer with the flag—which was, by the way, a towel of such cleanliness that I was then, as now, amazed that such a one could be found in the entire Rebel army—that he must proceed along to our left, where General Ord was stationed. With another abjectly stiff salute the officer with his milk-white banner galloped away down our line.

It was subsequently learned that General Ord was situated some distance away at my left with his troops of the Army of the James, comprising Gibbon's Second Army Corps and a division of the Twenty-fifth Army Corps. His line quite stretched across the Lynchburg Road, or "pike," as we called it then.

Well, as I have said, the flag of truce was sent to Ord, and not long afterward came the command to cease firing. The truce lasted until 4 o'clock that afternoon. At that time our troops had just barely resumed the positions they had originally occupied when the flag came in. They were expecting momentarily to be attacked again, and were well prepared, yes, eager, for a continuance of the battle.

And just then the glad news came that General Lee had surrendered. Shortly after that we saw pass before us that sturdy Rebel leader, accompanied by an orderly. He was dressed in the brilliant trappings of a Confederate army officer, and looked very inch the soldier that he was. A few moments after that our own beloved leader, General Grant, also accompanied by an orderly, came riding by. How different he was in appearance from the conquered hero. The one gay with the trappings of his army, the other wearing an open blouse, a slouch hat, trousers tucked into heavy, mud-stained boots, and with only the four tarnished golden stars to indicate his office! They passed us by and went to the house where were arranged the final terms of surrender. That work done neither leader stayed long with his command, the one hurrying one way, the other another.

That night we slept as we had not slept in four years. There was, of course, a great deal of unrestrained jubilation, but it did not call for much of that to be a sufficiency, and before long the camp over which peace after strife had settled was sleeping with no fear of a night alarm. We awoke next morning to find the Confederates peering down into our faces, and involuntarily reached for our arms, but once the recollections of the previous day's stirring events came crowding back to mind, all fear fled, and the boys in blue were soon commingling freely with the boys in gray, exchanging compliments, pipes, tobacco, knives and souvenirs.

Note: In the last days of fighting, which ended in Lee's surrender, General Chamberlain was wounded twice. That his service was gallant in the extreme may be judged when it is told that both General Sheridan and General Grant commended him personally. This the General cared to dwell on but little. But when it came to describing the final scenes of the war, the gray-haired army leader grew ardent with enthusiasm for his subject.

On that night, the 10th of April, in 1865, I was commanding the 5th Army Corps. It was just about midnight when a message came to me to report to headquarters.

I went thither directly and found assembled in the tent two of the three senior officers whom General Grant had selected to superintend the paroles and to look after the transfer of property and to attend to the final details of General Lee's surrender. These were General Griffin of the 5th Army Corps and General Gibbon of the 24th. The other commissioner, General Merritt of the cavalry, was not there. The articles of capitulation had been signed previously and it had come to the mere matter of formally settling the details of the surrender. The two officers told me that General Lee had started for Richmond, and that our leader, General Grant, was well on his way to his own headquarters at City Point, so called, in Virginia. I was also told that General Grant had decided to have a formal ceremony with a parade at the time of laying down of arms. A representative body of Union troops was to be drawn up in battle array at Appomattox Courthouse, and past this Northern delegation were to march the entire Confederate Army, both officers and men, with their arms and colors, exactly as in actual service, and to lay down these arms and colors, as well as whatever other property belonged to the Rebel army, before our men.

I was told, furthermore, that General Grant had appointed me to take charge of this parade and to receive the formal surrender of the guns and flags. Pursuant to these orders, I drew up my brigade at the courthouse along the highway leading to Lynchburg. This was very early on the morning of the 12th of April.

The Confederates were stationed on the hill beyond the valley and my brigade, the 3rd, had a position across that valley on another hill, so that each body of soldiers could see the other. My men were all veterans, the brigade being that which had fired the first shot at Yorktown at the beginning of the war. Their banners were inscribed with all the battles of the Army of the Potomac from the first clear through the long list down to the last.

In the course of those four eventful years the makeup of the brigade had naturally changed considerably, for there had been not alone changes of men, but consolidations of regiments as well. Yet the prestige of that history made a remarkably strong *esprit de corps*.

In that Third Brigade line there were regiments representing the States of Maine, Massachusetts, Michigan, and Pennsylvania, regiments which had been through the entire war. The Bay State veterans had the right of line down the village street. This was the 32d Massachusetts Regiment, with some members of the 9th, 18th, and 22d Regiments. Next in order came the First Maine Sharpshooters, the 20th Regiment, and some of the 2d. There were also the First Michigan Sharpshooters, the 1st and 16th Regiments, and some men of the 4th. Pennsylvania was represented by the 83d, the 91st, the 118th, and the 155th. In the other two brigades were: First Brigade, 198th Pennsylvania, and 185th New York; in the Second Brigade, the 187th, 188th, and 189th New York.

The First and Second Brigades were with me then, because I had previously commanded them and they had been very courteously sent me at my request by my corps and division commanders.

The arrangement of the soldiery was as follows: The Third Brigade on one side of the street in line of battle; the Second, known as Gregory's, in the rear, and across the street, facing the Third; the First Brigade also in line of battle.

Having thus formed, the brigades standing at "order arms," the head of the Confederate column, General Gordon in command, and the old "Stonewall" Jackson Brigade leading, started down into the valley which lay between us, and approached our lines. With my staff I was on the extreme right of the line, mounted on horseback, and in a position nearest the Rebel solders who were approaching our right.

Ah, but it was a most impressive sight, a most striking picture, to see that whole army in motion to lay down the symbols of war and strife, that army which had fought for four terrible years after a fashion but infrequently known in war.

At such a time and under such conditions I thought it eminently fitting to show some token of our feeling, and I therefore instructed my subordinate officers to come to the position of "salute" in the manual of arms as each body of the Confederates passed before us.

It was not a "present arms," however, not a "present," which then as now was the highest possible honor to be paid even to a president. It was the "carry arms," as it was then known, with musket held by the right hand and perpendicular to the shoulder. I may best describe it as a marching salute in review.

When General Gordon came opposite me I had the bugle blown and the entire line came to "attention," preparatory to executing this movement of the manual successively and by regiments as Gordon's columns should pass before our front, each in turn.

The General was riding in advance of his troops, his chin drooped to his breast, downhearted and dejected in appearance almost beyond description. At the sound of that machine like snap of arms, however, General Gordon started, caught in a moment its significance, and instantly assumed the finest attitude of a soldier. He wheeled his horse facing me, touching him gently with the spur, so that the animal slightly reared, and as he wheeled, horse and rider made one motion, the horse's head swung down with a graceful bow and General Gordon dropped his swordpoint to his toe in salutation.

By word of mouth General Gordon sent back orders to the rear that his own troops take the same position of the manual in the march past as did our line. That was done, and a truly imposing sight was the mutual salutation and farewell.

At a distance of possibly twelve feet from our line, the Confederates halted and turned face towards us. Their lines were formed with the greatest care, with every officer in his appointed position, and thereupon began the formality of surrender.

Bayonets were affixed to muskets, arms stacked, and cartridge boxes unslung and hung upon the stacks. Then, slowly and with a reluctance that was appealingly pathetic, the torn and tattered battleflags were either leaned against the stacks or laid upon the ground. The emotion of the conquered soldiery was really sad to witness. Some of the men who had carried and followed those ragged standards through the four long years of strife, rushed, regardless of all discipline, from the ranks, bent about their old flags, and pressed them to their lips with burning tears.

And it can well be imagined, too, that there was no lack of emotion on our side, but the Union men were held steady in their lines, without the least show of demonstration by word or by motion. There was, though, a twitching of the muscles of their faces, and, be it said, their battle-bronzed cheeks were not altogether dry. Our men felt the import of the occasion, and realized fully how they would have been affected if defeat and surrender had been their lot after such a fearful struggle.

Nearly an entire day was necessary for that vast parade to pass. About 27,000[1] stands of arms were laid down, with something like a hundred battleflags; cartridges were destroyed, and the arms loaded on cars and sent off to Wilmington.

Every token of armed hostility was laid aside by the defeated men. No officer surrendered his side arms or horse, if private property, only Confederate property being required, according to the terms of surrender, dated April 9, 1865, and stating that all arms, artillery, and public property were to be packed and stacked and turned over to the officer duly appointed to receive them.

And right here I wish to correct again that statement so often attributed to me, to the effect that I have said I received from the hands of General Lee on that day his sword. Only recently, at a banquet in Newtown, Massachusetts, of the Katahdin Club, composed of sons and daughters of my own beloved State, it was said in press dispatches that a letter had been read from me in which I made the claim that I had received Lee's sword. I never did make that claim even as I never did receive that sword.

As I have said, no Confederate officer was required or even asked to surrender his side arms if they were his personal property. As a matter of fact, General Lee never gave up his sword, although, if I am not mistaken, there was some conference between General Grant and some of the members of his staff upon that very subject just before the final surrender. I was not present at that conference, however, and only

---

[1]Reference may be made as to this statement to "Paroles of the Army of Northern Virginia," Vol XV, *Southern Historical Society Papers*, p.xxvii, communication of General Lee to President Davis: On the morning of the 9th, according to the reports of the ordinance officers, there were 7,892 organized infantry with arms.

know of it by hearsay.

But, as I was saying, every token of armed hostility having been laid aside, and the men having given their words of honor that they would never serve again against the flag, they were free to go whither they would and as best they could. In the meantime our army had been supplying them with rations. On the next morning, however, the morning of the 13th, we could see the men, singly or in squads, making their way slowly into the distance, in whichever direction was nearest home, and by nightfall we were left there at Appomattox Courthouse lonesome and alone.

Head Quarters 1st Brigade 1st Div. 5th Corps.
Appomattox Court House Va. April 10th 1865

Colonel:

I would respectfully recommend to you for promotion to the rank, if possible, of First Lieutenant, of Henry A. Kelsey of your Regiment for his conspicuous good conduct during all the engagements of this campaign. At the battle of "Lewis's Farm" on the 29th of March he was constantly on the line rallying the men, though only acting as my orderly, and I was an eye witness to his capturing an officer and five men out of the very line of battle in the enemy's ranks. At the battle of "White Oak Road" March 31st he really acted as aide de camp. At the battle of "Five Forks" his behavior was heroic. And at the battle of Appomattox Court.

House April 9th he dashed into the town in advance of the Skirmish line, & captured several Officers & men, besides rendering me important services in carrying orders to different parts of the field.

I am very desirous that such a distinguished instance of gallantry should be suitably rewarded.

I am, Colonel,

Very respectfully

Your obd. sevt.

J.L. Chamberlain

Brig. Genl Comdg

Colonel

Gustavus Sniper,

Comdg. 185 New York Vols.

Letter from General Joshua Chamberlain to Colonel Gustavus Sniper of the 185th New York Volunteers, mentioning all of the closing campaigns of the war in reference to a promotion request. This letter was written the day after the surrender, April 10, 1865.

H

ADDRESS TO THE SIXTEENTH MAINE VOLUNTEERS

General Chamberlain's response to the toast "Gettysburg" at a banquet in honor of the Sixteenth Maine Infantry and the Fifth Battery at the city of Gardiner, Maine.

Comrades of the Sixteenth and of the Fifth Battery:

It is an honor to be held worthy of your remembrance on an occasion like this. The reason of it is to be found in your own generous hearts. Something there may be in the suggestion that the flag of the Sixteenth in the field was finally furled within my own lines. In the closing days of our service, when all those varied experiences grouped under the wide and deep word, "casualties," together with the gradual expiration of terms of enlistment, brought men of the same state nearer and nearer together, it happened that the men of the Sixteenth left in the field (as had been those of the Second and the Sharpshooters) were consolidated with those of my old regiment, the Twentieth, and so were mustered out of the service in the division of which I was the commanding officer. I have evidence of my ability at that time to recognize merit in that I, forthwith upon the opportunity, invited one of your gallant field officers to a place on my staff.

Another thing which perhaps gives me footing here is that queer "back action" attraction by which "extremes meet." This is often from deep, underlying likeness, and not apparent antagonism. Here it is like service in opposite extremes of position. You were at one post of peril and responsibility; I was at another, the most remote from you in place, but so similar in circumstance, that I can understand and appreciate all your experience. With you, on the first day, the army put her right foot forward; with us, on the second, she put her left foot forward. She changed steps, but she stood.

You have given me a great theme. It is large enough to occupy our minds as many days as it held us, body and soul, breasting that tidal wave of July, 1863. I have not now, for this, so many minutes at my disposal. I pass it with a glance.

Gettysburg was a great battle;—its action, its tension, its hazards, its consequences. In it were involved questions of gravest import, the decision of which makes history; interests social, political, moral, personal; of gravest import for ourselves, for others, for our Country, for man everywhere;—for the present time, and for the future, for which also we hold a trust. The pressing question before us was whether we had a Country; whether we were a people, or only a populace; whether we were a mere chance partnership holding only by human will, or a Nation, constituted in the purpose and calling of Divine Providence, bound together for the noblest ends of living by ties of mutual interest and honor,—bonds both of love and of law. All the great ruling sentiments which have their vital source in this idea,—patriotism, loyalty, self-devotion for the sake of others,—nay, what we consider the supreme of earthly blessings,—largest scope for individual life, endowments, powers, genius, character,—these were the prize for which we wrestled in that terrible arena. More than this. Involved here, too, were widest human interests. We fought for the worth of manhood; for law and liberty, which mean freedom for every man to make the most of himself, with good-will of all others, without oppression or depression.

We had a deep, inward vision of this at the time, though unspoken and perhaps unclear; but no man even now can realize in thought, or recognize in fact, all the reach of good coming forth out of that struggle and that victory for the Country and for mankind. But I must leave that line of thought with you.

Looked at in its outward aspect, this battle will be a great example in military history,—a study in military science;—the strong features of the ground affording great variety of offensive and defensive measures, of grand and minor tactics, in a sudden and unplanned great battle; not without exemplification, too, of the tactics of the moral forces and the desperate strategy of sacrifice. In its inward aspect, example, also, of the value of character in the stress and strain of battle, where mature experience and intelligent comprehension have enforced the lesson that manly fortitude, heroic valor, and pride of honor must be organized into the habit of discipline and unquestioning obedience, without which all generalship is vain. But this thought, also, leading so far and so deep, I must leave for you to finish.

Many have claimed the honor of selecting the final standing-ground of our great defense. To this sudden change of position, some participants were "accessory before the fact," and some "after the fact." But if there was any selection here, it was a very "natural selection." Whether, in every instance, it led to the "survival of the fittest," there may be some question. The manner of its occupancy is not suggestive of deliberate premeditation, but our people certainly may be said to have chosen this ground and promptly taken it, in decided preference to matters and things they have found at the further front.

But who, let me ask, made it possible to select this ground but the men who on that first of July, all day long, held Lee's advance at bay, until our scattered corps could come up by forced marches and take advantage of the field? Who but John Buford with his cavalry, and Reynolds with his First Corps—you of his infantry and artillery,—with masterly skill, stubborn courage, and unexampled devotion, wrought that marvelous opening by which it was Meade, and not Lee, who secured that heart of hills made awful in memory and immortal in history? That magnificent fighting of the First Corps, I do not know where it was ever surpassed!

But my theme grows intense as it narrows and nears. I know how you of the Fifth Battery, after holding your salient angle at the front until it was an island in the raging sea of foes, galloped straight through their enveloping masses, through embarrassing masses of fugitives as well, and with your brazen throats calling a halt to the astonished enemy thinking to sweep away our right flank, where for a sublime moment you alone gave check to the battle tide.

I know what you men of the Sixteenth did, when your General of Division, seeing that it must be a stricken field, and that he must save what he could of his command by the last resort of falling back with his main body while a few should hold the fighting front, and that this could be done only by men who would make a stand equal in every test of character to the desperate charge of a "forlorn hope," calling to Colonel Tilden, said: "Take that hill and hold it at any cost!" I know how you stood, and where, and when, and at what cost! Your General knew what men you were. You knew perfectly well what your service was to be. It is a terrible duty, but a glorious honor. You saw what was coming, front and left and right. You saw the last of the Union army leave the field. You saw the blades of the great shears coming down and down, and closing in and in—and you knew they must meet, and cut and crush all that was between. But you stood; you fought it out to the last and "at any cost" indeed. Environed, enveloped, crushed, overwhelmed,—as truly heroic, as much to be held in highest honor and dearest memory, as if you had died at your posts, every man of you!

Some such example as yours, the great Apostle must have had in mind when he exhorts his followers to "put on the whole armor of God, that ye may be able to withstand in the evil day, and having done all, *to stand.*"

So many of you were captured,—not because you were placed in a false position, with flank unguarded and rear cut off; not because you were not well handled; not because you were "caught napping" or "cooking coffee"; but because you would not yield your post, though disaster and death swirled and swept around and over you.

Your colors, it was said, were lost. That word came to me when, on the morning of the second, I reached the crest far to the rear of that where you had stood; and I felt a shock, but not of shame. For I knew something terrible must have befallen, and that there could have been no dishonor where you were. But when I came to know the truth of it all, I saw that instead of your colors being lost, they were eternally saved! Not laid down, but lifted up; not captured nor surrendered, but translated,—the shadow lost in substance! The flag,—it is the symbol of the Country's honor, power, law, and life. It is the ensign of loyalty, the bond of brotherhood for those who stand under it; a token and an inspiration. Hence it is held sacred by the soldier; as in great moments it is also by the citizen. All which that flag symbolized you had illustrated and impersonated; had absorbed into your thoughts and hearts—if I should not rather say, itself had absorbed your thoughts and hearts,—your service and suffering into its own deeper meaning and dearer honor. Now it had done all a symbol could do; you had stood for all it stood for. Now the supreme moment had come. Nothing could be averted; nothing could be resisted; nothing could be escaped. That was an awful moment; passing that of death, it seems to me. Then the soul is born anew. No thought of yielding up the token of the Country's honor enters the heart of any one of you, though it has fulfilled its ends; though you are to go to prison and to death. Your Colonel, calm and dauntless,—commander still,—bids you break the staff that had borne it aloft, and tear that symbol single as your souls into as many pieces as you had bosoms, and shelter them with your lives, lest that flag be touched by hostile hand, or triumphed over by living man! And they went with you to prison. And these bars and stars next your hearts helped you to endure those other bars, besetting you because you were true; helped you to look up to those other stars, where we dream all is serene and safe and free. (Here the long repressed feelings of the hearers broke into wildest demonstration, in the midst of which a member of the regiment arose and took from his breast pocket a star of the old flag, at which the assembly lost all control of itself; and the General continued.) Yes, and through this tumult of cheers and tears, I see that you hold them still to your hearts, precious beyond words, radiant with the glory of service and suffering nobly borne; potent to transmit to other souls the power that has made them glorious!

Lost? There is a way of losing that is finding. When soul overmasters sense; when the noble and divine self overcomes the lower self; when duty and honor and love,—immortal things,—bid the mortal perish! It is only when a man supremely gives that he supremely finds.

That was your sacrifice; that is your reward.

I

ORATION ON THE ONE HUNDREDTH ANNIVERSARY OF THE BIRTH OF ABRAHAM LINCOLN

Ceremonies at Philadelphia, Pennsylvania
February 12, 1909

General Chamberlain's Address:

Great crises in human affairs call out the great in men. They call for great men. This greatness is of quality rather than quantity. It is not intensified selfhood, nor multiplied possessions. It implies extraordinary powers to cope with difficult situations; but it implies still more, high purpose—the intent to turn these powers to the service of man. Its essence is of magnanimity. Some have indeed thought it great to seize occasion in troubled times to aggrandize themselves. And something slavish in the lower instincts of human nature seems to grant their claim. Kings and conquerors have been named "great" because of the magnificence of the servitude they have been able to command, or the vastness of their conquests, or even of the ruin they have wrought.

But true greatness is not in nor of the single self; it is of that larger personality, that shared and sharing life with others, in which, each giving of his best for their betterment, we are greater than ourselves; and self-surrender for the sake of that great belonging, is the true nobility.

The heroes of history are not self-seekers; they are saviors. They give of their strength to the weak, the wronged, the imperilled. Suffering and sacrifice they take on themselves. Summoned by troubles, they have brought more than peace;

they have brought better standing and understanding for human aspirations. Their mastery is for truth and right; that is for man. Hence they are reverenced and beloved through the ages. If we mourn the passing of the heroic age, all the more conspicuous and honored is heroic example, still vouchsafed to ours.

There are crises yet, when powers and susceptibilities of good fevered with blind unrest and trembling for embodiment seem turned to mutual destruction. Happy then the hour when comes the strong spirit, master because holding self to a higher obedience, the impress of whose character is command. He comes to mould these elemental forces not to his own will, but to their place in the appointed order of the ongoing world. For lack of such men the march of human right has so many times been halted—hence the dire waste of noble endeavor; grandeur of martyrdoms uplifted in vain; high moments of possibility lost to mankind.

There came upon our country, in our day, a crisis, a momentous peril, a maddened strife such as no description can portray, nor simile shadow forth; volcanic eruption, earthquake, up-whelming seas of human force involving in their sweep agonies and destruction such as the catastrophes of Italy never wrought; not merely the measurable material loss, but the immeasurable spiritual cost; the maddened attempt to rend asunder this ordained Union, this People of the United States of America, a government by divine right, if anything on earth can be so. The shock was deep and vast. It was the convulsion of a historic and commissioned people. It was the dissolution of covenants that had held diverse rights and powers in poise; collision of forces correlated to secure unity and order,—now set loose against each other, working destruction. It was more than the conflict of laws, clash of interests, disharmony of ideas and principles. It was the sundering of being; war of self against self; of sphere against sphere in the concentric order of this great composite national life of ours.

For us the aggregate human wisdom had been found wanting. Conventions, Congresses and compromises had failed; the heights of argument, sentiment and eloquence had been scaled in vain; the mighty bond of historic memories, patriotism and Christian fellowship had been dissolved in that ferment. Had a committee of wisest men been chosen,—expert doctors of law, medicine and divinity,—nay the twelve apostles

themselves been summoned,—to determine what combination
of qualities must mark the man who could mount above this
storm, make his voice heard amidst these jarring elements,
and command the "law of the mind" to prevail over the "law in
the members," they could not have completed their inventory,
nor have found the man of such composition.

It was a divine providence which brought forth the man,
to execute the divine decree, in a crisis of human history.

It was a strange presentment and personality,—this
deliverer, this servant and master, this follower and leader of
the law;—strange, and not readily accepted of men. Out of the
unknown, and by ways that even he knew not, came to this
place of power, Abraham Lincoln.

He came mysteriously chosen; not by the custom of
hereditary descent, not by the concurrence of his peers, but by
the instinctive voice of a predestined people. Called because
he was chosen; chosen, because he was already choice. The
voice came to him as to the deliverer of old: *"Be strong, and of a
good courage, for thou must go with this people unto the land which the
Lord hath sworn to their fathers to give them. And thou shalt cause them
to inherit it!"*

This one man called to the task. Millions of them could
not meet it. He could. The order to be strong and of a good
courage came to him because he was that already. There was
that in him which this order appealed to and rested on. A
weak man could not even receive it.

So, this deliverer of ours. Courtly manners and culture
of the schools he did not bring. But moulded and seasoned
strength, calm courage, robust sense, he brought; and a heart
to humanize it all. His inherent and potential greatness was
his power of reason and sense of right, and a magnanimity
which regarded the large and long interests of man more than
the near and small of self. Strength and courage are much the
same; In essence, in action, and in passion,—the ability to
bear. These qualities were of the whole man;—mind, heart
and will. Intellect keen yet broad; able in both insight and
comprehension; taking in at once the details of a situation, and
also its unity and larger relations. He knew men in their
common aspects, and he knew man in his potential excellence.
Courage of will was his: power to face dangers without and
within; to resist the pressure of force or of false suggestion;
standing to his conviction; firm against minor persuasions;

silencing temptation. Courage of the heart; power to resolve, and to endure; to suffer and to wait. His patience was pathetic.

Courage of faith; belief in the empowering force of his obligation. Wise to adjust policies to necessity, he kept sight of his ideal. Amidst mockeries of truth, he was "obedient unto the heavenly vision." Through the maze of false beacons and bewildering beckonings, he steered by the star. Above the recalling bugles of disaster and defeat he heard the voice of his consecration, and held it pledge and prophecy. These qualities, coordinated and commanded by wise judgment, and sustained by a peculiar buoyancy of temperament, constituted a personality remarkable, if not solitary, among the great men of our time.

Before this assembly of the Loyal Legion it is natural to consider Abraham Lincoln as he was presented to our observation and experience in the military sphere; not as Chief Executive in the common phrase of ordinary times, but as representative of the nation before the world, and clothed with its power. That is, as Commander-in-Chief of the army and navy of the United States, in an insurrection so vast as to involve nations over the seas. A secondary title might be: The Revelation of the War Powers of the President.

The situation Lincoln confronted was without parallel; in magnitude, in complexity, in consequence. The immediate and pressing object was manifest. To overcome the embattled hostile forces; to quell the rebellion; to restore the honor and authority of the American Union; to preserve the existence of the people of the United States.

But this involved much more. There are no single lines in human affairs. Cross-currents of interest, sentiment and passion confused the motives, embarrassed the movements, and clouded the issues, of this new declaration that this people should be one and free.

Much had to be met that force could not manage; much that sharpest insight and outlook could not foresee. Not only the direct event of battle was involved, but the collateral effects and continuing consequences; the far-reaching interests of a great people yet to be; the interests of related nations, and of humanity itself.

Little experienced in administrative functions and unfamiliar with the art of war, he had to take the chief responsibility in both. He had much to learn, and was willing to learn it. But not in haste. In some matters he came slowly to the execution of his conviction, as possibly to the conviction itself. But his judgments were based on what was sincere in his nature, and large in motive. That he took no counsel from fear is manifest. Evading the assassins hired to waylay his path to the place of duty, and the no less infamous plots to prevent the counting of the electoral vote and the announcement of his election, he stood up and faced the menacing, cleaving masses in the beleaguered capital.

He chose his cabinet of official advisers in a novel way, and, one might think, hazardous; but it showed the breadth of his patriotism and the courage of his independence. Instead of seeking those of like thinking with himself, or likely to make a unity among themselves on public questions, he called men who were rival candidates or popular in their respective localities; even offering places to distinguished statesmen in Virginia and North Carolina. And Seward, Chase, Cameron, Welles, Bates, Blair and Smith, and afterwards Stanton,—what measure of agreement with him or each other, on any point of public policy, could be expected from a council like this! Most of these men, no doubt, at first thought slightingly of him. But he converted or over-awed them all. He went straight on.

He found more trouble in the military sphere. The popular, or political principle of appointment would not work so well here. It took some time and trial to rectify this, and make practical tests of ability the basis. It was unfortunate that it took so long to secure a nominal military chief, who had the soldierly brain and eye and hand to command the confidence of his subordinates as well as of his superiors.

But even among his generals in the field there was a lack of harmony and a redundance of personality. He had to overrule this. He was their responsible commander. He made himself their practical adviser. This latter function some of them undertook to make reciprocal. They did not gain much by it. His sharp rejoinders, winged with wit and feathered with humor,—as apposite as unexpected,—stirred the smiles of all but the immediate recipients. But they commanded the sober respect of all, as uncommon lessons of good common sense,—which is also and always good tactics.

We behold him solitary in the arena; surrounded by various antagonists and unsympathizing spectators. He had to deal with cabinet, Congress, committees, diplomatists, cranks, wiseacres, as well as the embattled enemy on land and sea.

Sorely tried by long delays in the field, he was vexed by the incessant clamor of the excited and unthinking, and of influential persons and papers that beset him with the demand to free the slaves, and the reckless cry, "On to Richmond," which may have forced campaigns of disaster. Perils from lurking traitors in the capital, pesterings of open or secret enemies and rash and weak advisers, augmented the difficulties of the momentous contention. All the while, with heart-crushing things to bear, which he would not openly notice,—nor let us, now! We cannot but wonder how he ever lived through, to crown his work with a death so tragic, an ascension so transfiguring.

But he was appointed for great ends; and this was his guaranty of life!

Let us note more particularly some of the difficulties which environed the president growing out of the magnitude and exterior complications of this great rebellion.

At first we looked upon the rebellion as a domestic insurrection, to be dealt with by the provisions and processes of municipal law. But facts forced us from that theory. Laws, no less than tactics, change with magnitudes. As the range and force of the rebellion grew, and conditions became more complex, the president had to enlarge his policy, and the grounds of its justification.

One of the first warlike acts of the Confederate States was to send forth armed cruisers, commissioned by "Letters of Marque" to prey upon our merchant-ships and commerce on the seas. We could not treat these cruisers as a domestic insurrectionary force, because they were operating on the "high seas,"—the road of the nations; nor could we treat them as pirates, and apply to their captured crews the summary process of a short rope at the yard-arm, because they were only "domestic enemies," and did not come under the "pirate" definition of international law, as "enemies of mankind." So we had to submit to their enjoying certain privileges recognized by the law of nations, and admit their captured crews to exchange as prisoners of war.

Nor could we treat the armed forces of the rebellion as a "mob," because they were in such force and form that they had to be treated under the laws of war,—presumed to be part of the law of nations. Yet we could not recognize the Confederacy as a nation, and a proper party to such agreement or practice.

Moreover, the president had instituted a blockade of Southern ports, a measure better known to international, than to domestic law. So it came about that the very magnitude of the rebellion, and its extent on land and sea, compelled us, both on grounds of public law and on grounds of humanity, to extend to our formidable antagonists some degree of the regulations known as "belligerent rights." But belligerents are presumed, in law at least, to be aliens to each other; not fellow-citizens. Hence great perplexity for the president.

But the situation now affected other nations. Here opens a painful chapter of that sad experience. And I have to ask your attention for a moment to difficulties outside the domestic sphere, which from the very first to the very last, were among the most trying of the president's experiences. He was confronted by an exterior circle of hostile intent and action in the strange unfriendliness of nations,—perhaps I should say, governments of nations, —historically and racially nearest to us, and professing principles and sentiments deeply accordant with our own.

The governments of England and France did not wait for a distinct good understanding upon international relations. They took the earliest possible occasion to declare their neutrality, and to put the insurgents on the full footing of lawful belligerents. They even denominated them as "States," thus ignoring their character as insurgents. This was the more trying because early in the discussion of the situation, our Government had distinctly declared to the British Government that "No proposition would be considered which did not regard this as a domestic insurrection, with which foreign nations had no concern."

This recognition by England and France, followed by other governments, gave the Confederate cruisers wide privileges on the "high seas," and in foreign ports, and a certain prestige to the Confederate claim before the world.

Then came the severe trial for the president when Captain Wilkes of our navy took from an English steamer on the high seas Messieurs Mason and Slidell,—diplomatic agents of the Confederacy for France and England,—and conveyed them to Boston in custody; our Secretary of the Navy officially congratulating Wilkes, and the House of Representatives voting him the thanks of Congress; the British Government in a rage; Lord Russell in imperious tones demanding an apology, the instant delivery of Mason and Slidell, and the dismissal of Wilkes from our service; forthwith embarking troops for Canada, and gathering vast munitions of war; engaging the whole power of the Empire to enforce his demand if it was not instantly obeyed. The wisdom and moral strength with which the president met this most difficult situation,—yielding in a manner appeasing England and not humiliating to our Country,—is of highest example.

Then during all the years of the war, England permitted the building and equipping within her jurisdiction and territory of ships intended as Confederate cruisers, and for the known purpose of warring upon the commerce of the United States. This went on in disregard of every protest, until the end of the war, we were in a position to ask England to consider the question of damages; and a Board of Arbitration awarded as a minimum, fifteen millions of dollars. Had the decision been otherwise, and England sustained, we probably could have borne it. But England, in case of a rebellion in some of her dependencies, would have been astonished at the fleets of rebel cruisers investigating her commerce on all seas.

At best, France and England were reluctant and perfunctory observers of neutrality, and anything but cordial well-wishers. All the while they were eager for a pretence of reason to recognize the independence of the Confederate States.

It was believed by us all in the army marching to the unknown field predestined to be immortal Gettysburg, that upon the issue of this battle hung the fate of the nation; that should Lee's army gain a decided advantage here, these two governments would seize the moment to declare the independent sovereignty of the Confederate States, and accord such recognition and support as would bring the end of our great endeavor. You may well believe that this conviction had part in the superhuman marching and fighting which made that a field of deathless glory. It gave us new devotion. It seemed to lift the whole scene and scale of the contention to a higher plane. We were fighting not only forces in the field, but with spiritual foes in high places, with "the princes of the powers of the air."

A serious flank-movement, which gave the president

much anxiety, was the occupation of Mexico by the French Emperor. After various vexing schemes, he chose the darkest hour for that Republic and ours, to send a French army to force a monarchy, with an Austrian arch-duke as Emperor, on the people of Mexico. Besides the direct effect on us, this scheme of planting a hostile monarchial power on our southern border, had an ulterior motive,—to gain a vantage ground from which, by some turn of tangled affairs, to recover a hold on the old Louisiana tract, and the control of the lower Mississippi. In his eagerness Louis over-reached himself. His formal proposal to the Confederates to cede to him, in the name of France, the great State of Texas, angered them, and lost him the game. But he kept his army in Mexico, fighting its people, with Maximillian as nominal head, or catapult, and under the increasing remonstrance of our far-sighted president.

Some of us remember, at the disbandment of the Army of the Potomac, being retained in the service and assigned to a mysterious Provisional Corps of veterans; the intent and mission of which, we were confidentially informed, was to go down with Sheridan to assist Louis Napoleon to get his French army out of Mexico. A personal reconnaissance of Sheridan in Mexico, and the virile diplomacy of Seward, deprived us of that outing. The French army with its monarchy vanished from the shores of Mexico, leaving a stain on the pride of France and a fearful fate for Maximillian and poor Carlotta.

Contemplate for a moment, what would have been the situation, if in any event, Louis had got his foothold in Louisiana under color of title; and what the task might have been for either the North or the South, or both together, to recover that holding and the control of the mighty Mississippi, sea-road for the commerce of half our Atlantic slope.

Let us now take a closer view, and consider the great embarrassments of the president in treating a domestic insurrection under the laws of war; when compelled to use the military forces of the nation, not in aid of the civil authority, and under its regulation, as in common cases, but to replace and supersede it.

In spirit war and law are opposed: the end of one is the beginning of the other. Still, upon occasion, they are made reciprocally supporting. War is brought to support law, and law is applied to regulate war. An armed rebellion is war, and all its consequences are involved. We did not realize this at first. Military force in time of war stands on a very different basis from that when it is called to the aid of the civil authority. The strict limitations in the latter case are much relaxed; indeed quite replaced. Military law regulates the conduct of armies, and is prescribed by the civil authority. Martial law is something beyond this; it is the arbitrary will of the commander, and operates upon civilians and citizens. This justifies itself by "necessity," which, it is said, "knows no law." So things have to be done which in time of peace are illegal; yet are justified by the inherent law of sovereignty,—the law of life.

I shall not attempt to enumerate all the consequences involved in the operation of belligerent rights. By the law of nations strictly speaking provinces or communities in revolt have no rights. Concessions to such are not made on their account, but from considerations of policy on the part of the dominant state, or of humanity.

Some of the privileges granted to recognized belligerents are well known; such as flags and passages of truce for occasions of need or mercy; exchange of prisoners; immunity of hospitals and perhaps of homes. But on the other hand, and for the larger range, there are corresponding liabilities involved in these "rights," and of a most serious nature. They follow the right to capture, confiscate and destroy enemy's property; to arrest, capture and imprison persons of the enemy; to employ and emancipate slaves of the enemy; to suspend or reduce civil and political rights of a community brought under the jurisdiction of arms, leaving them only the rights of a conquered territory under the laws of war.

This would seem to be enough to task the best ability and conscience in any case. But in a case of intensified and enlarged domestic insurrection, where the insurgents are claiming independent sovereign capacity, denied and resisted by the parent people, which on the other hand regards them as rightly and in fact part of itself,—how to concede belligerent rights and yet avoid acknowledgment of the competency of the antagonist to be a party to the agreement, is a task for tact and wisdom of no common order. And the necessity of applying the laws of war to fellow citizens must bring grievous problems to the head and heart.

Practical questions also were forced upon the president, beyond the sphere of ordinary peace or war, for the determination of which there was no precedent, nor certain warrant. Questions of statesmanship, of political ethics, and constitutional interpretation, such as kept our Congress and Supreme Court busy for years afterwards, had to be acted on practically and promptly by him.

He took to himself no credit for anything. After years of the struggle and many dark and discouraging aspects of the issue, just before the yet darker depths of the terrible campaign of '64, he writes this self-abasing sentence: "I claim not to have controlled events; but confess that events have controlled me." We can judge better about that, perhaps, than he could, enveloped in the mesh of circumstance. We know how disturbed were the polarities of compelling forces, and how firm the guidance, how consummate the mastery. To our eyes he sat high above the tumult, watching events, meeting them, turning them to serve the great purpose. So far and so far only, did events control him.

He felt himself upborne by the power of his obligation, as charged with a duty like that of the Roman consul: "to see to it that the Republic suffered no detriment." The rule of such emergency is that,—also Roman,—which constitutions involve but do not enunciate, warrantable only in the last extremity: *"Salus populi, suprema lex."* The salvation of the people is supreme law!

Take the instance of the Emancipation Proclamation. I remember well that many high officers of our army disapproved this in heart and mind, if they dared not in speech. They thought the president had no right to proclaim this intention nor power to carry it into effect. But they had not deeply enough studied the implications of the constitution of their country, or those of the laws of war. They had to take a post-graduate course in their own profession. Indeed, upon political matters the habitual thought of us all was related to a condition of domestic peace, and did not contemplate war at the center of life.

So our Congress, just before the breaking out of the rebellion, in the hope to avoid war and to save the Union, had unanimously passed a resolution that "neither the Federal government nor the free States had any right to legislate upon or interfere with slavery in any of the slave-holding States of the Union." This seems more like an utterance under duress, than a deliberate interpretation of the Constitution. They did not foresee the construction as well as the destruction involved in war.

Even for the president there was a progressive revelation. At his inauguration he had publicly affirmed that he had no intention, directly or indirectly, of interfering with the institution of slavery in the States where it existed. "I believe I have not the right, and I am sure I have not the desire," he adds. He was then viewing the matter under the precedents of peaceful times. The deep reach of his constitutional powers in time of supreme peril of the Country had not been brought to light as it was under the tremendous tests of a vast and devastating war. It came to him but slowly. He seemed reluctant to avail himself of it. Later we find him saying in effect: "My purpose is to save this Union. I will save it without slavery, if I can; with slavery, if I must."

When in the course of events the war-powers of the president emerged, they appeared with a content and extent not dreamed of before. He took them to a high tribunal. He almost made a covenant with God that if the terrible blow threatening the life of the country was broken at Antietam, he would emancipate the slaves in the territory of the rebellion. The thought was not new. The laws of war gave to commanders in the field the right to break down all the forces supporting the enemy; and two of his generals had declared the freedom of the slaves within their military jurisdiction. He promptly rebuked them and countermanded their proclamations. This was not work for a subordinate. So grave, so deep-reaching, so far-reaching, were its necessary effects, he reserved the prerogative for the chief commander and the last resort.

This was not because of immaturity of purpose, nor fear to act; but because he chose to wait until the terrible sufferings and cost of war made this measure seem a mitigation, and the right and necessity of it so clear that the Country and the world must acquiesce. He did this, not because slavery was the *cause* of the war, but because it was *a muniment of war* waged against the life of the people. He set the appointed time and conditions when, within the territory of the rebellion, the slaves should be freed. The time came,—and the proclamation, deep with thought as with consequence. This, the conclusion:

"And upon this act, sincerely believed to be an act of justice, warranted by the Constitution, upon military necessity, I invoke the considerate judgment of mankind, and the gracious favor of Almighty God!"

Observe the grounds of this: Justice, the eternal law of righteousness; political right, warrant of the constitution; military necessity, for the salvation of the people; the approving judgment of man; the confirmation of God. This justification of the act was the revelation of the man. Without precedent of authority, or parallel in history, but as it were, *"sub specie eterni"*—in the aspect of the infinite, he spoke freedom to the slave! That voice was of the ever-coming "Word" that works God's will in His World!

Lo! this the outcome of belligerent rights, and the wilful appeal to the arbitrament of arms! Astounding annunciation of the powers of the president for the people's defence; and the discovery that not only military law, but also the absolute authority and summary processes of martial law, are part of the Constitution, part of the supreme law of the land. Had the leaders in the arrogant pretension of self-sufficiency and the frenzied rush to war, understood the reach of this, they would have hesitated to commit their cause to the wager of battle. And any future plotter against the nation's integrity and truth, may well pause before waking that slumbering lion at the gates of her life!

It was, indeed, a "domestic problem" which Lincoln had before him,—a wide one, and a far one,—to save his country. We think it was worth saving. The world thinks so, too.

An outcome of Lincoln's heart and mind was the projection into military law of a deep and wide humanity. We well knew his sympathy and tenderness towards the young soldier and the all-surrendering mother. He often superseded the death sentence for sleeping on post, pronounced upon the new-coming youth unseasoned by discipline and the habit of hardship.

All the lessons drawn from that stern experience of his, are embodied in the famous General Order Number 100, published to the army in 1863.

It was a reconstruction, a regeneration, of the rules of war. The necessity of stern justice and rigorous discipline recognized; but all tempered by great-hearted recognition of the manhood of man! The notable thing about this is, that it has been adopted, word for word, by nation after nation, and is to-day part of the international law of the civilized world.

And the power of this nation's influence in the world to-day,—the reason why her intervention sets free an oppressed people, her word speaks peace to embattled nations, and her wish prevents the dismemberment of empires,—is not so much in the might of her fleets and armies, splendid as these are, but because of her character, the confidence of the nations in her justice, and truth, and honor! Look at her! Her mission is peace and light and liberty! Her flag speaks hope to man!

Who can tell what part in all this is Abraham Lincoln!

I would speak now of him as he was seen and known more intimately by the army in the field. We had often opportunity to see him,—for some occasions, too often. Sometimes he came for conference with commanders amidst actual conditions, where he could see for himself, and not through casual or official reports. Sometimes, from conferences with cabinet, or Congressmen, or ministers of other powers, holding suggestions of deep import.

But always after a great battle, and especially disaster, we were sure to see him, slow riding through camp, with outward or inward-searching eyes,—questioning and answering heart. His figure was striking; stature and bearing uncommon and commanding. The slight stoop of the shoulders, an attitude of habitual in-wrapped thought, not of weakness, of any sort. His features, strong; if homely, then because standing for rugged truth. In his deep, over-shadowed eyes, a look as from the innermost of things. Over all this would come at times a play, or pathos, of expression in which his deeper personality outshone. His voice was rich; its modulations, musical; his words most fitting.

I have scarcely seen picture or sculpture which does him justice. The swarm of caricaturists with their various motives and instructions, have given a very wrong impression of him,—unfortunately too lasting. There was something of him,—and the greatest and most characteristic,—which refused to be imaged in earthly form.

In his action there was a gravity and moderation which the trivial might misinterpret as awkwardness, but which came from the dignity of reserved power. Those who thought to smile when that figure,—mounting, with the tall hat, to near seven feet,—was to be set on a spirited horse for a ceremonial excursion, were turned to admiration at the easy mastery he showed; and the young-staff game of testing civilians by touch-

ing up the horses to headlong speed returning over a course
they had mischievously laid, with sudden crossings of old rifle-
pit and ditch, proved a boomerang for them, when he would
come out the only rider square in his saddle, with head level
and rightly crowned.

In familiar intercourse he was courteous and kindly.
He seemed to find rest in giving way to a strain of humor that
was in him. On a moot question, his good story, sharp with
apt analogy, was likely to close the discussion,—sometimes at
the expense of a venturesome proposer. There was a roll of
mischief in his eye, which eased the situation.

We were glad to see that facility of counterpoise in him;
for we knew too deeply well, the burden that was even then
pressing on his spirit, and our laughter was light and brief.

But always he wished to see the army together. This
had a being, a place, a power, beyond the aggregate of its
individual units. A review was therefore held, in completeness
and most careful order. Slowly he rode along front and rear of
the opened ranks, that he might see all sides of things as they
were. Every horse was scanned: that is one way to know the
master. We could see the deep sadness in his face, and feel the
burden on his heart, thinking of his great commission to save
this people, and knowing that he could do this no otherwise
than as he had been doing,—by and through the manliness of
these men,—the valor, the steadfastness, the loyalty, the devotion, the sufferings and thousand deaths, of those into whose
eyes his were looking. How he shrunk from the costly sacrifice
we could see; and we took him into our hearts with answering
sympathy, and gave him our pity in return.

There came a day of offering, not of his appointing. His
day came; and a shroud of darkness fell on us. The surrender
was over; the all-commanding cause triumphant. Lee's army
had ceased to be. That solid phalanx we had faced through
years of mortal struggle, had vanished as into air. The arms
that had poured storms of death upon us, had been laid at our
feet. The flags that had marked the path of that manly valor
which gave them a glory beyond their creed, had been furled
forever. The men who in the inscrutable workings of the
human will had struck against the flag that stood for their
own best good, were returning to restore their homes and
citizenship in a regenerated country.

We were two days out from Appomattox,—a strange

vacancy before our eyes; a silent joy in our hearts. Suddenly a foam-flecked, mud-splashed rider hands a telegram. No darkest hour of the dismal years ever brought such message. *"The President assassinated! Deep plots at the Capital!"* How dare to let the men know of this? Who could restrain the indignation, the agony, the frenzy of revenge? Whether they would turn to the destruction of every remnant and token of the rebellion around them, or rush to the rescue of Washington and vengeance upon the whole brood of assassins, was the alternative question. We marched and bivouacked with a double guard on our troops, and with guarded words.

Two days after, came from the War Department the order to halt the march and hold all still, while the funeral farewell was passing at the capital. Then why not for us a funeral? For the shadow of him was to pass before us that day, and we would review him!

The veterans of terrible campaigns, the flushed faces from Appomattox, the burning hearts turned homewards, mighty memories and quenchless love held innermost;—these were gathered and formed in great open square,—the battered flags brought to the front of each regiment; the bright arms stacked in line behind them; sword-hilts wreathed in crape; chief officers of the Corps on a platform of army-chests at the open face of the square,—their storied flags draped and clustered in significant escutcheon. The commander of the Division presiding,—the senior chaplain called beside him. The boom of the great minute-guns beats against our hearts; the deep tones echoing their story of the years. Catching the last note of the cannon-boom, strikes in the soulful German ballad, with that wondrous "Russian Hymn" whose music we knew so well:

> "God the All-terrible; Thou who ordainest
> Thunder Thy clarion, and lightning Thy sword!"

that overmastering flood of whelming chords, with the breath-stilling chromatic cadences, as if to prepare us for whatever life or death could bring.

A few words from the commander, and the warm Irish heart of the chaplain wings its eloquence through the hearts of that deep-experienced, stern, loving, remembering, impressionable assembly. Well that the commander was there, to check the flaming orator! Men could not bear it. You could not, were

I able to repeat it here. His text was thrilling: "And she, being instructed of her mother, said: 'Give me here the head of John the Baptist in a charger'!" Then the application. Lincoln struck down because so high in innocence, in integrity, in truth, in loyalty, in fidelity to the people. Then the love he bore to them, and they to him; that communion of sorrows, that brotherhood of suffering, that made them one with him in soul. Then the dastard hand that had struck him down in the midst of acts of mercy, and words of great-hearted charity and good will. The spirit of hate, that struck at his life, was the spirit that struck at the life of the people.

"And will you endure this sacrilege," he cried. *"Will you not rather sweep such a spirit out of the land forever, and cast it, root and branch into everlasting burning!"* Men's faces flushed and paled. Their muscles trembled. I saw them grasp as for their stacked muskets,—instinctively, from habit, not knowing what else, or what, to do. The speaker stopped. He stood transfixed. I seized his arm. *"Father Egan, you must not stop! Turn this excitement to some good!"* *"I will,"* he whispers. Then, lifting his arm full height, he brought it down with a tremendous sweep, as if to gather in the whole quivering circle before him, and went on. *"But better so! Better to die glorious, than to live infamous! Better to be buried beneath a nation's tears, than to walk the earth guilty of a nation's blood! Better,—thousand-fold, forever better, Lincoln dead, than Davis living!"*

Then admonished of the passion he was again arousing, he passed to an exhortation that rose into a prayer; then to a pæan of victory; and with an oath of new consecration to the undying cause of freedom and right, he gave us back to ourselves, better soldiers, and better men.

That was our apotheosis of Lincoln. He passed up through the dark gate we knew so well. And now when the eyes that were wont to see him in earthly limitations, behold him high amidst the deathless ranks marshalled on the other shore, he stands in unfolded grandeur. Solitary on earth; mightily companioned, there!

He stands, too, upon the earth:

"As some tall cliff that lifts its awful form,
Swells from the vale, and midway leaves the storm;
Though round its breast the rolling clouds are spread,
Eternal sunshine settles on its head!"

His magnanimity has touched the answering heart of the chivalrous South. To-day, all do him reverence.

There he stands,—like the Christ of the Andes—reconciler of the divided!

And more than this. A true fame grows. Contemporary antagonisms fall away. Prejudice and misconception are effaced by better knowledge. The pure purpose is revealed under broader lights. The unforeseen, far-reaching good effects are more and more acknowledged. The horizon widens; the image lifts. Land after land, year after year; nay,—century upon century, recognize the benefactor as they come to realize the benefaction.

So, more and more for the Country's well-being, will sound the symphony of that deep-themed second Inaugural, majestic as the second giving of the law; and that Gettysburg speech, from his open heart, glorious with devotion, sublime with prophecy. Beyond the facts which history can record,—the deliverance and vindication of a people in peril of its honor and its life, and the revelation of the stored-up powers vouchsafed to him who is charged with the salvation of his country,—there will be for this man an ever unfolding record.

More and more the consecrating oath of that great purpose: *"With malice towards none; with charity for all; following the right, as God gives us to see the right,"* will be the watch-word of the world. Coming time will carry forward this great example of the consecration of power, self-commanding, and so all-commanding, for the well-being of the people, and the worth of man as man. This example, lifted up before the nations, support and signal of the immortal endeavor,—the human return to God!

So we look forward, and not backward, for the place of Abraham Lincoln!

Governor Joshua L. Chamberlain, ca. 1868
(Courtesy Pejepscot Historical Society)

Joshua L. Chamberlain, ca. 1870
(Courtesy Pejepscot Historical Society)

MILITARY ORDER OF THE
LOYAL LEGION OF THE UNITED STATES.

COMMANDERY OF THE STATE OF MAINE.

In Memoriam.

JOSHUA LAWRENCE CHAMBERLAIN

Late Major-General U. S. V.

CIRCULAR NO. 5.
SERIES OF 1914.
WHOLE NUMBER, 328.

MILITARY ORDER OF THE
LOYAL LEGION OF THE UNITED STATES.

HEADQUARTERS COMMANDERY OF THE STATE OF MAINE.

PORTLAND, MAY 6, 1914

THE FOLLOWING TRIBUTE TO THE MEMORY OF

Companion
Joshua Lawrence Chamberlain,

LATE MAJOR-GENERAL U. S. V.

WAS ADOPTED AT A STATED MEETING OF THIS COMMANDERY, MAY 6, 1914.

> Nothing is here for tears, nothing to wail
> Or knock the breast; no weakness, no contempt,
> Dispraise or blame; nothing but well and fair,
> And what may quiet us in a death so noble.

Joshua Lawrence Chamberlain, a charter Companion of this Commandery, died at Portland, Maine, Tuesday, February 24, 1914. He was born in Brewer, September 8, 1828, the son of Joshua and Sarah Dupee (Brastow) Chamberlain. After a course in the public schools of Brewer he attended a military school in Ellsworth where he fitted for West Point. He entered Bowdoin in 1848 and graduated in 1852 with the highest honors. At his mother's instance he then took a three years' course at the Bangor Theological Seminary, fitting himself for the ministry. The master's oration delivered by him at Bowdoin in 1855 on "Law and Liberty" so impressed the officers of the college that they invited him to become an instructor in logic and natural theology. The following year he was elected professor of rhetoric and oratory. In 1861 he was elected to the chair of modern languages.

In his application to the Pennsylvania Commandery of the Military Order of the Loyal Legion of the United States for membership he gave the following brief statement of his services:

"Lieutenant Colonel, 20th Maine Infantry, Aug. 8, 1862; Colonel, June 13, 1863; discharged for promotion July 3, 1863. Brigadier General, U. S. Volunteers, June 18, 1864; honorably mustered out January 15, 1866. Brevetted Major General, U. S. Volunteers, March 29, 1865, for conspicuous gallantry and meritorious services in action on the Quaker Road, Va. Awarded the Medal of Honor under resolution of Congress for daring heroism and great tenacity in holding his position on the Little Round Top and carrying the advanced position on the Great Round Top at the battle of Gettysburg, Pa., July 2, 1863."

He was elected a member Nov. 1, 1865, Class 1, Insignia 62; transferred to Commandery of Maine, June 6, 1866, charter member.

Professor Chamberlain made several attempts to be relieved from duty at Bowdoin that he might enter the service of his country but it was not until the first of August, 1862, that he was enabled to do so through the permission of his college to take a leave of absence "for the purpose of visiting Europe." He then proffered his services for any military duty that might be assigned to him and thereupon received from Governor Washburn the appointment of Lieutenant Colonel of the 20th Maine Volunteer Infantry then being organized. He promptly accepted the appointment in spite of the efforts of the college to restrain him and was mustered in on the 8th of August and commanded the camp until Col. Adelbert Ames took command of the regiment near the close of the month. The 20th was at once ordered to the front and was assigned to Butterfield's "Light Brigade" of the 5th Corps, General Porter, of the Army of the Potomac.

It was in a good hour for himself and for his country that he entered the service under such conditions and auspices. He was at an age when enthusiasm is still quick and inspiring and the judgment has been drilled into coolness and leadership by some experience in life and duty. With the docility of youth he had the independence and self-reliance of manhood.

Ames, the colonel, but recently from West Point, could not rest until he had advanced his regiment to as close an approximation of his ideals as the exigencies of active campaigning permitted. He found an able second in his Lieutenant. Under such instruction and leadership the 20th, composed, officers and men, of the best Yankee stock, was not long in becoming a soldierly entity to be relied upon and to be reckoned with in the day of battle. The 5th Corps was generally considered the "pet" corps of the army, partly because it included the division of regulars, and was thought to be in a little closer touch with headquarters than any other corps. The superior officers of the 5th and other corps with whom Colonel Chamberlain

came in contact, officially and socially, were predisposed in his
favor by the knowledge of the vocation he had left at his country's
call, and by the inference of scholarly ability naturally accompanying that knowledge, and also by his marked and agreeable personality and the soldierly qualities he displayed.

The 20th immediately on joining was marched away to the
Maryland Campaign. The 5th Corps was not actively engaged in
the battle of Antietam but occupied a position of "watchful waiting"
and smelt the battle from afar off. The first engagement in which
the 20th took part was a reconnoissance at Shepherdstown Ford on
the 20th of September. On the 12th of October Chamberlain led a
reconnoissance to a pass of South Mountain. He took part in the
action at Fredericksburg, Dec. 13, and was slightly wounded in the
right cheek. He commanded the regiment, Colonel Ames being on
other duty, the night of the evacuation and covered the retreat of
the army from the advanced position on the heights in rear of the
city. In all the affairs in which the regiment took part that winter
Colonel Chamberlain was present. The 20th did not take part in
the battle of Chancellorsville because it had been isolated through
the prevalence of small-pox in its ranks. Upon Colonel Chamberlain's request for some duty the 20th was assigned to the protection
of the signal and telegraph lines of communication. On the 20th of
May, 1863, he was appointed Colonel of his regiment. On that date
the 20th was strengthened by the assignment to it of a hundred and
twenty men of the 2nd Maine, a two-years' regiment, whose term
had expired.

At the battle of Gettysburg, on the 2d of July, 1863, Colonel
Chamberlain rendered a service which ranks among the most conspicuous and brilliant in all history of battles and earned for him
the popular title of "Hero of Little Round Top." That height was
a boulder-strewn hill on the left of our line and had not been occupied. When General Warren, Engineer in Chief on Meade's staff,
discovered that fact and that a strong force of the enemy was
evidently preparing to move forward and take possession of it and
thus gravely compromise our whole line of battle, he hastily gathered
for its defence such troops as he could reach, among them Vincent's
brigade in which was the 20th Maine. The brigade hastily mounted
the hill and formed in line near the crest, the 20th Maine on the
left of the line, barely in time to meet the onset of Law's brigade of
Hood's division. The rebels came on as if determined to take
possession of the crest and were met by the determination of its
defenders to hold it. The opposing lines were but a few yards
apart and in some instances there were hand to hand encounters.

Colonel Chamberlain, discovering that a force of the enemy was
moving towards his left flank and rear, promptly changed the front
of his left wing and extended the line by taking intervals and forming in single rank. The enemy made fierce onslaughts time after

time but had to fall back before the stout resistance of this thin line. At length the situation became so desperate through the persistence of the enemy and the lack of ammunition that Chamberlain ordered a charge. The "pine swung against the palm" and overcame it. The enemy was driven down the hill and to complete his discomfiture Captain Morrill with his company, ordered to the left front on the arrival of the 20th, as skirmishers, formed behind a wall and with a few sharpshooters who had joined them, poured such a hot fire into the flank and rear of the fleeing enemy that those who did not surrender stayed not upon the order of their going. It is no wonder that Longstreet reported "Hood's left was held as in a vise," and that Chamberlain received the personal and official thanks of his commanding officers. The importance of the stand made by Chamberlain and his men of Maine has never failed of recognition by any military student or historian of the battle.

In the shades of evening Chamberlain was ordered to take possession of Great Round Top and he skilfully carried out the order.

Soon after Gettysburg, General Chamberlain was assigned by General Griffin to the command of the 3d brigade, 2d division of the 5th corps, and was retained in it for a long time in spite of attempts to replace him by some general officer. He took part in the Culpepper and Centreville campaign and at Rappahannock Station his horse was shot under him.

A severe malarial fever culminated in such prostration that he was sent to Washington for treatment in November, 1863. When recovered sufficiently to perform the duty he was assigned by the Secretary of War to service on an important court-martial sitting in Washington. His efforts to go to the front were not successful until after the Wilderness. He resumed command of his brigade and half an hour after he was ordered to take seven regiments and make a charge on the works in front of the Court House at Spottsylvania. It was deferred, however, until evening when it was successfully executed. On the first of June, 1864, a brigade was formed by the consolidation of two brigades of Pennsylvania troops of the 1st Corps and Chamberlain was assigned to the command by General Warren, commanding the corps. At Petersburg, on the 18th of June, he led an attack on a strong position from which a heavy artillery fire was directed on his advance. Many of his men were swept down and Chamberlain's horse was killed by a shell. The attack was pushed with vigor and while leading it on foot Chamberlain fell, shot through by a ball which passed through the body from hip to hip severing arteries and fracturing bones. He was carried from the field and taken to hospital at Annapolis where for two months he lay at the point of death.

After the General had been taken to the field hospital the regular surgeon in charge declared the case hopeless. Companion

A. O. Shaw, surgeon of the 20th Maine, after an exhausting day's labor, rode through the woods at night and finding the General, remained with him, watching and caring for him and performing a surgical operation he found necessary, until his patient seemed out of immediate danger. His friends who were cognizant of the case have always felt General Chamberlain's life was saved by Dr. Shaw's skill and faithfulness.

In his last illness, Dr. Shaw attended his old chief with the same faithfulness he had shown in caring for him so many years before.

At the end of five months, and before he could mount a horse or walk a hundred yards, he resumed command of his brigade. Before he was taken from the field he was assured of his promotion. After his arrival at Annapolis he received a telegram as follows:

HEAD QRS. ARMY OF THE U. S.
June 20, 1864.

To COL. J. L. CHAMBERLAIN,
20th Maine Infantry.

Special Order No. 39. 1st—Col. J. L. Chamberlain, 20th Maine Inf'y Volunteers, for meritorious and efficient services on the field of battle and especially for gallant conduct in leading his brigade against the enemy at Petersburg on the 18th inst., in which he was dangerously wounded, hereby, in pursuance of the authority of the Secretary of War, is appointed Brig. Gen. of U. S. Volunteers to rank as such from the 18th day of June, 1864, subject to the approval of the President.

U. S. GRANT,
Lieut. Gen.

This is the only instance in the war of promotion on the battlefield. The terrible wound received on the 18th of June, 1864, caused him suffering throughout his life and at intervals incapacitated him for work of any kind.

Resuming his command under conditions that would have amply excused him from active service he was at once employed in operations along the Weldon Railroad. His condition was so severely affected by the hardships of duty and the inclemency of the weather that at the end of a month his corps commander insisted on his going North for treatment. While recuperating he declined many offers of attractive positions in civil life. After a month in the care of surgeons he stole away from them and leaving his room for the first time made the painful journey to the front and took command of a new brigade composed of New York and Pennsylvania regiments.

On the 29th of March, 1865, the final struggle between the Army of the Potomac and the Army of Northern Virginia began. The honor of the advance was given to General Chamberlain. With his brigade and a battery, after a long and severe battle against vastly superior numbers, in which every one of Chamberlain's mounted officers was either killed or wounded, he himself wounded in the breast and arm and his horse shot under him, he drove the enemy from his position and opened the way to the Boydton Plank Road. For this action he was brevetted Major General by President Lincoln.

On the second day after, General Chamberlain, in spite of all his wounds, was summoned to the command of the extreme left to resist an attack being made in force. He not only did this successfully but gallantly and skilfully made an assault on the works, drove the enemy, captured many prisoners and effected a lodgment on the White Oak Road.

At the battle of Five Forks on the following day Chamberlain commanded two brigades on the extreme right. The 20th Maine was now in his command and occupied the post of honor. In this severe action Chamberlain's own brigade, the smallest in the division, captured 1050 men, 19 officers and five battle flags,—one-half the captures of their division.

The next day in the advance on the South Side Railroad he still had the advance. He drove Fitz Hugh Lee's division of cavalry across the railroad, captured a train, and routed the enemy from his position. In the subsequent pursuit he took many prisoners and a large quantity of material. He marched all night and arrived at Appomattox Court House to aid the cavalry which was being hard-pushed by the opposing infantry. He formed under General Sheridan's eye, other troops formed on his left and the line went forward driving the enemy through the town until the flag of truce came in and put an end to hostilities.

General Chamberlain was designated to receive with the division he then temporarily commanded the formal surrender of the arms and colors of Lee's army on the 12th of April, 1865.

The description of this historic ceremony by Gen. Morris Schaaf in his "Sunset of the Confederacy," in its vivid and picturesque language, seems so well suited to the occasion and the chivalrous character of the principal actors, Chamberlain and Gordon, that we quote it:—

"I believe," he says, "that the selection of Chamberlain to represent the Army of the Potomac was providential in this, that he, in the way he discharged his duty, represented the spiritually-real of the world. And by this I mean the lofty conceptions of what in human conduct is manly and merciful, showing in daily life consideration for others and on the battlefield linking courage with magnanimity and sharing an honorable enemy's woes. Chamberlain's troops, facing westward and in single rank formation, having gained their position were brought to an 'order arms.' The Confederates, in plain view, then began to strike their few weather-worn scattered tents, seized their muskets and for the last time fell into line. Pretty soon, along Chamberlain's ranks the word passed: 'Here they come.' On they come and Gordon is riding at the head of the column. On he leads the men who had stood with him and whose voices had more than once screamed like the voices of swooping eagles as victory showed her smile; but now he and all are dumb. They are gaining the right of Chamberlain's line; now Gordon is abreast of it; his eyes are down and he is drinking the very lees for he thinks that all those men in blue, standing within a few feet of him at 'order arms' are gloating over the spectacle. Heavy lies his grief as on before the lines he rides, and now he is almost opposite Chamberlain who sits there mounted, the Maltese cross, the badge of the 5th Corps, and the Stars and Stripes displayed before him: lo a bugle peals and instantly the whole Federal line from right to left comes to a 'carry,' the marching salute.

"General Chamberlain has said: 'Gordon catches the sound of shifting arms, looks up, and taking the meaning, wheels superbly, and making with himself and his horse one uplifted figure, with profound salutation as he drops the point of the sword to the stirrup; then facing his own command, gives word for his successive brigades to pass us with the same position of the manual—honor answering honor. On our part not a sound of trumpet more, nor roll of drum; nor a cheer nor word nor whisper of vainglorying; nor motion of man standing again at the order, but an awed stillness rather, and breath-holding, as if it were the passing of the dead.'

"Great in the broad and high sense, was the cause battled for and spontaneous and knightly was this act of Chamberlain's, lending a permanent glow to the close of the war like that of banded evening clouds at the end of an all-day beating rain. It came from the heart and it went to the heart; and when 'taps' shall sound for Chamberlain I wish that I could be in hearing, hear Maine's granite coast with its green islands and moon-light reflecting coves taking them up in succession from Portland to Eastport, and as the ocean's voice dies away, hear her vast wilderness of hemlock, spruce and pine repeating them with majestic pride for her beloved son.

"It was not mere chance that Chamberlain was selected and that he called on the famous corps to salute their old intrepid enemy at the last solemn ceremonial. Chance, mere chance? No, for God, whenever men plough the fields of great deeds in this world, sows seed broadcast for the food of the creative powers of the mind. What glorified tenderness that courtly act has added to the scene! How it, and the courage of both armies, Lee's character and tragic lot, Grant's magnanimity and Chamberlain's chivalry, have lifted the historic event up to a lofty, hallowed summit for all people. I firmly believe that Heaven ordained that the end of that epoch-making struggle should not be characterized by the sapless, dreary commonplace; for with pity, through four long years, she had looked down on those high-minded battling armies, and out of love for them both, saw to it that deeds of enduring color should flush the end."

General Chamberlain's account of the surrender read at a re-union of his old brigade some years ago, is appended to "The Attack and Defense of Little Round Top," by Oliver Willcox Norton.

After the surrender Chamberlain was assigned to the command of a division and with it occupied a long portion of the South Side Railroad for some time. He led the triumphal entry into Richmond and in the Grand Review in Washington. When the army was broken up he was assigned to another command; but active operations being over, he declined, and on the 24th of August,

1865, he repaired to his home for the surgical treatment and rest which his war-worn and war-torn frame required. In the January following he was mustered out. Immediately after the surrender, General Griffin, his corps commander, addressed a special communication to headquarters urging General Chamberlain's promotion to the full rank of Major General for distinguished and gallant services on the left, including the White Oak Road, Five Forks and Appotomattox Court House, "where," says General Griffin, "his bravery and efficiency were such as to entitle him to the highest commendation. In the last action, the 9th of April, his command had the advance, and was driving the enemy rapidly before it when the announcement of General Lee's surrender was made." The recommendation was cordially approved by Generals Meade and Grant and forwarded to Washington where assurances were given that the promotion should be made.

The limitations of this memorial permit only the mere outline of General Chamberlain's services. It would require a volume to do them justice. Much information in regard to them may be found in the official reports, in published lives and letters of participants in the war and in the many papers, lectures and addresses of the General. The many expressions of his superior officers prove how highly he was regarded as a soldier and a leader—always praise, never blame or criticism.

In 1866 he was made the candidate of the Republican party for governor and was elected by a majority of nearly thirty thousand. Three terms in succession followed. Respect and admiration for the soldier-governor were not limited by party lines. His four years of service were an "era of good feeling." His messages were admirable documents. They breathed of loyalty and state pride and his recommendations were made with care and full consideration and had only in view the welfare and advancement of the state and people. All the duties of his office and the many functions to which he was called by the people were performed with thoroughness, grace and dignity and to the enhancement of the great love and consideration in which he was held. His reputation as a statesman was worthy of that he had made as a soldier.

In 1871 Bowdoin claimed the professor who had left the college for so long a "leave of absence" and elected him president. He retained that position twelve years. While his scholarly and executive abilities were of great value to the college it would be difficult to measure the value to the young men under him of having constantly before them a man who in so many fields had achieved the highest success, who was an inspiration and an object-lesson illustrating the many-sidedness which the scholar might hope to attain.

He was appointed to represent the state on "Maine Day" at the Centennial Exposition in Philadelphia in 1876. In the performance of that duty he delivered a valuable address on the State of Maine which was published in book form. In 1878 he was appointed a commissioner to the Paris Exposition and in the execution of that duty rendered a full and interesting report.

General Chamberlain was elected Major General of the militia in 1876 and was thus enabled to render the state great service at the "Count-out" in 1880. His presence and wise and prudent counsels on that occasion no doubt averted disaster and perhaps a bloody civil strife.

After resigning at Bowdoin he engaged in business enterprises and was for some time in Florida. In 1890 he was appointed by President McKinley Surveyor of Customs for the port of Portland and retained that position by successive re-appointments during the remainder of his life.

He was greatly and actively interested in all soldier societies and associations. He attended the reunions of the men who had been under his command in regiments from many states and his lecture on "Little Round Top" was repeated before delighted thousands throughout a widespread territory. He was early a member of the Grand Army of the Republic and was for a term Commander of the Department of Maine. When the Society of the Army of the Potomac was organized in the city of New York in 1869 he was selected as orator of the occasion and delivered an eloquent address on "The Army of the Potomac" before a large audience which included many officers of high rank.

Here are extracts from the official report:—

"With admirable tone and manner, and frequently interrupted by the appreciating and enthusiastic plaudits of a brilliant audience, General Chamberlain then delivered the first annual oration before the Society as follows:—

"'Comrades: You bid me speak for you. What language shall I borrow that can hold the meaning of this hour? How translate into mortal tongue the power and glory of immortal deeds. Where can I find a strain to sound these depths of memory, or sweep these heights of harmony ' Rather would I stand mute before the majesty of this presence, while all the scene around—token and talisman—speaks the unfathomable, unending story. Visions trooping on me in solemn, proud procession overcloud the present, till it drifts away to dream and shadow, and they alone are the living and unchanged. Emotions struggling up through the dark and bloody years choke down my utterance. No! Rather do you speak to me; you, who return my greeting, and you, unseen and silent to mortal sense, comrades in soul to-night! and drown my faltering words in your vast accord.

    *   *   *   *   *   *   *

"'God be praised that in the justice of his ways this same much suffering old Army—scoffed at for not moving but never, that I have heard, for not dying enough—should be the chosen one to push the Rebellion to its last field, and to see its proudest ensigns at its feet.

    *   *   *   *   *   *   *

"'So it rises and stands before me, the glorious pageant—the ranks all full—you the living, they the immortal—swelling together the roll of honor; that great company of heroic souls that were and are the Army of the Potomac! Let me borrow the prophet's tongue rapt with celestial vision: "These are the living creatures that I saw under the God of Israel, by the river of Chebar, and the likeness of their faces were the same faces which I saw by the river; and they went everyone straight forward." '

"At the close of the oration General Chamberlain was greeted with prolonged cheers."

General Chamberlain was President of the Society of the Army of the Potomac in 1889 and at the meeting in Orange responded to the greeting of the Governor of New Jersey in part as follows:—

"*   *   *   *   And now pardon me a word in behalf of those for whom I am to return your greeting. I desire that the friends with us to-day, especially the younger portion, who may not be so familiar with the history of the country in its details, may be reminded of what manner of men these are before you. When his Excellency the Governor mentioned that space of twenty-five years ago I could not help thinking, comrades and gentlemen, of that dark and bitter year, 1864, when the hearts of almost all men, and I don't know but of some women, were filled with fear at the aspect of things for our country's honor and the hopes of all seemed trailing in the dust; when all the newspapers here were filled with foreboding and (the gentlemen of the press will forgive me) almost upbraiding us of the army at times that we were not in Richmond; while in Washington even prominent members of Congress were beginning to forsake the great President and form plans other than his and when the issue of our great cause seemed to have settled down as in a cloud upon almost every heart in the country; and I desire to say here to-day that in this Army of the Potomac whose suffering and losses were such in that same year of 1864 that we were not called upon or permitted to report our casualties during that whole campaign from the Rapidan and Rappahannock to the James and Appomattox, for fear the country could not stand the disclosure, in this army there was no faltering nor thought of dispair. These men before you and their comrades alone of all men I ever heard of, kept up their heart and hope and loyalty to the President and the great cause, holding up their bleeding and shattered forms, and protesting that never, while one man of them could hold the field, should that flag be sullied in the dust or the honor of the country go down in shame. I want these honorable gentlemen to bear in mind, and these beautiful and sympathizing ladies, and these youths, that it was the word character, as well as the physical force of these men of the Army of the Potomac that made them patriots and saviours of their country. These are the men for whom it falls to my honorable and happy lot to speak to-day, and to respond for to your welcome, and say that they are deserving of it."

On the 22nd of February, 1866, he delivered an address on "Loyalty" before the Pennsylvania Commandery. The only record there is of this address is in the papers of the day.

In the "War Papers" published by this Commandery there appear the following papers by General Chamberlain: in Volume I, "The Military Operations on the White Oak Road, Virginia,

March 31, 1865," read December 6, 1893; in Volume II, "Five Forks," read May 2, 1900; in Volume III, "Reminiscences of Petersburg and Appomattox, October, 1903," read March 2, 1904, and "The Grand Review of the Army of the Potomac," read May 2, 1906. Among the papers in the hands of the Publication Committee awaiting publication is one by him entitled "Abraham Lincoln Seen from the Field in the War for the Union," read before the Commandery of the State of Pennsylvania, February 12, 1909, and subsequently read before this Commandery. It is needless to add that all these are carefully prepared and highly interesting papers and most valuable to the history of the war. Companions will recall the many impromptu addresses made by him at meetings of the Commandery when talking to his companions on the themes suggested by the papers that had been read, when he was at his best and spoke "winged words" that thrilled the hearts of his hearers.

In person General Chamberlain was of medium height; his form was perfectly proportioned, well-knit, neither slender nor stout, and always erect and graceful. His finely shaped head and face of classic features and beauty was nobly borne, with an air well fitting the chivalrous spirit within. His voice was pleasing, strong and resonant and used with perfect art, oftentimes thrilling with tones suited to his utterances.

In the State Library there is a marble bust of him executed in Florence by Jackson, a Maine sculptor, and presented to the state by a number of friends when he was Governor. It is a fine work of art and a perfect likeness. Jackson said that when it was on exhibition at his studio it elicited the highest admiration from his visitors.

The funeral exercises, February 27, were simple but impressive. At the request of the family a committee of the Loyal Legion had charge of them. Companion Gen. John T. Richards was designated by that committee to have immediate charge of the ceremonies. The Portland battalion of the National Guard performed escort duty. The casket was taken to the City Hall and placed in front of the stage, and around it stood a squad of honor from the National Guard. The hall was filled with dignitaries, officials, soldiers and representatives of many associations. Bosworth and Thatcher Posts of the Grand Army were present in great force and there was a large representation of the Loyal Legion. Governor Haines, who had made a worthy proclamation to the State, and members of his staff, the collector of the port and many officials of the custom house, delegates from the Society of American Wars, officers of Bowdoin College, and many friends from many parts of the State, were there to honor the illustrious dead. Ex-Gov. John C. Bates, Maj. Henry L. Higginson and Gen. Morris Schaaf represented Massachusetts at the request of the Governor in the communication which follows :—

"BOSTON, February 26, 1914.
HON. JOHN C. BATES,
    73 Tremont Street, Boston, Mass.
My Dear Governor:

It has occurred to me that it would be most fitting and proper that the Commonwealth of Massachusetts should be represented at the funeral of the late Gen. Joshua L. Chamberlain which is to be held at Portland, Me., to-morrow, and I sincerely trust that you will find it possible to attend. I have made a similar request of Maj. H. L. Higginson and Gen. Morris Schaaf.

The great public services rendered to his country and to New England by General Chamberlain would seem to make it desirable that some representatives of this commonwealth who knew him during his lifetime and were familiar with his public record should be present to indicate the affection and regard that the people of Massachusetts had for him as a commanding officer in the Civil War, as Governor of the State of Maine, and as president of a great college.

The commonwealth will be grateful to you for representing her at the last ceremonies in honor of this great man, before his remains are consigned to the earth.

            Yours very sincerely,
                    DAVID L. WALSH."

An eloquent and appreciative address was delivered by Rev. Jesse Hill, D. D., and several solemn and beautiful selections were rendered on the organ. The remains were then borne from the hall and escorted to the railroad station, through streets lined with respectful throngs, and placed on a car for transportation to Brunswick. At that place they were taken by the appointed local bearers and escorted by the Brunswick company of the National Guard, Vincent Mountfort Post of the Grand Army, the student body and members of the faculty of Bowdoin College, to the First Parish Congregational Church where services were conducted by Rev. Chauncey W. Goodrich and a eulogy was delivered by President William DeWitt Hyde. Many distinguished and representative citizens from all parts of the State were in attendance at these exercises.

Our great and beloved Companion has passed from us and the scene of his high achievements to a goodly company and further service. How great a factor in assuaging "the immortal woe of life", confirming and enhancing the dignity of man and strengthening faith in the belief that the human lot is not common with that of the beasts that perish, is the memory of the great and good exemplars of our race! The lofty souls that have appeared here and there in the long procession of humanity still march with us. We look to them and feel in our hearts some kindling of sparks of the noble attributes that in them shone with clear and resplendent light. We seek their guidance in times of storm and stress when we grope to find the true path of action, and when we find the way that they have trod we go forward with confidence and glad assurance. How noble a company it is and with what joy the world welcomes every accession to its mighty brotherhood!

When the faithful Douglas, keeping his promise to his beloved king, bore the heart of the great Bruce in sacred pilgrimage to deposit it in the soil of the Holy Land, voyaged with a noble attendance of goodly knights on entering a port of Spain they heard "the clash of the atabals and the trumpets' wavering call" and learned that a contest with the Moors was going on. They alighted from their ship and proffered their Scottish spears to King Alfonzo. When the Moors were pressing them heavily the Douglas, standing in his stirrups, held high the casket that contained his precious charge and, flinging it far ahead, cried,

> "Pass thee first thou dauntless heart
> As thou wast wont of yore."

And then

> "the spears of Spain came shivering in
> And swept away the Moor."

So in future years, in contests of arms or principles, the heart of Chamberlain will go before and arouse new zeal in the breasts of its followers. But the cause must be true and righteous or that heart will be no talisman of victory.

General Chamberlain married at Brunswick, December 7, 1855, Caroline Frances Adams, a gracious and accomplished woman. She died October 18, 1905. Their children were Grace Dupee, wife of Harold G. Allen of Boston, a lawyer, and Harold Wyllys, a Companion of this Commandery, a lawyer residing in Portland. This Commandery tenders its profound sympathy to the daughter, son, and grandchildren and assures them that their illustrious parent will always be held dear by his surviving Companions and that his name and fame will be a precious legacy to his countrymen.

Respectfully submitted,

SELDEN CONNOR,
FRANKLIN M. DREW, } *Committee.*
ABNER O. SHAW,

By order of

LIEUT. GEORGE D. BISBEE, U. S, V.,
COMMANDER.

HORATIO STAPLES,
FIRST LIEUTENANT, U. S. V.,
RECORDER

OFFICIAL:
RECORDER.

14

Bibliography

The sources in this bibliography appear in the same order in which the subject matter appears in this book. Every item included herein was authored, in its original form, by Joshua Lawrence Chamberlain.

"My Story of Fredericksburg." *Cosmopolitan Magazine.* New York, December 1912.

"Through Blood and Fire at Gettysburg." *Hearst's Magazine.* New York, June 1913.

"Reminiscences of Petersburg and Appomattox." *Bangor Daily Commercial.* Bangor, March 3, 1904. Also, *War Papers. Read before the Commandery of the State of Maine, Military Order of the Loyal Legion of the United States.* Portland, 1903.

"Military Operations on the White Oak Road." *War Papers. Read before the Commandery of the State of Maine, Military Order of the Loyal Legion of the United States.* Portland, 1897.

"Five Forks." *War Papers. Read before the Commandery of the State of Maine, Military Order of the Loyal Legion of the United States.* Portland, 1902.

"Appomattox." *Personal Recollections of the War of the Rebellion: Addresses Delivered before the Commandery of the State of New York, Military Order of the Loyal Legion of the United States.* New York, 1907.

"The Grand Review of the Army of the Potomac." *War Papers. Read before the Commandery of the State of Maine, Military Order of the Loyal Legion of the United States.* Portland, 1908.

"Dedication of the Twentieth Maine Monuments at Gettysburg, October 3, 1889." Waldoboro, 1891.

"Dedication of Maine Monuments at Gettysburg." *Maine at Gettysburg.* Portland, 1898.

Colonel Chamberlain's Report on the Battle of Gettysburg. *War of the Rebellion: A Compilation of the Official Records of the Union and Confederate Armies*. Washington, 1880-1901.

Colonel Chamberlain's letter describing the Battle of Gettysburg to Maine Governor Coburn.

General Chamberlain's Report on the White Oak Road and Five Forks Campaign. *War of the Rebellion: A Compilation of the Official Records of the Union and Confederate Armies*. Washington, 1880-1901.

"The Third Brigade at Appomattox." *The Attack and Defense of Little Round Top*. New York, 1913.

"The Last Salute of the Army of the Northern Virginia." *Southern Historical Society Papers*. Richmond, 1876-1919. Also, *Boston Journal*. May 1901.

Address to the Sixteenth Maine Volunteers. *Maine at Gettysburg*. Portland, 1898.

"Oration of the One Hundredth Anniversary of the Birth of Abraham Lincoln." *War Papers. Read before the Commandery of the State of Maine, Military Order of the Loyal Legion of the United States*. Portland, 1915. Also, *Commandery of the State of Pennsylvania Military Order of the Loyal Legion of the United States*. Philadelphia, 1909.

Index

Suggested reading list:

"Bayonet! Forward": My Civil War Reminiscences by General Joshua Lawrence Chamberlain

The Passing of the Armies: The Last Campaign of the Armies by Joshua Lawrence Chamberlain

Lee: A Biography by Clifford Dowdey

Crisis at the Crossroads: The First Day at Gettysburg by Warren Hassler

The Great Invasion of 1863 or General Lee in Pennsylvania by Jacob Hoke

A Diary of Battle: The Personal Journals of Colonel Charles S. Wainwright 1861-1865 edited by Allan Nevins

The Attack and Defense of Little Round Top, Gettysburg, July 2, 1863 by Oliver W. Norton

Sickles the Incredible: A Biography of General Daniel Edgar Sickles by W.A. Swanberg

Soul of the Lion: A Biography of General Joshua Lawrence Chamberlain by Willard Wallace

Through Blood and Fire at Gettysburg: My Experiences with the 20th Maine Regiment on Little Round Top by Joshua Lawrence Chamberlain

At Gettysburg: What a Girl Saw and Heard of the Battle by Tillie (Pierce) Alleman

Maine at Gettysburg—Maine Gettysburg Commission

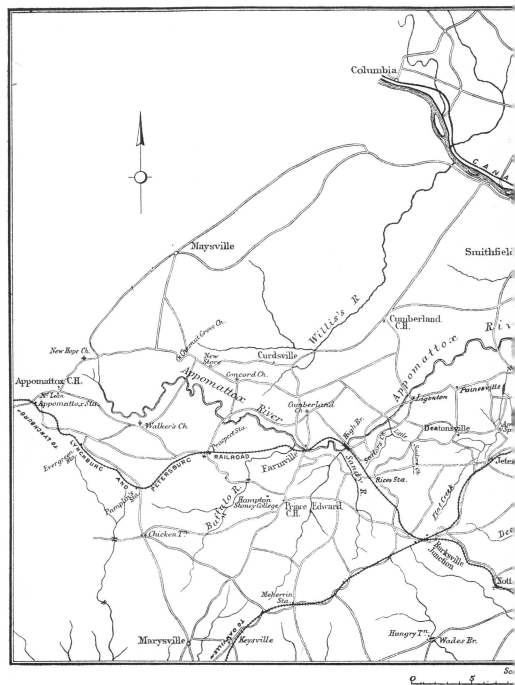

Columbia

Smithfield

Willis's R

Maysville

Cumberland
C.H.

River

Chestnut Grove Ch.
New Hope Ch.
New
Store
Curdsville

Appomattox
Ligonton
Painesville

Appomattox C.H.
Concord Ch.
Cumberland
Ch.
Deatonsville

McLean
Appomattox Sta.
River
High Br.
Sailor's Ck.
Little
Sailor's Ck.

Walker's Ch.
Prospect Sta.
RAILROAD
Sandy R.
Rices Sta.
Flat Creek
Jetes

Evergreen Sta.
LYNCHBURG AND
PETERSBURG
Farmville

Pamplin's Sta.
Buffalo R.
Hampton
Stoney College
Prince Edward
C.H.

Chicken Tn.
Burksville
Junction

Meherrin
Sta.
Nott

Marysville
Keysville
Hungry Tn.
Wades Br.

0   5   Sc